LASER CUTTING AND 3-D PRINTING

FOR RAILWAY MODELLERS

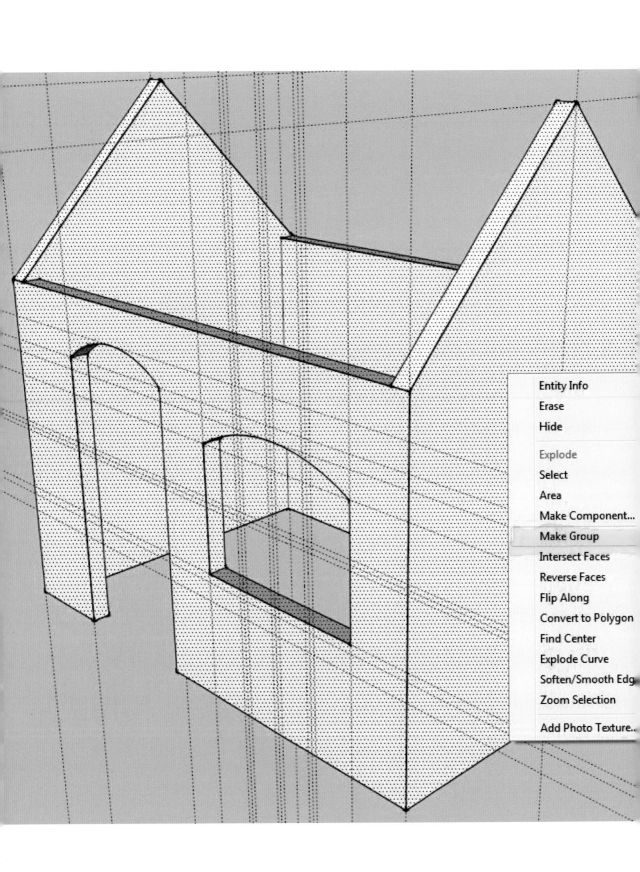

Entity Info
Erase
Hide

Explode
Select
Area
Make Component...
Make Group
Intersect Faces
Reverse Faces
Flip Along
Convert to Polygon
Find Center
Explode Curve
Soften/Smooth Edg
Zoom Selection

Add Photo Texture..

LASER CUTTING AND 3-D PRINTING

FOR RAILWAY MODELLERS

BOB GLEDHILL

THE CROWOOD PRESS

First published in 2016 by
The Crowood Press Ltd
Ramsbury, Marlborough
Wiltshire SN8 2HR

www.crowood.com

British Library Cataloguing-in-Publication Data
A catalogue record for this book is available from the British Library.

ISBN 978 1 78500 226 7

Acknowledgements
My thanks to those members of Manchester Model Railway Society
who were the first to see and try out the first few chapters on their
'improvement' course, and to Ralph Robertson in particular who gave
me detailed feedback and many helpful comments after reading the
entire script.

   I would also like to express my gratitude to Ken Shipley for his
help and support in the early stages of writing Part II: Laser Cutting.
Finally my thanks to my wife, who has had to endure a winter of
discussion on writing and chapter headings instead of the usual chat
about 'what I have just made'. Her support and proof reading have
been invaluable.

Disclaimer
The author and the publisher do not accept any responsibility in any
manner whatsoever for any error or omission, or any loss, damage,
injury, adverse outcome, or liability of any kind incurred as a result of
the use of any of the information contained in this book, or reliance
upon it. If in doubt about any aspect of laser cutting, 3-D printing and
railway modelling, readers are advised to seek professional advice.

Designed and typeset by Guy Croton
Publishing Services, Tonbridge, Kent
Printed and bound in Malaysia by Times Offset (M) Sdn Bhd

CONTENTS

PREFACE

I have always been fascinated by technology, and sometimes a technology comes along that will change the way we work. Thus it was that in 1983, I bought a second-hand Sinclair ZX81 and started to learn how to program it and find out what it could do. Now computers are part of everyday life, but back then this was a marvellous and novel little machine. There were several computer magazines that had in them printed programs for games you could type into your computer and then play. Many didn't work the first time, and most of the fun was trying to 'de-bug' the instructions and get them to work.

I returned to 4mm-scale (or strictly speaking 00-scale) railway modelling when I retired, having had a Triang TT layout in my youth, and found it an absorbing hobby with so many different skills to be learnt and models to be made. As you can imagine from the above, I quickly embraced DCC and computer control (via an ESU ECos controller and the excellent Traincontroller program).

I then met a member of the G-scale group, who meet at Keighley Model Railway Club, and joined, so now also have a G-scale garden layout. You will see examples of both scales throughout the book.

One of the members brought a cardboard tree, cut out on his wife's 'Craft Robo Cut' machine. Thinking this might help with the making of cardboard buildings I did a search of the internet for 'cutting machine', and among the listings was a laser cutting/engraving machine.

Once I discovered I could actually purchase and own a laser cutting machine, and from a company only four miles away, I became really excited again! The prospect of being able to draw and design something on the computer screen and then actually cut it out to sub-mm precision was a thrilling prospect. Not only could I hope to produce professional-looking items, but I could produce them in quantity.

For me, learning CAD (computer-aided design) was done on an adrenalin rush of excitement and anticipation. I bought CorelDraw and spent many enjoyable hours learning how to use it, laser cutting items as I did so.

My greatest reward was in discovering the techniques required to enable me to laser engrave realistic-looking stonework on to ordinary mount card. I could make realistic 'Northern'-looking stone-built houses, retaining walls and so on, without having to use paint or plastic sheet. Not only that, but as a bonus, the laser-engraving technique gave the surface a textured finish. The output might not have been finescale, but it was certainly better than anything I could have produced by painting plastic sheet.

More recently, and for over twelve months, I absorbed the news of each new 3-D printer with growing anticipation and excitement. I sent off for samples, read reviews, and eventually took the plunge and bought a Makerbot Replicator2. This proved to be a good 'starter' machine, as Makerbot had made the printer driver software very user-friendly, and the machine itself worked without too many problems.

Whilst looking at these machines and deciding when to buy one, I realized that CorelDraw would not cope with 3-D drawing, so I downloaded trial versions of about six different 3-D drawing programs and tried each one for a couple of hours. I chose Sketchup as the program I seemed to get on best with. It is very different in the way it works to CorelDraw, even though many of the concepts are the same (drawing rectangles, circles, straight lines and specifying dimensions). It also had the advantage that the Sketchup Make version of the program was – and still is at the time of writing – free.

I have therefore chosen to use Sketchup Make as the CAD package in this book, and which is therefore illustrated the most, but the reader needs to be aware that there are other programs around, some of which may better suit your learning style. This one program will produce both 2-D drawings for the laser cutter and 3-D for the 3-D printer.

Since purchasing the Makerbot Replicator2, I have built a couple of other 3-D printers from kits as 'Christmas present' (to myself!) projects (Printerbot Simple and Renkforce RF1000), and have bought a cheaper, semi-kit printer to evaluate for club use, the Hobbyking Print-Rite DIY printer (also advertised as the Colido DIY 3-D Printer). I illustrate and discuss these printers in Part III, the 3-D section of this book.

As you may have gathered, I find CAD drawing and the production of models via the laser cutter or 3-D printer an absorbing hobby in itself. I do now tend to look at kits in model shops and think 'I could make that'.

True to 'Sod's Law', three weeks before I was approached with a view to writing this book I had dismantled my 4mm railway to begin another, so many of the photographs in the book are of isolated items, rather than showing them 'in situ' on a layout.

If you simply want to continue to model in traditional ways and enjoy doing so, then this book may not be for you. If, however, like me, you enjoy learning new skills and techniques and embracing new technologies, or just like to see how many bought items are made, then I hope some of my knowledge and personal experience of laser cutting and 3-D printing machines will be of interest.

Bob Gledhill, 2016

INTRODUCTION

This book shows you how laser cutting and 3-D printing machines can be used to enhance our railway modelling hobby. It sets out to explain how these machines work, with copious examples of what they can produce, and the pros and cons of ownership. If you are thinking of buying a machine, have just bought one, or are simply interested in how they work and what they can make, then this book will prove of interest.

These are highly adaptable machines, and my examples show how a wide range of model railway items, in various scales, can be produced including window and door frames, fencing and walls, platforms, entire wagons including wheels, complete buildings, various brackets for servo-controlled points and signals, and even ultra-lightweight baseboards.

The book takes you through the stages of getting started with CAD (computer-aided design) so you can draw the items you require in a format suited to laser cutting/engraving and/or 3-D printing. After reading this book you should be well on the way to understanding the basic processes involved, and be able to produce items of your own.

For many of these I will take you through the stages necessary to do the actual working drawings, for others I will simply give some useful information on how they were produced. I have tried to assume no previous knowledge of using a CAD drawing program.

The book is arranged in three major sections:

Part I: CAD (computer-aided design): This section takes you through the various steps required to get

Various 3-D printed items in 4mm and G-scale. These are printed in different coloured filaments (plastic), with one of the huts and platform suitably weathered and/or spray painted. 4mm items include signal heads with feather, ladders, huts and platform. G-scale items include the signal lever frame, window frames, roof tiles and guttering. The odd-looking object to the left in front of the platform is a servo mount for operating semaphore signals.

Laser-cut and engraved mountboard, Mylar and Rowmark (styrene) used for retaining walls, fencing and platform awnings on the author's 4mm layout, now dismantled.

both 2-D (two-dimensional – flat) and 3-D (three-dimensional – a solid object) drawing programs installed, with a step-by-step guide to the basic knowledge needed to do your first drawings with Sketchup Make (the free version).

Part II: Laser Cutting: This section gives an explanation of how these machines work and what they can produce in different materials, with plenty of examples and 'hints and tips'.

Part III: 3-D Printing: This covers similar sections as above, but for 3-D printing machines.

You might like to 'browse' through Parts II and III to see the possibilities of laser cutting and 3-D printing before tackling the CAD section and learning the skills needed to produce your own drawings. If you follow the tutorials in the CAD section on your own computer or laptop then you should be able to draw

and cut out or print all the worked examples shown in the latter sections.

Note that laser cutting machines can also engrave, but to describe them as 'laser cutting and engraving' machines throughout the book would be somewhat cumbersome, so I will refer to them simply as 'laser cutting' machines. I do explain, however, with examples, how laser cutting machines can be used to engrave from both drawings and photographs.

COMPUTER-AIDED DESIGN (CAD) – IS IT NECESSARY?

Most of us use machines of one sort or another in our hobby, even if it is just a drill or a rotary tool to sand something down. In the past model engineers bought lathes, milling machines and other tools to work in metal (often making locomotives in larger scales), and those working in wood used lathes, circular saws and routers.

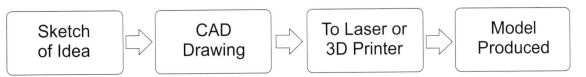

The CAD (computer-aided design) drawing is a vital stage in the production of your model on either a laser-cutting or 3-D printing machine.

Laser cutters and 3-D printers are their modern equivalent, only much, much more adaptable in that they can work with multiple types of material, and can produce multiple identical copies at the press of a computer key or click on a mouse button. However, whilst lathes, milling machines and circular saws can be worked by hand, laser cutters and 3-D printers cannot: they can *only* be worked via a computer. Furthermore with either machine 'If you can't draw it, you can't make it': you are limited to producing what others have drawn and shared on web sites such as Thingiverse (www.thingiverse.com).

The new skill required is CAD (computer-aided design), which does also require using a computer to draw things. Many shy away from this on the basis that it is too difficult or expensive, or of no use in our hobby. This book sets out to show that anyone can master the basics of CAD provided they have a suitable computer, and that once mastered, there are many items of use in our hobby that can be produced at little cost.

THE COMPUTER/SOFTWARE YOU WILL NEED

Many modellers will already own a suitable computer, but if not, a full size, reconditioned laptop or computer (you will need at least a 15in screen) running Windows can be bought at reasonable cost. You will also need a three-button mouse (or more accurately, two buttons and a scroll wheel), as the usual track pad or control button on a laptop is *not* suited to CAD.

You then need a drawing package, and the example used for the majority of drawings in this book is 'Sketchup Make'. I have chosen this program as one I am familiar with, but also it is *free* and is suited to both 2-D CAD drawing for the laser cutter and 3-D CAD for the 3-D printer. Widely

used, Sketchup Make is also very well supported with advice, forums and tutorials on the internet.

Note that the free version of Sketchup Make is for personal, non-profit use only.

At the time of writing there are many other CAD programs around, and if you are already familiar with one of those then you may skip the CAD section altogether and adapt the instructions on how to design the various models shown to your own preferred CAD program.

Note that this book is not a user guide to Sketchup Make, which would take a book in itself. It does, however, take you through the installation and early steps of using the program, with helpful hints and tips and worked examples for railway modellers.

For those new to Sketchup Make, an introduction to CAD and a step-by-step guide to installing, setting up and using Sketchup Make can be found in the first part of this book – Part I: CAD (Computer-Aided Design).

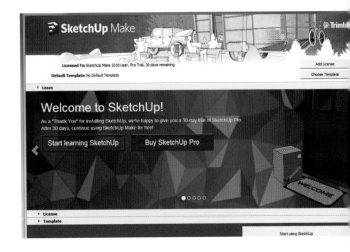

Sketchup Make is the (currently – 2016) free version of Sketchup and allows you to do the CAD drawings for both laser cutters and 3-D printers.

QUALITY

Can you produce commercial quality items with a 'hobby' laser cutter or 3-D printer? For laser cutters the answer is probably a 'yes', but for 3-D printers a 'no'. Let me explain.

LASER CUTTING MACHINES

The 'hobby' laser works like any other laser, but with a smaller cutting area (the author's is A4 size – 200 x 300mm) and less power. The focal length of the lens is also less than larger, more powerful machines, resulting in a slightly more angled cut, but in practice, unless you are regularly cutting 3mm-thick material this will be of little consequence.

So provided your models can be made out of pieces that fit the cutting area (usually A4), and the material you are working with is reasonably thin (up to 3mm Perspex, MDF or plywood), then a hobby laser can produce anything that the professionals can with their machines, albeit a little more slowly. I have made some very large G-scale models with careful use of sheets that are less than A4 in size. Joins can be disguised in a number of ways, for example, by changes in contour or by overlapping or hiding them behind features such as downpipes.

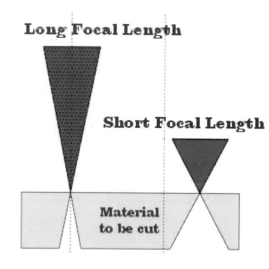

ABOVE: **The laser beam is focused on the workpiece and is never able to cut at a true 90 degrees, but in practice the slight angle of the cut is never a problem on thinner material. The longer the focal length of the lens the better.**

BELOW: **This large G-scale building is laser-cut MDF 2mm thick. The joins in the A4 sheets are hidden by horizontal details, and the vertical by rainwater downpipes. Window frames are added as a second layer after painting white. Brickwork is laser cut into the MDF and a red 'wash' applied.**

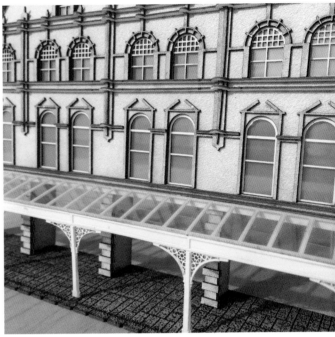

An extreme close-up of scrollwork for a shopping-arcade awning in 4mm scale. It is laser cut out of thin Mylar, then spray painted white; the central circle is just 1.5mm in diameter.

Scrollwork in context. The building is made up of laser-cut layers of mount card, whilst the awning is Mylar in order to get the fine detail required. The shop fronts are yet to be made. 4mm scale.

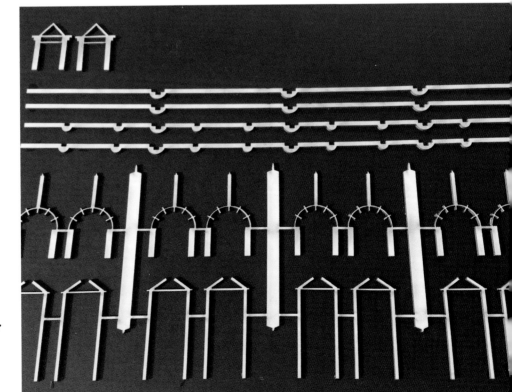

Fine detail for the building above, laser cut out of mount card.

3-D PRINTING MACHINES

3-D printers are different from laser cutting machines in that professional 3-D printers often use different technology and printing techniques than those used by 'hobby' machines (see Part III: 3-D Printing for details of the different types of 3-D printing). The vast majority of hobby 3-D printing at the time of writing is done on FDM (fused deposit modelling) machines, which build up a model layer by layer from a spool of filament. Imagine a hot glue gun building up layers, each on top of the previous one. FDM 3-D printers work on the same principle, but with much finer control.

Each layer shows on the finished article, and although typically only 0.1mm (100 microns) thick, this produces a banding effect on vertical surfaces. Also the top surface is even worse as it is formed of lots of parallel threads, each of which cannot be narrower than the hole from which it was extruded, usually 0.4mm or 0.5mm.

Often the surface can be made to look better by the use of a high-build grey plastic primer as sold for use on plastic car bumpers, but the more paint you apply, the more the fine detail disappears.

The larger the scale the more useful 3-D printers are for producing the final item. So whereas a G-scale wagon can be produced in its entirety, including wheels, and at very little cost (about £4 each for the plastic filament), and maybe a 0-gauge wagon (but not wheels) could be produced to an acceptable standard, a 00- or N-gauge wagon probably could not. The resolution and detail required to produce these wagons in the smaller scales would be difficult to achieve on a typical FDM printer.

BELOW: *G-scale wagon prototype in white produced entirely on a 3-D printer (only the axles and axle bearings are metal). The slight banding on the sides of the wagon in this scale looks quite acceptable. Even the 3-D printed wheels are functional. The body top is printed in one part and is 230mm long.*

This picture attempts to show the difference between 4mm-scale signal heads produced on a Makerbot Replicator2 FDM machine at home (right), and those produced, from the same drawings, by Shapeways, the 3-D print bureau on their professional machine (left). The Shapeways prints are smoother (especially the top surface) and better defined. These are tiny parts, however, and many would deem the home-produced prints acceptable, particularly printed in black and sprayed matt black, when some of the banding would be less obvious.

3-D PRINT BUREAUS

The hobby printer is an excellent tool for producing prototypes in the smaller gauges, and then, once the final design is correct, drawings can be uploaded to a 3-D print bureau for final printing. Used in this way a reasonably priced 3-D printer allows a design to be test-printed several times at reasonable cost until the design is finalized, when it can be sent off for a much more expensive, but better quality print at the 3-D print bureau.

Typically a batch of items such as the signal heads shown would cost less than 5p in plastic and electricity to print at home. From a 3-D print bureau including postage and packing, they would cost about £12+ (though it would be cheaper buying in bulk).

In the future as the professional 3-D printing processes are adopted by cheaper hobby machines, the home or club production of commercial quality items will become a possibility. Obviously you will also need to be able to produce commercial quality CAD drawings for this to happen.

WHERE DO I START?

It is obvious, but don't purchase an expensive laser cutter or 3-D printer until you have mastered at least the basics of CAD drawing or you will only be able to

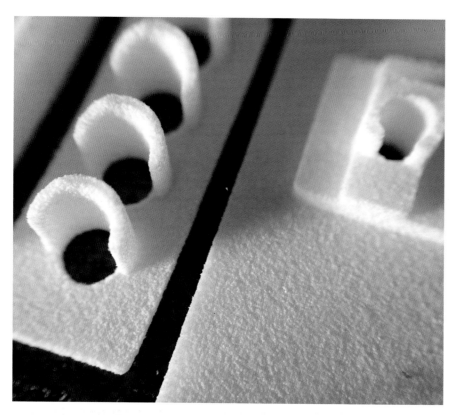

Shapeways 3 D prints of the 4mm signal head in extreme close-up (the signal-head back plate is 9mm wide). When using a 3-D print bureau it is important to note carefully their minimum thickness for walls and so on, which will vary from material to material.

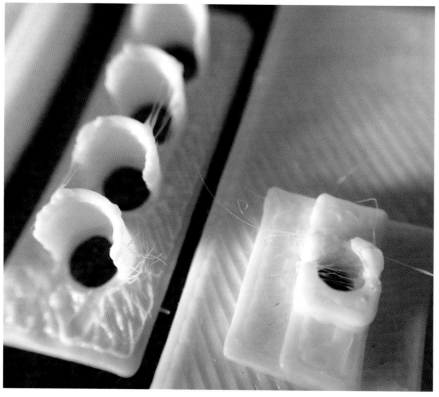

Makerbot Replicator2 prints of the 4mm signal head in extreme close-up.

produce what others have designed. This will prove both frustrating and very limiting.

Most recent Windows computers and laptops will load and run Sketchup Make, the free CAD program described in this book. The larger the screen, the better, and you will need a two-button mouse with a scroll wheel. A Macintosh version of the program is available, but note that this book describes and illustrates only the Windows version, and on the Macintosh the program may have a different look and feel.

There are hundreds of free 'how to' videos on line, covering every aspect of using Sketchup Make. However, be aware that some will describe features only available in the professional, and not the free version!

Given the computer and at least an ability to draw basic shapes in Sketchup, then a reasonably priced 3-D printer is a good starting point. At the time of writing (2016) £250 should suffice, and this book shows examples of two such printers. These are perfectly adequate for prototyping and producing useful small items that do not require a very fine surface finish.

If you do find your first machine useful, then progression to a larger 3-D printer or laser cutter is possible. Also dotted around the country are fab labs, makerspaces and hackerspaces, where you can potentially use 3-D printers and laser cutters for free, enabling you to 'try before you buy' and to obtain some helpful advice.

I suggest you have a quick browse through the laser cutting and 3-D printing sections of this book to see what can be produced on these machines before setting up your computer and tackling the CAD section. By the time you have seen the many examples in the last two sections, you will appreciate the basics that must be learnt step by step.

Once you have mastered the basics and are producing your own window frames, fencing and so on, do be prepared for a steady stream of club members approaching you with a rough sketch and the query 'Could you just make some of these for me on your machine please?'

Fab Labs, Makerspaces and Hackerspaces

Fab labs, makerspaces and hackerspaces are organizations that offer free access to help and equipment.

All fab labs (fabrication laboratories) are likely to have laser cutting and 3-D printing facilities, and allow 'community' use of their facilities for free, or for a small charge to cover material and running costs. See their website for up-to-date information, and to find out if they have a centre near you (www.fablabsuk.co.uk).

Makerspaces and hackerspaces are other organizations based in the community and are for people interested in making things. Their resources vary from group to group. See www.hackspace.org.uk.

For makerspaces, use an internet search engine to find one near you.

These are all good places to see these machines working and to get advice from those who use them.

Finally, I would add that this book is not an academic thesis, nor is it a comprehensively researched piece of writing covering all the intricacies and finer points of CAD, laser cutters and 3-D printers – rather, it is based on my own experience of using these machines to produce items for my own model railway. As such, I have concentrated on the practical issues you are likely to encounter in using either of these technologies to make things that are useful models.

Learning CAD and using these machines is about practice. It may seem daunting at first, but after you have produced your first few items, some of which would have been either impossible, or very difficult to produce by hand, you will find a whole new hobby in making unique and professional-looking items for your model railway. You will not simply be putting together kits, but making the kits themselves.

Good luck with the learning!

PART I: CAD

1 INTRODUCING CAD

In this section of the book you will install Sketchup Make and the required plug-ins, and learn the basic skills to begin drawing with it. You can refer to this section when drawing the 'Projects' items for both the laser and 3-D printer.

The book has been checked against the version of Sketchup Make (2016) available at the date of publication, but it is the nature of computer software to be constantly updated so you may find some of the details below have changed in the version of Sketchup Make that you are using.

CAD (computer-aided design) is the process of drawing things on the computer screen. Think of it as a word processor for drawings. The CAD program makes it possible to draw rectangles, circles and other shapes to exact dimensions in order to build up the design of a model on the screen. Adding, deleting and altering parts of the

drawing are catered for, as well as saving the drawing so it can be reloaded. The drawing can also be saved in the file formats required for laser cutting or 3-D printing.

Just as you save a file from a word processor which includes details of typeface, bold sections and other formatting, so the CAD file saves information about the drawing. You do not need to know any technical details about the file format, just which type(s) to use. These are explained in the relevant sections of this book.

Before you can use the programs you must install them to your computer. The programs are available from the internet, so you must also have access to the internet to download them, or download them to a memory stick to install from that. If downloading and installing programs is not your thing, then you may have to ask a computer-literate friend for help.

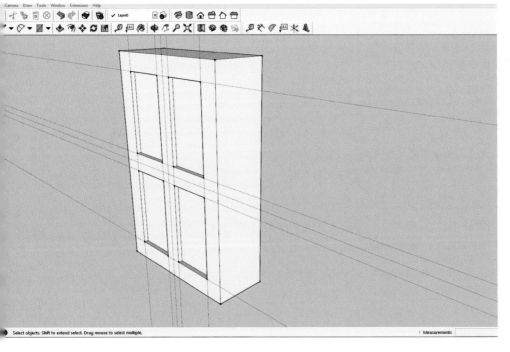

The Sketchup Make drawing screen with a 3-D (solid) object being drawn, in this case a wardrobe as part of the series of furniture items explained later in Part III, the 3-D section of this book. The icons (small pictures) at the top of the screen are used to select different shapes, measuring tools and lines, and so on, to produce the CAD drawings.

2 INSTALLING AND SETTING UP SKETCHUP MAKE

It is important that Sketchup Make is set up to load and run with the template as outlined in this book, otherwise you will be confused when your screen looks nothing like my examples.

These instructions relate to the Windows version of Sketchup Make 2016 only. The Macintosh version may have alternative icons and methods of working, though the basic procedures will be similar.

If you have Sketchup Make 2016 already installed on your computer, then you can skip to the next section, 'Setting up Sketchup Make 2016 for Use'.

NOTE: The current version of Sketchup Make requires Windows 7 or later on a PC, however Sketchup 2014 will run on Windows XP machines, and can still be found at the time of writing on the internet for download from Sketchup's official web site. Note that Sketchup 2014 may not look exactly like the version illustrated in this book.

Browse for the latest version of Sketchup Make and find the download screen. You may need to go to the Products menu and select Sketchup Make. These instructions refer to Sketchup Make 2016, and may differ for later versions. They are valid for both 2-D laser cutting and 3-D printing.

At various stages Windows asks for permission to alter your computer to continue you must give it by selecting 'yes'.

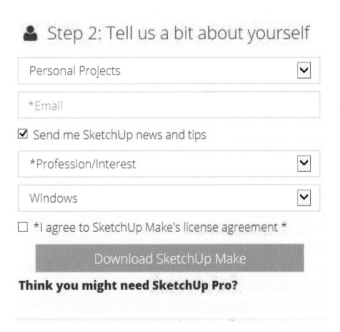

Main download screen of Sketchup Make 2016.

Complete the information boxes as required.

Click on Download, then 'run' once downloaded. Your computer may ask if it is OK to install. Click 'Yes'.

Complete the Setup Wizard using the defaults (unless you require otherwise).

SETTING UP SKETCHUP MAKE 2016 FOR USE

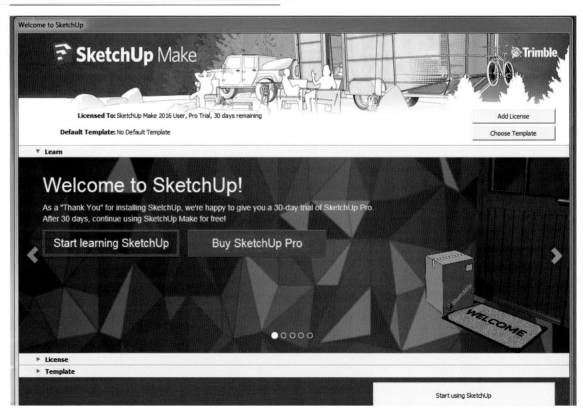

The first time you run Sketchup Make it will ask you to select a template.

Now use *Select a Template...*

... *and choose 'Architectural Design – Millimetres'*

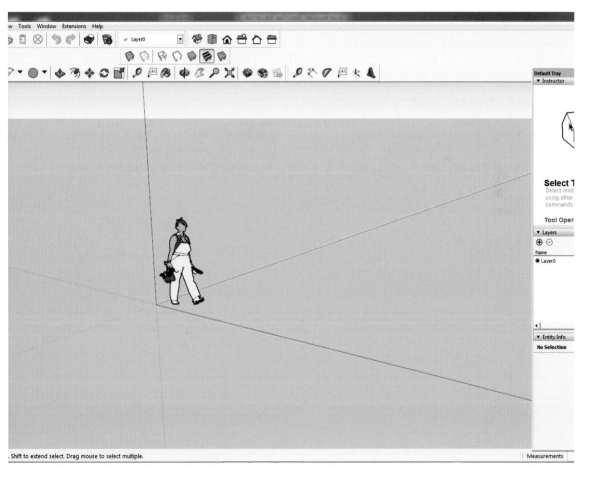

The opening screen should look like this.

SETTING UP A DEFAULT TEMPLATE

Before you begin drawing it is important that your screen looks like those I have illustrated in this book. Sketchup allows the screen to be configured in many ways to suit both beginners and professional users.

The steps opposite and below enable you to set up the screen to match the ones shown in this book and save it as a 'Laser3-D Template'. This will make it easier for you to follow my instructions.

Look at the bottom of the screen. If the Dimensions/Measurements box (it can be called either) is not showing, then add it on via the View>Toolbars menu, and tick the Measurements box.

Select Window >Default Tray, and select Layers and Instructor as shown opposite (you may have to re-select the menu after each change). The Instructor shows you how to use each tool as it is selected. The Layers menu is used in the Advanced CAD chapter at the end of Part I.

Select the figure (hold the left mouse key and pull a rectangle around to include the figure top left to bottom right) as shown: it will turn blue. Tap the Delete key to remove the figure.

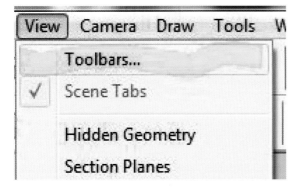

ABOVE: *Select the Toolbars option from the View menu (printed as 'View >Toolbars' throughout the book).*

RIGHT: *Ensure only the following toolbars are ticked:*
* Construction; * Getting Started; * Layers;
* Standard; * Views.

Scroll down the list to see all the options. This determines which icons are visible at the top of the screen. Once chosen, click on Close.

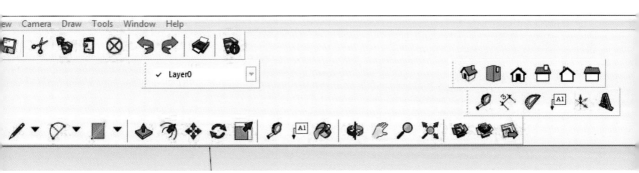

The icons as they first appear. You can move each set of icons by hovering with your mouse pointer over the left-hand end of the set and obtaining a cross. Hold the left mouse button down to move the group of icons. Use this technique to move the icons to the positions shown in the next screen shot.

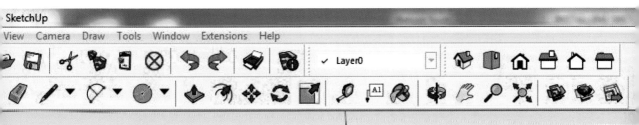

Your icons should now look like the ones above. This will make it easier to follow the instructions throughout the rest of the book.

The Tray option determines what you see down the right-hand side of your Sketchup screen. To begin with you only need two, Layers and Instructor.

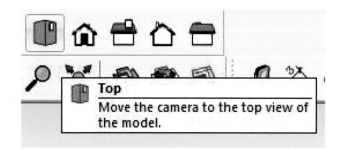

Top
Move the camera to the top view of the model.

Find the house icon above (the second house from the left) and click on it. This puts the 'view' into 'Top-Down' view. We will begin most of our drawings in this top-down view.

BELOW: *Your opening screen. Your screen should look like the one above with icons along the top and Instructor and Layers menus down the right-hand side. Only two axes (red and green) are shown, as you are in top-down view.*

You should see the red and green axis in the centre of your screen as shown. The third, blue axis in this view is coming out of the screen directly towards you. 3-D drawings have three axes: left, right and up/down. Do not confuse these axes with lines you have drawn – they are there as guides only.

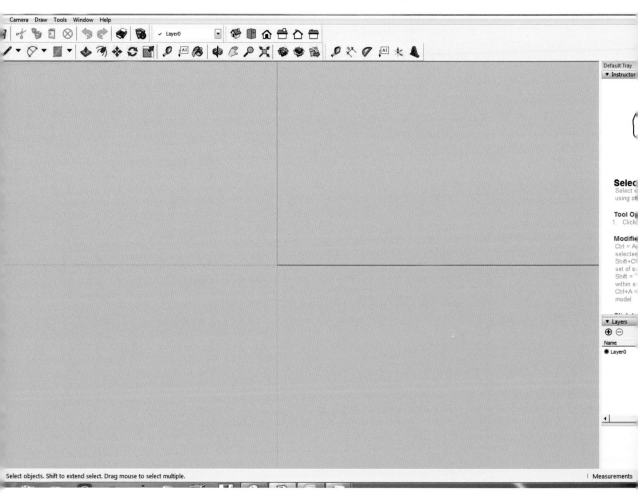

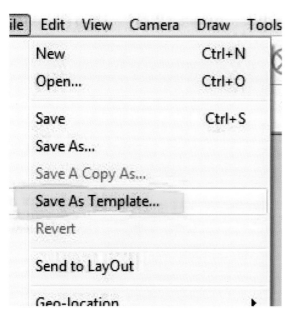

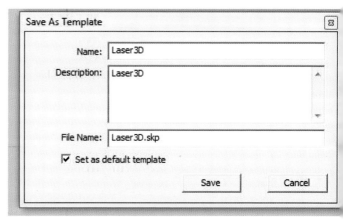

Laser3-D set as your template. Ensure that 'Set as default template' is ticked.

installs the .STL plug-in, but the one from the Extension Warehouse (see below) can be easier to use.

Having set the screen up as you require it, you must use the 'Save As Template' option from the 'File' menu (File >Save As Template).

Enter your template name as Laser3-D, and enter this also in the Description box as shown. 'Set as default template' is ticked. Click on 'Save'.

Close Sketchup Make and re-run it using the Choose a Template option, and select Laser 3-D Template before clicking on Start Using Sketchup to check you have your opening screen set up as described above (select 'Yes' if you get a Windows user account message). This should be in Top-Down view, with the Instructor and Layers menus to the right of the screen. Ensure you have the Laser3-D Template selected each time you run Sketchup. Normally this will load by default.

If the 'Laser3-D Template' is not there, then you need to repeat this section.

INSTALLING PLUG-INS

Plug-ins in Sketchup Make are additional pieces of computer code which enable Sketchup to do extra things.

For 3-D printing install the .STL plug-in, as described next.

For laser cutting skip the next section and go to the .DXF plug-in installation instructions. Bizarrely this also

INSTALLING THE .STL PLUG-IN FOR 3-D PRINTING

If you are only ever going to use Sketchup Make for 3-D drawing and printing, then install only this plug-in. There are a few steps to follow to install the plug-in.

NOTE: You need access to the internet in order to access the Extension Warehouse and install this plug-in.

RIGHT: *From the Window menu select Extension Warehouse (Window >Extension Warehouse).*

From the 'Top Extensions' list choose Sketchup STL. This is usually at the top, but you may have to search for it using the search box at top left.

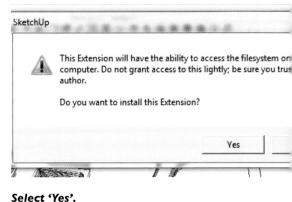

Select 'Yes'.

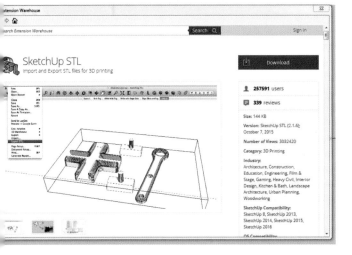

Select 'Download'. At some point you may also get a screen with 'Install' shown. Select it and click 'Yes' to it.

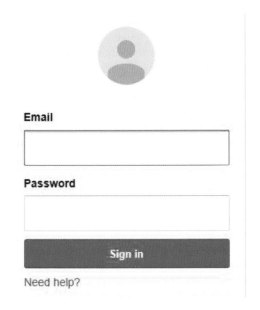

You may need to sign in or create a Google account to use the plug-in with Sketchup Make.

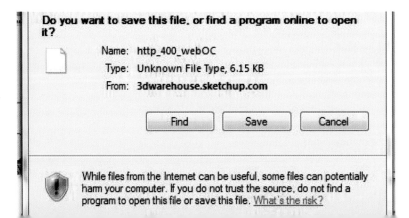

Click 'Save' to save this file in your Downloads folder on your computer.

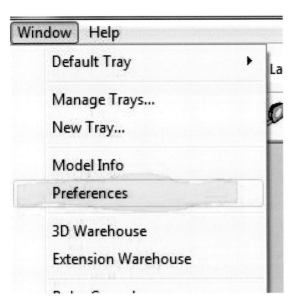

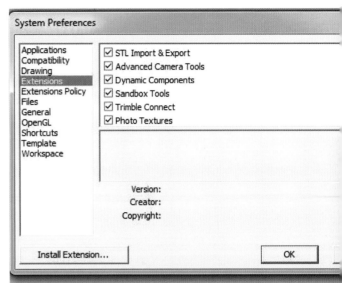

Run Sketchup Make and select 'Preferences' under the Window menu.

Select 'Extensions' in the left-hand menu, and then 'Install Extension' at bottom left.

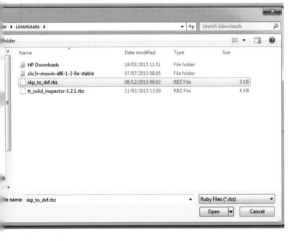

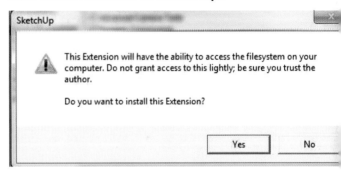

Select 'Yes' to install.

Navigate to your Downloads folder and select the file just saved. It will have an .rbz extension.

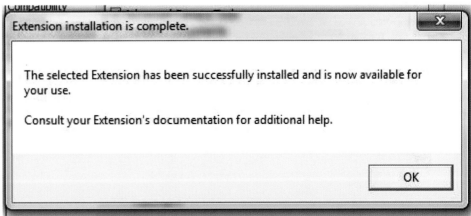

Successful installation.

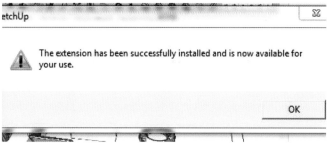

ABOVE: *You should eventually see this message to indicate success.*

RIGHT: *The Export STL option from the File menu confirms you have installed the .STL plug-in.*

To check you have successfully installed the >STL Export plug-in, go to the File menu and you should see 'Export STL'. This will be greyed out until you have drawn something.

USING THE EXPORT .STL FUNCTION FOR 3-D PRINTING

Always save your work frequently using the 'Save As' option from the File menu. This will be printed in this book as File >Save As >xxxxxx.skp, where 'xxxxx' is the filename. This saves your entire Sketchup drawing in Sketchup format.

To export your file for 3-D printing you need to export it as an .STL file. Select the item(s) you wish to export (they turn blue), and then use the Export .STL option from the File menu, printed in this book as File >Export STL >xxxxx.stl, where 'xxxxx' is the file name.

You will see an Export Options box: choose Centimeters as your export unit, and ASCII as your file format.

INSTALLING THE .DXF PLUG-IN FOR LASER CUTTING

This plug-in is not required for 3-D printing. Installing this plug-in is slightly more involved as it is not currently available in the Extension Warehouse but has to be located on the internet. I have successfully used the following website:

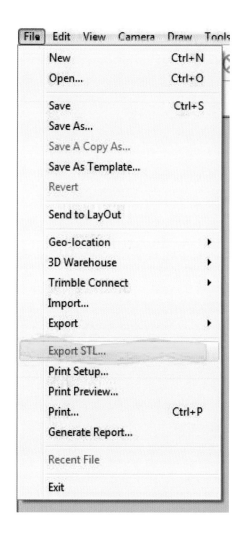

http://www.guitar-list.com/download-software/convert-sketchup-skp-files-dxf-or-stl

Then choose the file with the .rbz extension.

Alternatively, do a search for '.DXF plug-in for Sketchup Make', and choose one of the other variants. These plug-ins install as printer drivers and it is wise, therefore, to ensure your virus software is up to date prior to installing them. Also be aware that some of the download sites try to install other applications at the same time, some of which are less than desirable!

Download the relevant plug-in and save it in your 'Downloads' folder (ensure it is the correct version for your version of Sketchup Make) with an .rbz extension.

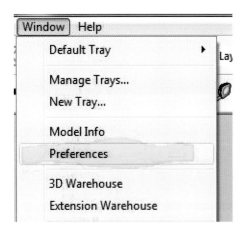

Run Sketchup Make and select 'Preferences' under the Window menu.

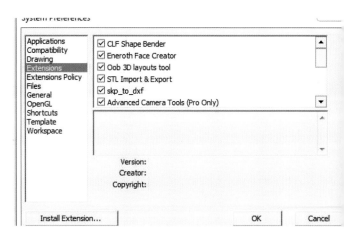

Select 'Extensions' in the left-hand menu and then 'Install Extension' at bottom left.

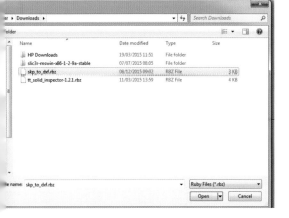

Navigate to your Downloads folder and select the file just saved. It will have an .rbz extension.

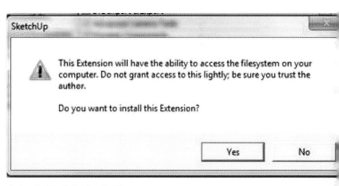

Select 'Yes' to install.

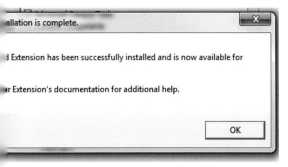

Successful installation.

A new option under the File menu. Note that in earlier versions of Sketchup this 'Export to DXF' or 'Export to STL' option appeared under the Tools menu.

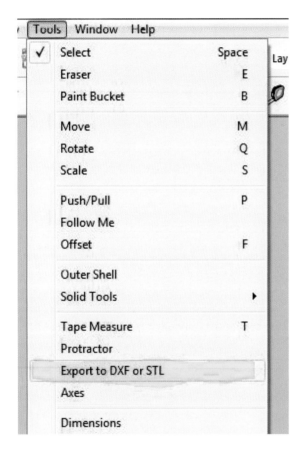

...It may also be under the Tools menu.

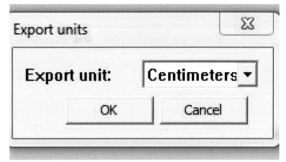

You will see an 'Export Options' box: choose 'Centimeters' as your export unit...

USING THE EXPORT .DXF FUNCTION FOR LASER CUTTING

Always save your work frequently using the 'Save As' option from the File menu. This will be printed in this book as File >Save As >xxxxxx.skp, where 'xxxxx' is the file name. This saves all your drawing in Sketchup format.

To export your file for laser cutting you need to export it as a .DXF file. Select the item(s) you wish to export (they turn blue), and then use the 'Export to DXF' or 'Export to STL' option from the File menu, printed in this book as File >Export to DXF >xxxxx. dxf, where 'xxxxx' is the file name.

Finally add your filename (ensure it has .dxf after it, as some early export programs did not put this in automatically). Add .dxf if required.

..and 'Lines' as the entities to export. The laser cuts along these lines.

3 INSTALLING AND USING NETFABB

Netfabb is only required for 3-D printing.

WHAT IS NETFABB?

Netfabb is a computer program capable of 'repairing' 3-D designs so they will 3-D print correctly. Simple designs will normally print perfectly well, but once designs become more complex, they can have small imperfections in them, perhaps where curved lines don't quite meet, leaving small 'holes' in your drawing. Once saved as an .STL file and sent to your printer, your printer 'slicing' software will not be able to understand it and you will get an error message – 'not solid', or 'unable to slice', or similar.

Netfabb can analyse and correct your 3-D drawings, filling in any small gaps and imperfections so that your printer slicing software can understand what to do.

The Basic Netfabb program is free. Search for Netfabb (www.netfabb.com) and download it to your computer.

USING NETFABB

After exporting your drawing from Sketchup as an .STL file, run Netfabb and open this file in Netfabb. You should see your drawing displayed. Click on it to select it – it turns green. The 'hole' in the box has been repaired and will now 3-D print as a solid box.

Click on the red cross ('Repair') to the right of the menu bar at the top of the screen.

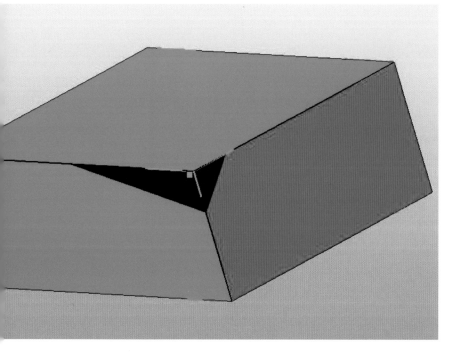

This box has been deliberately 'broken' by removing a corner. The walls of the box have no 'thickness' and would not 3-D print.

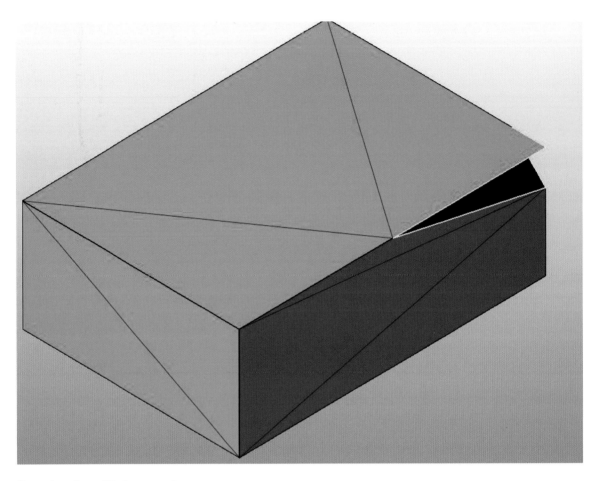

Your drawing will change colour.

Click on 'Automatic repair' (at the bottom left of the screen).

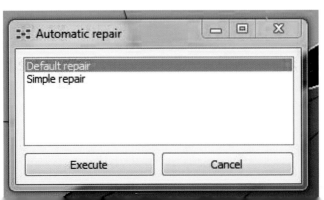

A box opens. Select 'Default repair'.

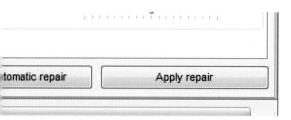

Click on 'Apply repair' at the bottom right of the screen.

A new box opens. Click on 'Remove old part'.

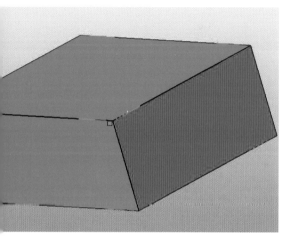

Your repaired box in green.

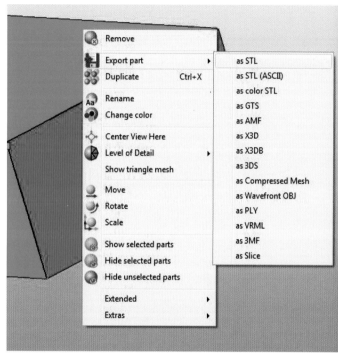

Right-click on your drawing and select 'Export part' and 'as STL'.

If you use the default Netfabb filename it will add some figures and '(repaired)' to your original filename. Since I run all my projects through Netfabb, I tend to click on my original filename and use that.

Note that sometimes Nettfabb will fill in a hole or opening that you intended to be there. I find that the sequence of drawing openings and holes sometimes has an effect on this. Also complex drawings where I have added and deleted items will also be 'over-repaired' by Nettfabb. In these circumstances you can try either printing without repairing your object with Nettfabb, or redrawing it using a different sequence.

4 2-D CAD BASICS

In this chapter you will learn the basics of drawing 'flat objects' with Sketchup; these basic skills are required for both laser cutting and 3-D printing. After completing this section you will have the skills to make the most of the laser cut examples in the section 'Laser Cutting Projects' in Part II.

Work your way through the instructions below, slowly and in order. Don't try to learn too much at once: several half-hour sessions can be better than a six-hour marathon. You will need to repeat the instructions from the beginning until you can draw the basic examples at the end without referring back to them.

These instructions assume you have the Sketchup Make program installed, and that the Laser3-D drawing template has been defined and saved as shown previously. Also that you are using a mouse with two buttons and a scroll wheel.

A mouse with two buttons and a scroll wheel. It is easier to use the scroll wheel if it has 'click points' as you move it, rather than just turning freely.

Obtaining More Help

If you are having difficulties understanding any of the drawing tools below, then try entering 'Sketchup Make (*problem*)' into your computer search engine. For example 'Sketchup Make: drawing circles' will bring up a host of tutorials and videos. Some of these can be helpful, *but* there are a number of issues you need to be aware of.

The Sketchup tutorial(s) shown may do the following:

• show a different version of Sketchup to yours
• be set up with different icons
• be in 3-D rather than 2-D view – or the reverse
• be adding complex features you really don't need yet
• confuse rather than clarify

There are hundreds of tutorials and videos on the internet showing how to use aspects of Sketchup and Sketchup Make. You will find them of most use once you have mastered the basics and when looking for better ways to do things.

There are also many books on Sketchup. Some describe the professional version, others are aimed at architects and other professionals. Even the beginners' guides will illustrate 3-D drawing (which is not required for laser cutting). I would advise a trip to a book shop so you can judge for yourself whether a particular title would help you progress

For laser cutting you do not need to progress to the 3-D drawing section, as all your drawings will be 2D and therefore flat.

If you get hopelessly lost at any stage then it is best to simply close the program and re-run it, when it should re-load the 'Laser3-D' template, your 'opening screen'.

As you select an icon, the 'Instructor' gives help on its functions. Further help is available at the bottom of each Instructor page if you are connected to the internet.

NOTE: Throughout this book the text showing you *what to do* is printed in bullet points, with the various tools (icons) that are used in bold, below the diagram showing it being done. Look at the photograph or diagram and read the text underneath it first before attempting the procedure or activity.

Run Sketchup Make 2016, and by default it should now load the Laser3-D Template set up after installing it. Your screen should have a Top-Down view with the Instructor and Layers menus to the right.

Help at the Pointer

Point to an icon (small picture) at the top of the screen: keep your mouse pointer still, and a context-sensitive help panel will explain what the icon does. As you select different icons by clicking on them, your pointer changes shape to reflect the icon you have currently selected. Try selecting some (left mouse click), then move the pointer down to the work area to see the effect.

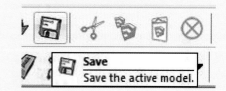

Each icon at the top of the screen has its own function. For laser cutting and 3-D printing you will not use them all.

RECTANGLES

To draw a rectangle, select the Rectangle tool from the Shapes menu as above and, holding down your left mouse button, drag a rectangle top left to bottom right. Try drawing a few rectangles and even overlapping them. Note how they are depicted in light blue with lines for overlapping rectangles.

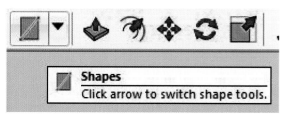

The Shapes menu shows which shape is currently selected. Click on the small 'down' arrow to switch to other shapes such as a circle.

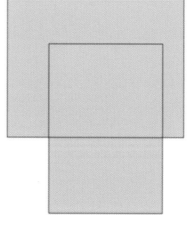

Overlapping rectangles drawn using the Rectangle tool.

Rectangles are used so often that a keyboard shortcut is available: just tap the letter 'R' on your keyboard.

SELECT

• Click on the Select tool – it shows a normal mouse pointer. To select a line just drawn, point to it and click the left mouse button. The line will turn blue

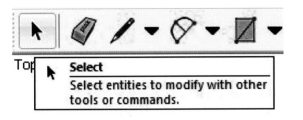

The Select tool allows you to select parts of your drawing.

• To select an area or object, for example a rectangle or circle just drawn, click above the top left of the object, hold down the left mouse button, and drag to below the bottom right. The object must be inside the 'selected' rectangle. Lines turn blue and areas dotted blue when selected

All the horizontal lines of the two left-hand rectangles have been selected by clicking on them (hold Shift whilst selecting to select more than one item at a time), whilst the entire right-hand rectangle has been selected by pointing above the top left of it, and dragging it to below the bottom right with the left mouse key held down. This draws a 'Selection Box' around the object, which then turns blue and dotted.

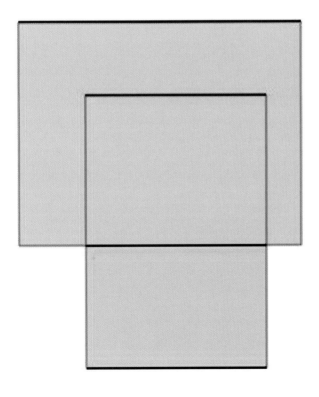

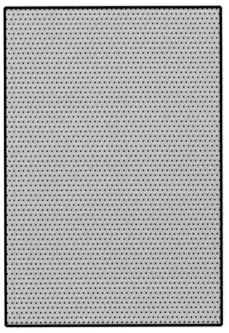

Overlapping rectangles with horizontal lines and right-hand rectangle 'selected'.

- To de-select, simply click anywhere on the background
- To delete selected lines/areas, select them with the Select tool (they turn blue) and tap the Delete key on your keyboard

Practise drawing some more rectangles and selecting just some sides or entire rectangles. Delete parts, or all of them.

The spacebar on your keyboard can also be used to select the Select tool.

ZOOMING IN/OUT

Use the scroll wheel on your mouse to zoom in and out when the Select tool is selected (your pointer is a pointer!). *Do not move your mouse whilst zooming.* Try drawing some more rectangles and zoom in and out on them. Note that you always zoom in/out at the pointer position. Draw a rectangle at top right, and should you wish to centre it, place your pointer bottom left and zoom out, the rectangle will become smaller and more central. Now place your pointer inside the rectangle and zoom in: it will become larger but stay centred. Practice makes zooming and moving objects around the screen easier.

Note that zooming in and out with the scroll wheel does not change the dimensions of the actual object, just its size on the screen. It enables small fine details to be viewed full screen if required.

CIRCLES

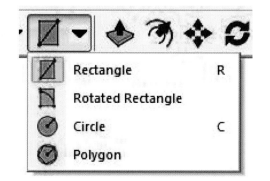

The Shapes drop-down menu allows a choice of rectangle and circle shapes.

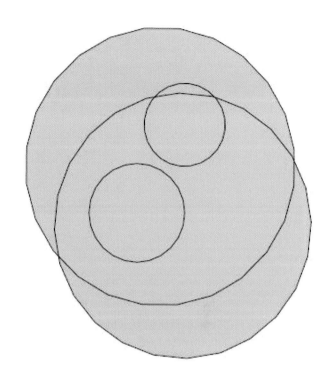

Overlapping circles.

OVERLAPPING CIRCLES

- Use the drop-down menu by the Rectangle symbol (the small down arrow) to select the Circle tool. Your pointer will change to a small circle shape
- To draw a circle, click on where you would like the centre to be, then hold down the left mouse button and drag it to the size required. Draw a few overlapping circles as shown. Try selecting and deleting some

Circles in Sketchup are always made up of straight lines and default to just twenty-four sides. Later you will learn how to change this.

Circles are used so often that a keyboard shortcut is available: just tap the letter 'C' on your keyboard.

LINES

There are two ways of drawing a line and it is worth understanding them both.

- Select the Lines tool (the pencil shape)

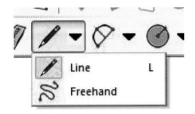

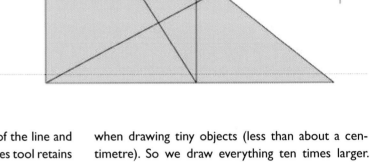

ABOVE: *The Lines tool menu. Your options are straight lines or freehand. For all our drawings we will need the Straight Lines tool, shown as a pencil above.*

RIGHT: *Lines. Note how the enclosed areas are tinted light blue.*

- The first way is to click at the start of the line and click at the end. Done this way the Lines tool retains its function and you can click on several points and lines will be draw between them. Click on Select or Escape to stop drawing
- The second way is to hold the left mouse button down at the start of the line and drag the line to the point where you want it; then release the mouse button and the Lines tool stops drawing

Try drawing several lines. Note how Sketchup tries to align lines with the axis – vertical and horizontal – and with other lines as you draw. This makes line drawing easier to do when drawing a complex model. This is called 'inference' by the program's authors. Also if your lines make an enclosed area, triangle or multi-sided, Sketchup colours the inside of the area light blue.

The Lines tool can be selected from your keyboard using the 'L' key.

DIMENSIONS (X 10)

So far you have drawn without reference to size. To draw objects to an actual size in Sketchup is easy, but it was devised originally for drawing buildings and engineering items that are much larger than the average model railway item, and it gets confused when drawing tiny objects (less than about a centimetre). So we draw everything ten times larger. When we save our work there is a really easy way of scaling everything down again – see under the 'Saving Your Work' heading later in this chapter.

Suppose we require an item to be 25 x 4.5mm: then simply add a nought and/or move the decimal point, and draw it 250 x 45mm.

- Select the Rectangle tool (under the Shapes drop-down menu) and draw a rectangle, any size, with the mouse, and you will see its dimensions are shown in the Dimensions box at bottom right
- *Immediately* – before touching any other key or moving the mouse – enter the dimension required (for example 250, 45 – just as numbers separated by a comma) into the Dimensions box (remember this is x 10), and tap the Enter key on your keyboard. The rectangle will change shape to reflect the dimensions entered
- You may then need to zoom in to the rectangle (best done with the pointer inside the rectangle) by holding down the scroll wheel on your mouse and moving it
- Try doing similar with lines and circles. They only require one number, and for circles this is the radius, not the diameter

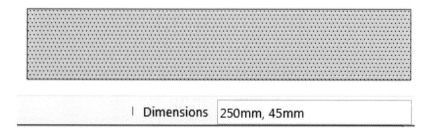

| Dimensions | 250mm, 45mm |

Rectangle drawn to specific dimensions in the box at the bottom of your screen. Sketchup adds the mm to the numbers. For circles the number is the radius, not the diameter! Note the Dimensions box is also called 'Measurement' or 'Length', depending on which tool you have selected.

It is really important that you master the Dimensions box in Sketchup as it allows you to draw items of an exact size, and move objects to precise positions. Practise with all the shapes learnt so far. Draw the shape and lines, and *immediately* enter the dimension required into the Dimensions box, then tap the Enter key. For rectangles, two numbers are required separated by a comma; for circles and lines just one number, then tap the Enter key on your keyboard.

Immediately after tapping the Enter key you can change the number(s) by entering it again and tapping Enter. Try it. Remember throughout always to draw x 10 larger than you actually require.

BETTER CIRCLES AND POLYGONS

Sketchup draws circles with straight lines. It defaults to just twenty-four, but you can change this:

- Select the Circle tool from the Shapes drop-down menu
- *Immediately* after selecting the Circle tool you will see a number twenty-four in the Dimensions box (bottom right). Change this to the number of lines you require for circles – I generally use ninety-six. Remember to tap the Enter key to confirm your change after entering the ninety-six

This stays at ninety-six until you re-run the program. Your circles, particularly large ones, will now look smoother on screen and when cut out or 3-D printed.

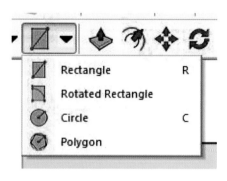

The circle and polygon menu.

The number of sides of polygons can be determined in a similar way.

MEASURING

The Tape Measure tool draws dotted guidelines enabling you to place items exactly. The guidelines can be placed exactly using the Dimensions box just described.

- Begin by drawing a rectangle 500 x 200mm using the Rectangle tool and adding the dimensions into the Dimensions box (and tap the Enter key)
- Now zoom in (scroll wheel) until the rectangle nearly fills the screen. This will take some practice! Remember the screen always zooms in and out from the cursor position
- Select the Tape Measure tool, and point to the left-hand rectangle edge until you obtain a small red square (a small box appears at the pointer position – 'On Edge') at the pointer position. This indicates that the Tape Measure tool has selected this line

Tape Measure Tool

Measure distances, create guide lines or points, or scale the entire model.

The Tape Measure looks like... a tape measure!

• Hold down the left mouse key and drag to the right. You can now move a dotted line to the right. This is the guideline. With the dotted line to the right of the original, let go of the left mouse button and enter '50' into the Dimensions box (bottom right) and tap Enter on your keyboard. The dotted line should move 50mm from the left-hand edge of the rectangle

• Repeat the process, drawing guidelines 50mm from the right-hand edge and also top and bottom as shown.

To obtain a guideline actually on another line such as the rectangle edge, double-click when pointing to it with the Measuring tool.

Try marking out other guidelines on the rectangle. For example, to find the centre draw two guide lines, either from opposite corners (small green circle – end point – at the pointer position), or along from the centre of the sides (blue circle – midpoint). Practise using these guidelines to draw more rectangles and as the centre of circles.

Try your own variations, adding rectangles, lines and circles to make several new shapes. Delete and add new lines, rectangles and circles. These are the

By selecting each side of the rectangle in turn and using the Measuring tool you have a rectangle with guide lines 50mm in from each edge.

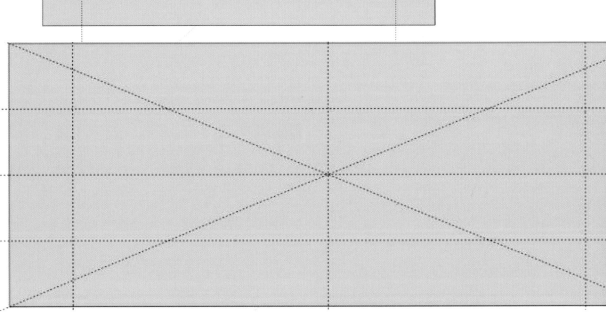

Guidelines to find the centre of the rectangle, and guidelines along the centrelines.

building blocks of all your drawings in Sketchup so they are worth practising until you are familiar with them and ready to move on to more advanced techniques.

You can also tap 'T' on your keyboard to change to the Tape Measure tool.

UNDO/REDO

The Undo and Redo arrows allow you to do just that – to undo a previous action or series of actions, or redo them. Do a drawing consisting of several features – rectangles, circles and so on – and then try the Undo and Redo icons.

The Undo and Redo icons allow you to correct mistakes as you draw.

MOVE

- By using the Select tool to select just one line of a rectangle you can move just that line and the rectangle will stretch or get smaller
- By holding down the arrow keys immediately after selecting the Move tool, you can move in the direction of the axis as follows: up arrow key = blue axis; left arrow key = green axis; right arrow key = red axis

The Move icon allows you to move selected items (they turn blue when selected) around the drawing.

Practise drawing some objects and moving them around the screen. Note that in 2-D mode (Top-Down view) the blue arrow moves the item in and out in the direction of yourself.

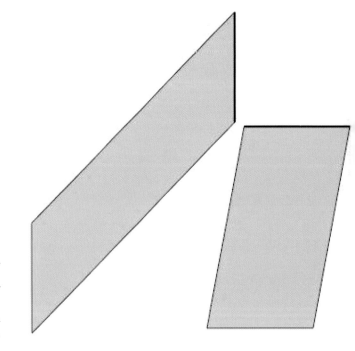

Two rectangles with the top lines selected and moved to produce parallelograms. Selecting whole objects moves them en masse.

MOVE AND COPY (MOVE+)

Being able to copy greatly speeds up the drawing of models that have repeated shapes such as awning boards, fencing, window openings.

- Use the Rectangle tool to draw a rectangle 600 x 400mm and give it a pointed end (any size) with the Line tool as shown
- Remember to use the Tape Measure tool to find the centreline of the rectangle, and to mark the bottom of the point. Use the Line tool to draw the point
- Select the entire object (Select tool, drag from top left to bottom right). It should be light blue
- Now select the Move tool. The cursor will change shape to reflect this. Tap the Ctrl key on your keyboard to get a small + by the Move cursor. This indicates the object is to be copied when moved

By copying the object to the right by the width of the object, using the Dimension box, an awning edge can be drawn.

- Click in the centre of the object, and holding your left mouse button down, move the object slightly to the right
- Enter 600 into the Dimensions box and tap the Enter key (the width of the object), and it should be copied to the position shown above. If not, click on Undo and try again
- *Immediately* after the copy (Move +Ctrl key) and Dimensions box number (600) has been input, enter *10 into the Dimensions box and the copy will be done ten times. (*25 would have copied it twenty-five times)

Awning edges, fencing, brickwork and so on, can be drawn very quickly using this technique. The sequence is to copy the object by a set amount as input into the Dimensions box, and immediately put a * and the number of copies required.

Throughout the rest of the book I shall use Copy (Move+) to describe this process of tapping the Ctrl key with the Move tool.

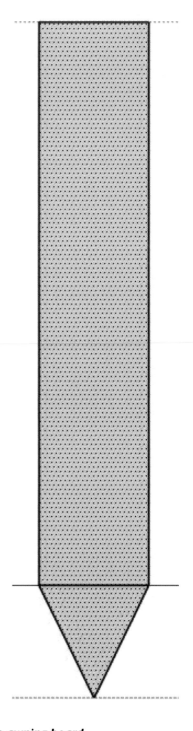

A single awning board.

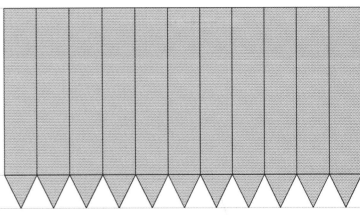

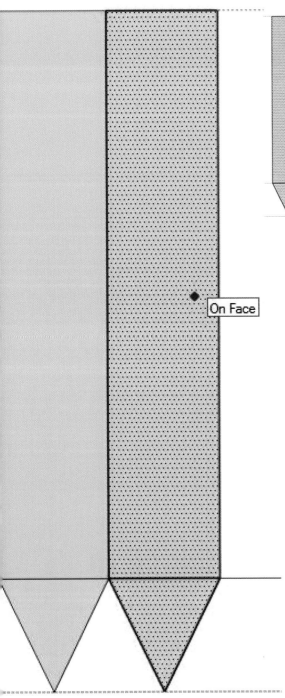

On Face

Object copied to the right.

Repeat copies are easy in Sketchup once the Move+ (Copy) command has been mastered. Here we have our finished awning.

SAVING YOUR WORK

At each stage of drawing you need to save your work using the File menu Save As option (shown from now on as File >Save As >Filename.skp. This will save your entire drawing in Sketchup format .SKP file so you can re-load it at a later date.

2-D CAD BASICS

You have now covered all the basics required to begin drawing the first examples in Part II: Laser Cutting. If an example states you need to draw it, then you must also have worked through the further skills described in the last chapter of Part I '2-D AND 3-D Advanced CAD'.

For 3-D printing you must now also get to grips with 3-D drawing, described in the next chapter '3-D CAD Basics'.

KEYBOARD, ICONS AND MOUSE REFERENCE

Bookmark this section if you require a reminder of how to use the icons and mouse. Note that some are only used for 3-D drawing for 3-D printing.

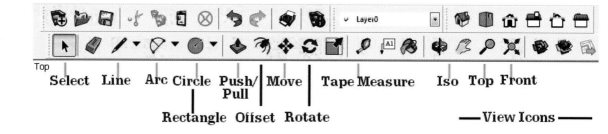

Top

Select Line Arc Circle Push/ Move Tape Measure Iso Top Front
Pull

Rectangle Offset Rotate ——View Icons——

Basic Sketchup icons.

Throughout the book I have used bullet point lists where input is required on the drawing, with the various tools (icons) in bold. For example:

• Use the Select tool to select the object
• With the Rectangle tool draw a rectangle 400 x 500mm

KEYBOARD AND ICONS

The following describes the function of each icon (with the keyboard shortcut, if any, in brackets after each):

Select (Spacebar): Click on a single item to select it. Hold down Shift whilst selecting for multiple items. Drag a box to encompass an object to select it and all its parts.

Line (L): Draw a straight line.

Arc (A): When first selected, Dimensions box can be used to determine the number of sides in an arc: the default is only twelve. Ninety-six is a useful number of sides to give reasonably smooth arcs.
Draw an arc. Most used is the two-point arc. Click on one end of the arc, then the other, and 'pull' the arc into a curve. Dimensions box can be used to determine the amount of offset in the arc. Click again to fix the arc once it is finished.

Rectangle (R): Click on start, and drag to form rectangle. Dimensions box can be used to determine the exact size of the rectangle.

Circle (C): When first selected, Dimensions box can be used to determine the number of sides; the default is only twenty-four. Ninety-six is a useful number of sides to give reasonably smooth circles.
Click on the centre of the circle (it is always best to mark the centre with guides or lines) and drag away from centre. Dimensions box can be used to determine the exact radius.

Push/Pull (P): Pushes and pulls flat surfaces into 3-D solid shapes. Once selected, moving the Push/Pull tool over a suitable surface will turn that surface blue and dotted. Hold the left mouse button, and drag the surface in or out (forwards or backwards). Dimensions box can be used to determine the exact amount of push/pull.

Offset: Draws a line inside or outside a shape. Once selected, hovering over a suitable line displays a small red box and an 'on edge' message. Hold down the left mouse button, and drag inside or outside the shape to draw the offset line. Dimensions box can be used to determine the exact amount of offset. It is useful for drawing frames around irregular objects (for example, a frame for a window with a curved top).

Move/Copy (M): Select the object(s) you wish to move with the Select tool; it (they) should turn blue. Click on the Move icon and hold down the left mouse button to move the object(s). Dimensions box can be used to determine the exact amount of movement.

To copy an object, first select Move, then tap the Ctrl key to get the + symbol by the cursor.

Hold down the arrow keys to determine the direction of move/copy:

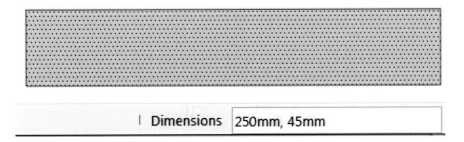

| Dimensions | 250mm, 45mm |

Dimensions box at the bottom of the screen (it can appear on either side).

Up arrow = blue axis
Left arrow = green axis
Right arrow = red axis

Rotate: Select the object(s) you wish to rotate. Select the Rotate tool and click on the rotation point. Move the cursor to the right or left, and pull it up or down to rotate. Dimensions box can be used to determine the exact amount of degrees of rotation.

Tape Measure (T): Used for measuring and drawing dotted guidelines. Once selected, hovering over a line displays a small red box. Hold the left mouse key down, and drag to draw a parallel guideline. Dimensions box can be used to determine the exact position.

DIMENSIONS BOX

This box is found at the bottom right of the screen and changes its name depending on the function you are performing: thus for lines it is Length, for circles Radius, and so on. It enables you to draw and place objects to an exact measurement. Throughout the book it is simply called the Dimensions box.

Simply enter your number(s) (two should be separated by a comma for rectangles) and tap the Enter key. Just numbers are required, Sketchup adds the mm.

VIEW ICONS (HOUSES)

This changes your view of the model.

Groups: To make a group, select it all, then right-click and select Make Group from the menu. To edit, double-click on Group. To close after editing, click anywhere on the background.

Layers: Add a Layer name in the Layers menu at the right of the screen. Assign a Group to a Layer by selecting Group and clicking on its name in the drop-down Layers menu at the top of the screen.

MOUSE USAGE

Zooming: Holding the mouse still, rotate the mouse wheel to zoom in and out from the position of the cursor.

Orbit: Hold the mouse wheel down and move the mouse to orbit the drawing and change your point of view, or use the Orbit icon.

Panning: As for orbiting, hold the mouse wheel down and also the Shift key whilst moving the mouse, or use the Pan icon.

SAVING AND EXPORTING YOUR WORK

Use the File menu and 'Save As' to save your drawing in Sketchup format. Always save in this format to enable drawings to be re-loaded into Sketchup.

Exporting for Laser: Select what you wish to export (it turns blue). Use the DXF plug-in to export to DXF. Choose Centimeters and Lines. Add .dxf to the end of the filename.

Exporting for 3-D Printer: Select what you wish to export (it turns blue). Use the STL plug-in to export to STL. Choose Centimeters as your scale.

5 3-D CAD BASICS

Before working through this chapter, you should be familiar with skills learnt in the last chapter, 2D CAD Basics. You can then do many of the drawings in the laser cutting sections of this book. Where new skills are needed for a particular model, I will introduce them as I describe the drawing for the model.

For 3-D printing, however, there is more: the wonderful world of 3-D drawing!

PUSH/PULL TOOL

Now you have mastered the basic skills of drawing 2D (flat) drawings in Sketchup, I am going to introduce you to the Push/Pull tool, which enables you to draw in 3-D.

Re-start Sketchup by re-running it. You are in Top-Down view.

• Use the Rectangle tool to draw a rectangle 1,000 x 800mm

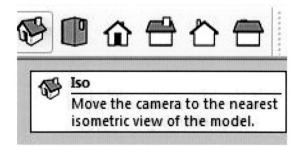

The Iso tool enables an isometric (3-D) view of the drawing.

Look at the house icons at the top of the screen. Note they are all different views of the same house: from left to right they are an Isometric (perspective or 3-D) view, a Top-Down view, and then the four side views. Clicking on these changes your view of

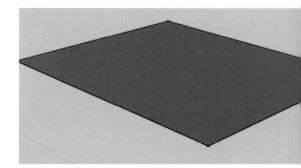

Your rectangle viewed in Iso (isometric) view.

your drawing. So far we have worked in Top-Down view, but we now need an Iso view.

• Click on the Iso view icon. Notice how your rectangle is now a different shape, as though you were looking at it from above one of its corners. This is a 3-D or perspective view

Now that we have an Iso view of our rectangle we can pull the top surface up, making a solid shape by using the Push/Pull tool.

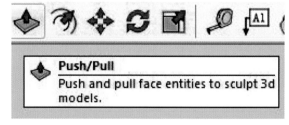

The Push/Pull tool enables you to push and pull surfaces into 3-D models.

• Select the Push/Pull tool and hover over the rectangle's surface. It turns into blue dots

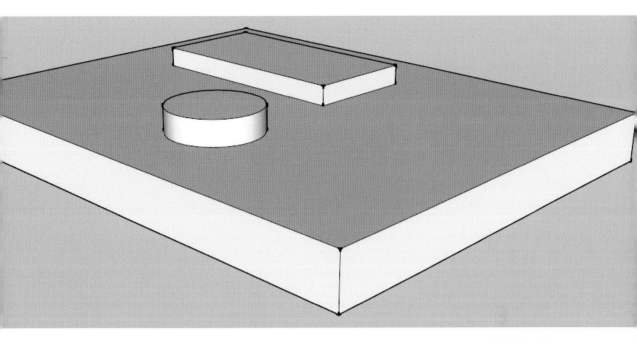

A rectangle and circle pulled up from the surface of the first rectangle. You have a solid 3-D object.

• Now, holding down the left-hand mouse button, slowly pull the surface of the rectangle upwards. Let go of the left-hand mouse button when you have pulled it up sufficiently

Draw another rectangle (any size) on the surface of the first. Pull this up a little.

Now draw a circle (any size) on the surface of either rectangle and pull this up.

The keyboard shortcut for the Push/Pull tool is 'P'.

Now try drawing your own lines, rectangles and circles on the surface of the shape above, and then use the Push/Pull tool to see what happens when you push or pull them.

MOVING AROUND 3-D DRAWINGS

Use your mouse scroll wheel to move your object around the screen:

• Move the scroll wheel backwards and forwards to Zoom

• Hold the scroll wheel down and move the mouse to Orbit
• Hold the scroll wheel and Shift key to Pan
• Click on the Iso icon for the standard perspective view

Try each of these on the basic shape just drawn.

ZOOM EXTENTS

The Zoom Extents icon as shown is really useful in making your drawing full size on the screen. This is especially helpful when working on multi-object drawings in different 3-D planes. Try it.

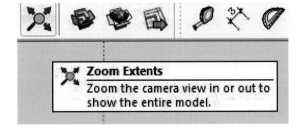

The Zoom Extents icon always makes your current drawing full size on the screen.

DIMENSIONED PUSH/PULLS

The next stage is to draw dimensioned objects in 3-D. Begin by closing down Sketchup and re-running it to get the default screen.

- Use the Rectangle tool to draw a 1,000 x 2,000mm rectangle (add 1000,2000 into the Dimensions box and tap Enter)
- Select the Iso view (perspective)
- With the Push/Pull tool, pull up the rectangle to 150mm. Use the Push/Pull tool and begin pulling up the surface, then enter 150 into the Dimensions box (and tap Enter) immediately after the pull-up. The surface should move so your shape is now 150mm thick.
- Select the Tape Measure tool, and begin by marking the top surface with guidelines as shown, 500m in from each end and 400mm in from each side. It does take a little practice to get used to drawing in 3-D
- Once you have the four guidelines drawn on the top surface, use the Rectangle tool to draw a rectangle to the guidelines
- With the Push/Pull tool, pull the rectangle on the surface up to a height of 100mm (Dimensions box 100 and tap Enter)
- Use the Tape Measure tool to draw two guidelines, 75mm down and 200mm along from the front corner
- Use the Circle tool to draw a 50mm radius circle centred where these guidelines cross
- With the Push/Pull tool, pull this circle out 100mm, as shown

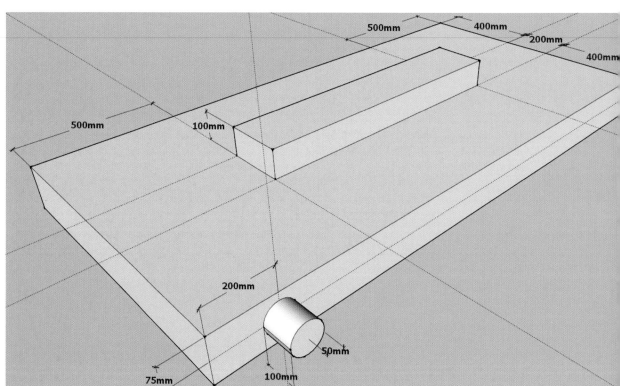

A basic shape with other, measured shapes drawn on it.

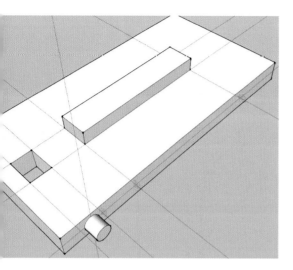

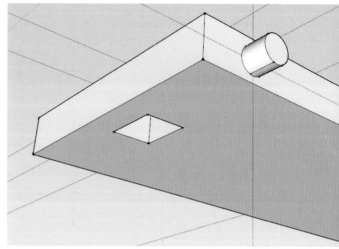

A square hole 'punched' in the object by pushing a rectangle down by the thickness of the object. Note that the guidelines highlighted in yellow look as if they cross on the edge of the object. In fact they don't: move the object around using the Orbit tool to see why. You need to view your drawings from different viewpoints to see exactly what you have drawn, and where.

The underside of the object showing the rectangular hole punched through it.

PUNCHING HOLES

To create a hole in an object, simply push a shape through it using the thickness of the object as the dimension.

• Take the shape just drawn and use the Tape Measure tool to add the two further guidelines, as shown above

• With the Rectangle tool, draw a rectangle using the new guidelines along with the existing ones, as shown above

• Use the Push/Pull tool to push the rectangle down 150mm. (Use the Push/Pull tool to begin pushing down the rectangle, then enter 150 in the Dimensions box and tap Enter.) Sketchup usually recognizes that if you push a shape into an object by the thickness of the object you require a hole. Move the object above around to check you have a square hole in it. Remember to use the Iso icon if you get lost! Note that sometimes Sketchup will draw the hole on the underside but leave a thin

'membrane' on the underside of the hole. This can usually be deleted.

Holes can be deleted by drawing across both their faces with the Lines tool, which creates a surface. The lines can then be deleted. Try it.

This technique of punching holes works for any shape drawn on the surface of the object, but only on flat objects. Try some more, including circular holes along the edge punched through the width (1,000mm) and length (2,000mm). Note that if your holes intersect, then they may fail, and you will need techniques more advanced than those described in this book to draw them (because you can't normally push/pull a curved surface).

CREATING A NEW SURFACE TO PUSH/PULL

Sometimes you need to tell Sketchup that you want to do something outside the 'normal' rules – for example, joining several posts together with a bar, as shown in the illustration. Begin by closing Sketchup and re-running it.

The stages in drawing (left to right) are as follows:

• Use the Rectangle tool to draw a rectangle 900,300

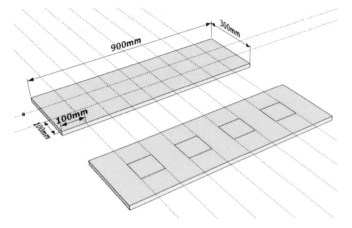

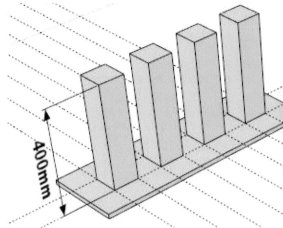

Stages in drawing the posts. Begin with the rectangle and guidelines.

Rectangles pulled up to 400mm.

- With the Push/Pull tool, pull the rectangle up to about 20mm (remember Iso view first)
- Use the Tape Measure tool to mark out a 100mm grid as shown
- Draw around each of the four squares produced by the guideline grid with the Rectangle tool
- With the Push/Pull tool, pull the first square up 400
- Double click on the other squares and they will be pulled up by a similar amount

- Use the Tape Measure tool to draw a line across the front face of your front post 100mm down
- Use the Lines tool to draw a line across the face of the front post using the guideline just drawn
- With the Push/Pull tool, try pushing this line back and see the result (left-hand post above)
- Undo (with the Undo icon) the push just done, and now try pushing with the Push/Pull tool – but after selecting the Push/Pull tool and *before* pushing, tap

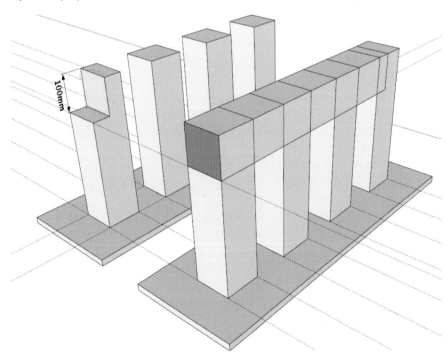

The difference between a 'normal' push (left), and a push after tapping the Ctrl key (right).

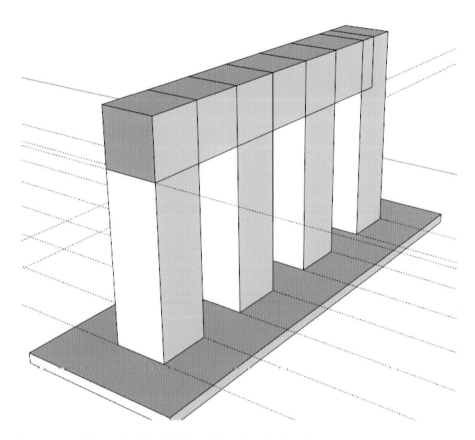

Horizontal bar created by using Push/Pull + (plus the Ctrl key).

the Ctrl key to get a + by the Push/Pull tool cursor: this indicates that you wish to create a new surface to push. Push to the centre of the far post (the right-hand post above)

You should now have a bar running between the posts.

Using the Push/Pull tool with the Ctrl key leaves the existing surface where it is and creates a copy to Push/Pull.

OFFSET TOOL

Sometimes you will need to draw a second line within a shape to make a frame, as, for example, when drawing a window with a curved top. The Offset tool allows you to do this.

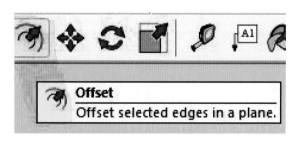

Icon for the Offset tool.

USING THE OFFSET TOOL TO DRAW A LINE WITHIN A SHAPE

The top shape shows how the Offset tool cursor has been positioned on the top line to show a small red box and the 'On Edge' box.

• Begin by re-running Sketchup to get your Laser3-D Top-Down opening screen

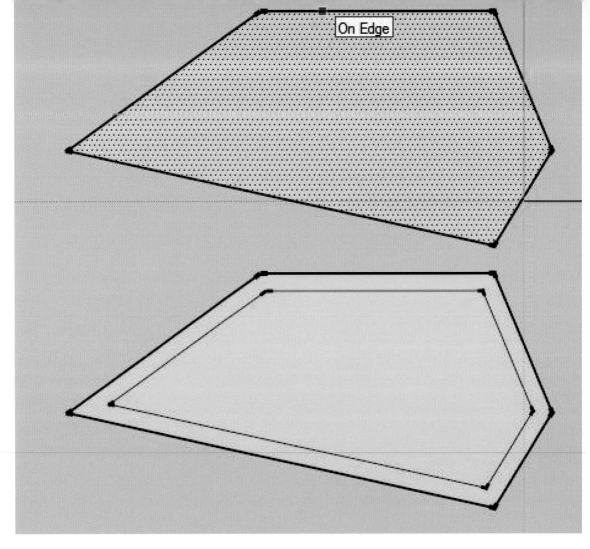

On Edge

Using the Offset tool to draw a line within a shape. The top shape shows how the Offset tool cursor has been positioned on the top line to show a small red box and the 'On Edge' box.

- With the Lines tool, try drawing several straight lines to enclose a space as above (the inside shape should turn blue)
- Select the Iso view icon and Zoom in to your shape(s)
- Select the Offset tool and hover over one of the lines to get a small red square and the 'On Edge' box
- Hold down the left mouse button and 'drag' the cursor inside the shape
- Enter the amount of offset required into the Dimensions box (in this case fifty). This will be the thickness of your border/frame
- You can now try the Push/Pull tool on this border to pull it up. These could be the walls of a house?

You now have all the skills required to begin the 3-D projects section! A good way to begin would be to draw and print the 3-D test pieces.

Where additional skills/knowledge of icons are required I have detailed these in the relevant section.

EXPORTING THE FILE FOR 3-D PRINTING

Use the File >Save As xxxxxx.skp option to save all your drawing in Sketchup format (where xxxxx is the filename).

Use File >Export STL, then Centimeters and xxxxxx.stl to save in .stl format for the 3-D printer (where xxxxx is the filename).

6 2-D AND 3-D ADVANCED CAD

Before tackling this section you should understand and have practised the commands in the two previous chapters, 2-D CAD Basics and 3-D CAD Basics (for 3-D printing). From now on I will assume that, for example, the instruction 'draw a rectangle 500 x 300mm with a 300mm diameter circle at its centre' makes sense to you, and that you know how to do it. If this causes you problems, please return to the 2-D CAD Basics chapter and re-do that section.

ROTATE

It is often useful to be able to rotate objects, and used with the Ctrl key as just described with the Move command, we can rotate and then copy that rotation as required. This is useful for spokes on wheels, window frames with arched tops and suchlike.

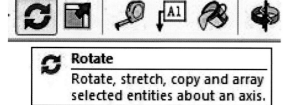

Use the Rotate tool to rotate objects, or items such as lines within objects.

• With the Rectangle tool draw a rectangle

The Rotate tool rotates the selected lines or objects from the centre of the protractor. The left-hand shape above illustrates what happens if just part of the rectangle is selected when rotating: the object distorts.

• Use the Select tool to select all your rectangle (it turns blue)

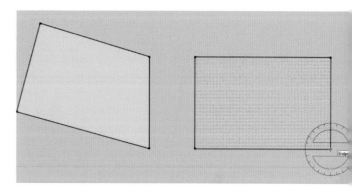

The protractor indicates that the Rotate tool has been selected. The right-hand rectangle will be rotated about its bottom right corner as it is all selected.

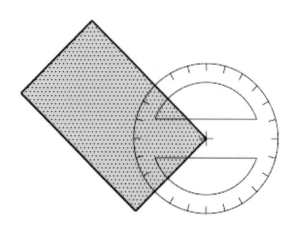

The rotated rectangle.

• Select the Rotate tool and click on one corner of the rectangle. This determines the point of rotation
• Click to the right or left of the protractor and then move the cursor up or down to rotate the object
• Entering a number (degrees) into the Dimensions box enables you to control the degree of rotation

ROTATE AND COPY (ROTATE+)

When working with circles it is important to know where the centre is. If drawn freehand, the centre disappears. The circle above is drawn from where the axes cross (red, blue and green lines when you first run Sketchup). If drawing elsewhere it is useful always to draw the centre point with two guidelines (or actual lines) *before* drawing the circle.

• Use the Circle tool to draw a circle centred on the intersection of the axes; it can be any radius
• Use the Lines tool to draw a line from the centre to the outside of the circle, as shown above
• Select this line so it turns blue

You are now going to copy the line twenty times around the circle (think bicycle spokes). The sequence is as follows:

• Select the Rotate tool and tap the Ctrl key on your keyboard to get a small + symbol by the cursor

(protractor). This indicates that the line should be copied and not just rotated
• Rotate the line 18 degrees by clicking with the left mouse button with the Rotate tool on the centre of the circle to locate rotation, then click again about halfway along the line and pull downwards to begin the rotation
• *Immediately* enter eighteen into the Dimensions box and tap the Enter key
• *Immediately* after tapping the Enter key to complete the number of degrees of rotation, enter *20 into the Dimensions box and tap Enter. The line rotation will be copied twenty times round the circle as shown

This repeated rotation can be very useful when drawing spokes on a wheel or complex rounded window frames.

I advise some practice on this with different shapes until you can do it without having to look at the sequence of instructions each time.

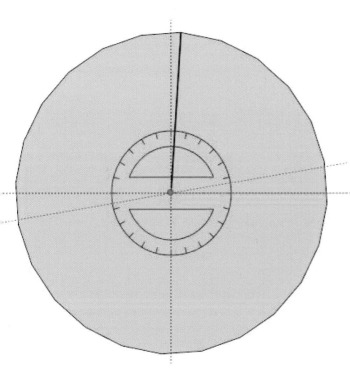

A circle with a line drawn from the centre.

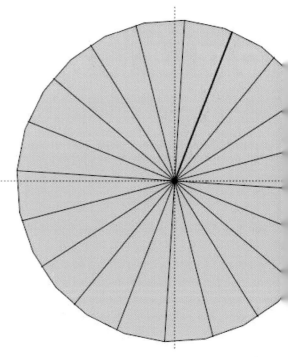

Here the line has been copied and rotated 18 degrees (using the Rotate tool, Ctrl, and the Dimensions box).

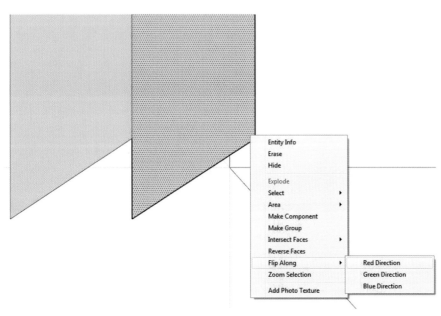

The Flip command is found by right-clicking on a selected object to get the menu shown above. You can Flip along the red, green or blue axis by holding down the relevant arrow key whilst flipping.

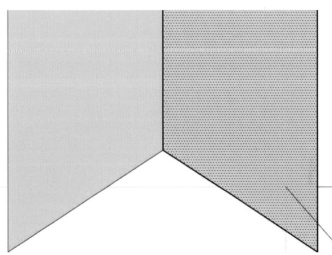

The right-hand side is flipped to make a perfect chimney stack part-fitting the roof apex, where both sides must be equal in size and shape.

FLIP

If you have an object which is the same on both sides, it can sometimes be useful to draw just one side, and copy it to the other (Move+) – then, with it still selected (or re-selected), right-click on it and from the menu presented, Flip it.

Here is part of a chimney stack being drawn. By Move+ (copying) an object and then right-clicking on it, a menu is revealed which allows, among others, you to Flip the object. Here the Red direction is chosen. Practise to find the Flip direction.

Even more time can be saved with more complex shapes. Try drawing the left-hand part of the chimney above (use your own dimensions) and using the Move+ (copy) and Flip commands.

SAVING YOUR WORK

In the next exercise there are several steps to a final drawing, and it is advisable to keep saving your work in case you make a mistake. If you save using the same filename you may find that you have saved your mistakes!

Saving Your Work

I use a simple method for saving files which enables me to go back to a previous stage, but also lets me see immediately which is the latest version.

Using File >Save As, I save the first drawing file as xxx (where xxx describes the file, for example terraced house). The next time I save the drawing file using File >Save As, I save it incremented with a letter of the alphabet:

a Terraced house
b Terraced house
c Terraced house
d Terraced house

These are sorted in order by the computer, and it is easy to see what the file is about, which file was saved last, and which file you require if you need to go back one or more stages.

So instead of just using Save when saving your work, use Save As and increment the letter in front of the filename. This means that if you have saved several versions of a drawing, when you come to export the .STL file for printing, give this the same name as the current version. For example:

f drawing.skp = the Sketchup version
f drawing.stl = the exported filename for the .stl print file

This way you can easily see which printing file relates to which version of the drawing.

Saving your work with Save As from Sketchup Make saves your entire Sketchup drawing. We need to save in a different format (which allows individual Layers to be saved) for laser cutting or 3-D printing, and this is explained in the relevant sections later in the book.

Remember, use the File >Save As menu to save your work.

Note: Throughout the next exercise I have put reminders about saving.

GROUPS AND LAYERS

This is a long section, so give yourself adequate time to work through it. Think of each Layer as a drawing on a sheet of tracing paper which can be placed over the base Layer or not, and be used in different combinations.

When working with complex objects it is sometimes useful to be able to add objects to existing ones without having to re-measure or re-draw everything. Sketchup Make allows you to do this by using Layers. Layers turn on and off the visibility of objects on the screen.

Also, when your objects get quite complicated it is not easy to select just certain parts of it to move, rotate or copy, and often other sections of other objects are inadvertently selected. By making each object a Layer, its visibility can be turned on and off, enabling complex objects to be broken down into a series of parts.

To illustrate the use of Layers our example is that of the fronts of three terraced houses with doors and windows. You will also practise the skills learnt so far. Note that there are two Layers menus, and it is easy to confuse them.

Begin by closing down Sketchup and re-running it using the Laser3-D template set up earlier.

Drop-down Layers menu at the top of the screen.

The drop-down Layers menu and icon is at the top centre of the screen and shows a list of Layers you have added. Click on the small 'down' arrow to see your Layers once they are set up.

The Laser3-D template you set up and should be using includes the Layers menu at the right-hand side of your screen. Note the distinction between

Making and Using Groups and Layers

Groups are a way to keep related entities (lines, circles, shapes) together in a drawing. You can edit a Group without affecting objects and the entities behind them. Layers control the visibility of objects.

To Make a Group

• With the Select tool, select all the entities (lines, circles, rectangles) that you wish to include in your Group
• Choose Edit>Make Group from the menus, or right-click on the selected entities and select Make Group from the menu that appears. Groups appear in a blue 'frame' when any part of them is selected; this indicates they are a Group

To Edit/Change a Group
• Double-click on the Group to edit it. Once changed, click anywhere on the background to close it

To Make a Layer
• Add a Layer name to the Layers menu (on the right-hand side of the screen)
• Draw your object
• Select all your object (it turns blue), or click anywhere on your Group
• Click on the Layer name in the drop-down Layers menu (top of screen) to add the Group to a Layer

To Change the Visibility of Layers

• Click on the tick box to remove the tick against the Layers name in the Layers Menu at the right of the screen to make the Layer invisible
• Click again on the tick box to make the Layer visible

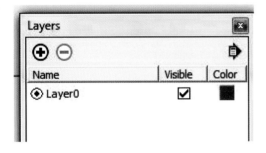

The Layers menu is at the lower right-hand side of the screen. If it is not, use the Window >Default Tray menu to turn it back on.

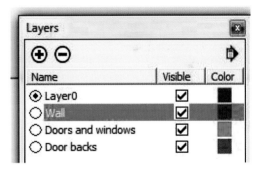

Layers menu with object titles added.

the drop-down Layers menu at top centre, and the Layers menu on the right-hand side.

The terraced house example will have Groups on three Layers: Wall, Doors and windows, and Door backs.

• Add the titles of the objects required by clicking the + sign at the top of the Layers Menu and entering

the name. Repeat until your Layers Menu looks like the one above. Ignore the ticks and colours for now

Note: Note the dot by Layer0. This is the current drawing Layer. This should never be moved and it should always be ticked as visible. All our drawing is done on Layer0. This is really, really important.

The Layers drop-down menu (at the top of the screen) enables you to make each object a separate Layer. Click on the small arrow to view it.

- Use the Rectangle tool to draw the wall of the house as a rectangle 1,780mm x 750mm (remember, just numbers and comma between in the Dimensions box).
- Select all your rectangle using the Select tool (it should turn to blue dots and lines)
- Right-click on the rectangle and choose Make Group
- Use the drop-down Layers Menu at the top of the screen as shown, and click on Wall. This makes your rectangle Group 'Layer Wall'

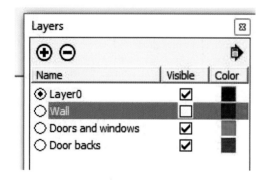

Each Layer can be made visible or invisible. Here, 'Layer Wall' has been made invisible – tick 'removed'.

- In the Layers Menu click on the tick against Wall. The tick will disappear and so should your wall!
- Now click again, and the tick should reappear with your wall

Each Group of objects can have its own Layer and be made visible or not. Imagine you have drawn your

wall on a sheet of tracing paper. This can be really useful.

Note: I shall refer to all Layers throughout the rest of the book as 'Layer xxx', 'Layer yyy' and so on, to distinguish them from general discussion about Layers.

Also note that the dot is still in the Layer0. This must remain so. Check it frequently. The dot signifies the active Layer. Do not draw on any other Layer.

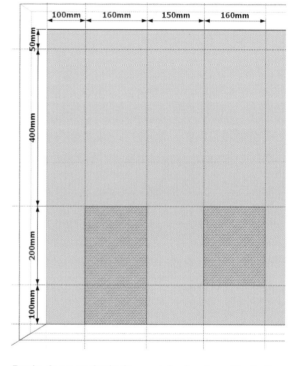

Basic door and window marked out on the left-hand end of terraced houses. Note the grey 'frame' around the drawing to show that this is a Group being edited.

The next stage is to add door and window openings to the Layer Wall:

- Double-click on the rectangle (Layer Wall) to make it editable (a 'frame' opens around it to show you it is a Group)
- Use the Tape Measure tool to draw guidelines on the left side of the Layer Wall, as shown above

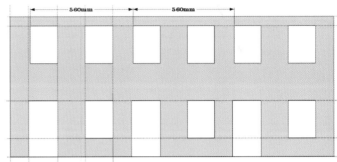

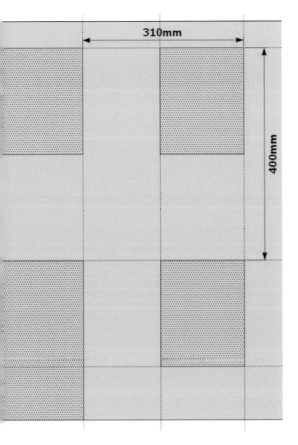

Basic rectangles for the door and three windows of one terraced house.

• With the Rectangle tool draw a rectangle for the door and window using the guidelines

Save your work as File >Save As >a Terraced house. skp

• Select the bottom right window (drag from top left to bottom right)
• Copy it (Move + Ctrl key) upwards 400mm (400 into Dimensions box)
• Next, Copy it to the left 310mm (Move + Ctrl key again, then 310 in Dimensions box)

Note how Sketchup tries to help you align vertical and horizontal moves. If it goes wrong, remember you can use the Undo icon or re-load your saved file.

The finished wall with door and window openings. This is all now 'Layer Wall'. I have removed the blue background for clarity.

• Save your work as File >Save As >b Terraced house. skp

Finally, you need to copy all three windows and the door twice to the right:

• Select the three windows and door (click above the top left of the top left window and drag to just below the wall and to below the right of the bottom right window). All windows and the door should turn blue
• Copy (Move + Ctrl key) all four 560mm to the right (560 into Dimensions box)
• Tap Ctrl again to get Move+ and repeat. Remember, once you have begun your direction of movement, entering 560 into the Dimensions box will complete the move for you
• With the Select tool, click inside each door and window rectangle in turn and tap Delete. This deletes the blue background. Your drawing should now match that of mine above
• Click anywhere on the background outside the rectangle with the Select tool to close Group Layer Wall

Now the whole rectangle together with the door and window openings (the Group) is Layer Wall. Check this by unticking the box next to Layer Wall in the Layers menu. The drawing should be made invisible. Re-tick the box to make it visible again.

• Save your work as File >Save As >c Terraced house. skp

You now have a wall that you can cut out on the laser or easily modify (by giving it a thickness) for 3-D printing. It is independent of the window and door styles. It is also of a length that will easily fit in a hobby laser or most 3-D print beds. The wall layer can be of a material suited to the outside wall.

Now you need to draw a door and window layer. You can use the Layer Wall as a guide for these.

• With the Layer Wall visible, use the Rectangle tool to draw a new rectangle round all the outside edges of the entire wall, over the existing rectangle

You have drawn this new rectangle *over* the Layer Wall, but not on it. Imagine each Layer as separate pieces of tracing paper. You have just drawn on the equivalent of a piece of tracing paper, using your original drawing as a guide.

Using the Layer Wall as a guide, draw guidelines for the door and window frames. This is easier if you zoom in.

• Use the Tape Measure tool to draw guidelines for the outside frames (I used 12mm width in from the door and window openings, with 24mm for the door bottom)
• Draw guidelines for the vertical and horizontal centrelines and then one each side to make up the width (I used 6mm each side)
• Use the Rectangle tool to draw four rectangles for the door and four for the window, using the guidelines as shown highlighted in blue above. These are the door panels and window panes

Do not draw a fifth rectangle around the whole door frame, or around the window.

Remember, you are drawing everything x10 size so the frames will be 1.2mm wide, or about 4in in 4mm scale when cut out.

Imagine you have just drawn on a piece of tracing paper sitting on the Layer Wall. You have used the Layer Wall as a guide but have not actually drawn on it.

• Now make the Layer Wall invisible by unticking the box next to it in the Layers menu. You should have a drawing similar to that above

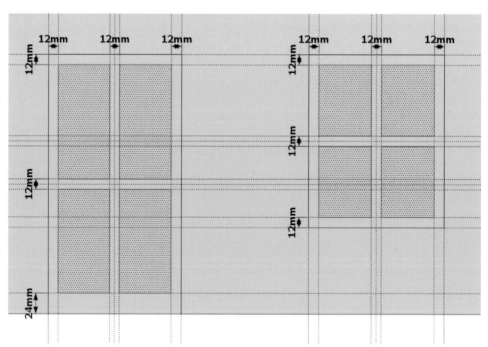

Guidelines drawn using the Layer Wall.

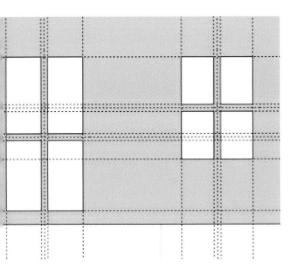

One door and one window ready for the Doors and windows Layer.

• Click inside each window and door rectangle with the Select tool, and tap Delete to remove it. This makes the drawing clearer, as above

Save your work as File >Save As >d Terraced house. skp

• Zoom out so you can see the entire wall
• As before, select and Move+ (Copy) the window up 400mm and then to the left 310mm

• Now select your three windows and door and Move+ (Copy) them twice 560mm to the right
• With the Select tool, select inside each door and window rectangle in turn and tap Delete (this is not necessary but it does improve the clarity of the drawing)

You should have the drawing as shown in the illustration.

• Use the Select tool to select all the drawing
• Make this a Group >Edit >Make Group (or right-click on it and Make Group)
• With the drawing still all selected, click on Doors and Windows in the drop-down Layers Menu (at the top of the screen) to make it Layer Doors and Windows

Try turning each Layer on and off to see the result and to check it against my examples.

When the two Layers are cut out of mount card (or other thin material) using the laser cutter and one placed behind the other, the window and door frames are set back by the thickness of the card, and the frames show as they are 1.2mm inside the door and window openings (10 x smaller than drawn).

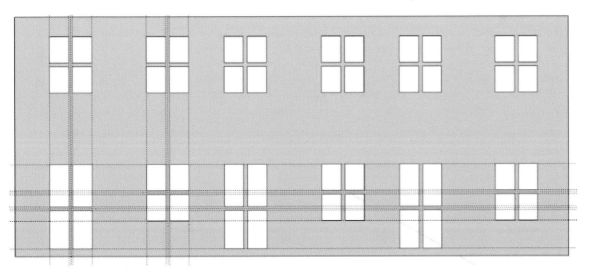

The complete Doors and windows Layer. The grey lines are the guidelines. I have removed the window panes and door panels for clarity.

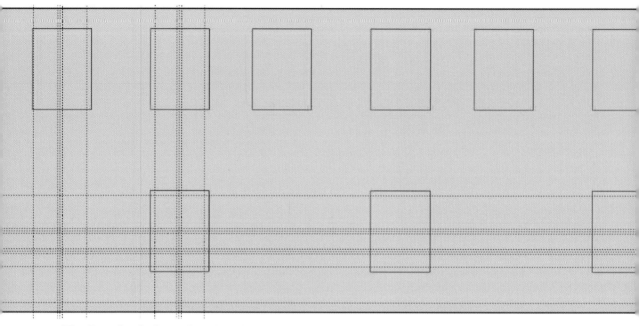

The Door backs Layer has the windows drawn to cut out, but not the doors.

You have one problem remaining: the doors can be seen through! You need a final layer, the Door backs Layer.

You now need to draw a layer for the door backs. This will have the windows cut out but not the door. Begin by making the Layer Doors and Windows invisible and the Layer Wall visible.

- Use the Rectangle tool to draw a rectangle over the outside rectangle of Layer Wall
- Use the Rectangle tool to draw a new rectangle over each window

Make the Layer Wall invisible (we no longer want the door openings). Your drawing should now look like the one in the illustration, where the window openings are cut out but not the door openings.

- Use the Select tool to select all the drawing
- Make this a Group by clicking >Edit >Make Group (or right-click on it and use Make Group)
- With the drawing still all selected, click on Door Backs in the drop-down Layers menu (at the top of the screen) to make it Layer Door Backs

You should now be able to turn each Layer on and off separately. If you can, well done, you are well on your way to mastering layers. If not, try repeating this exercise until you can. Remember the Re-do and Undo icons.

- Save your work as File >Save As >e Terraced house. skp

Should you add further Layers and detail at a later date, you can then add the next letter prefix and 'Save As'.

In the laser cutting section of this book I take this exercise further by developing brickwork and an alternative set of window and wall styles, together with lintels and windowsills. Using Layers enables you to re-use your drawings to make different models.

You now need to save your work in a format suited to laser cutting. These need to be as three separate files so that each can be cut out of mount card separately!

Make each Layer visible in turn, select it all with the Select tool (it turns blue), and then export as .DXF files, selecting Centimeters and Lines in the saving box. For example:

ABOVE: *The three Layers glued together. The top Layer (red card) has been covered in brick paper printed from a Scalescenes (www.scalescenes.com) download. It is easy to add a layer of transparent film for the windows underneath the Doors and windows Layer – it just needs the doors cutting out. This can be cut by the laser and would be another Layer to design.*

LEFT: *The terraced house example cut out in different coloured mount card, giving a contrast between the colour of the wall, the window and door frames, and the door panels. The model will also be incredibly strong, built up out of Layers like this. Also by drawing it this way, if you require different windows or doors you can achieve this by simply drawing another Doors and windows Layer.*

WORKING WITH GROUPS AND LAYERS

Making Groups visible and invisible via Layers is an important part of working with Sketchup. If you make a Group visible and draw on it, what you draw is separate from the Group (like drawing on tracing paper over the Group).

To actually alter the Group: Right-click on it and select Edit Group from the drop-down menu (or simply double-click on it). You should see a 'frame' around the Group to show that it is indeed a Group. Once selected like this any lines drawn on the Group object become part of the Group.

To close the Group: simply click anywhere on the background.

File >Export As DXF >e terrace house wall layer. dxf
File >Export As DXF >e terrace house doors and windows layer.dxf
File >Export As DXF >e terrace house door backs layer.dxf

Each of these filenames describes what the drawing is and what it will cut out on the laser cutter. The 'e' suffix denotes the version of the drawing as saved in Sketchup format so that you can easily refer back to the original drawing if required.

Select these filenames in turn in your laser cutter software, add mount card each time (or cereal packet for prototypes), and cut them out.

PART II: LASER CUTTING

7 ENHANCING YOUR HOBBY WITH A LASER CUTTER

Railway modellers have always embraced new technologies, some rather more than others. The move from three-rail to two-rail, from DC to DCC, DCC with sound, and to the ultimate of computer control as at the extensive 'Miniatur Wunderland' model railway in Hamburg (www.miniatur-wunderland.com), shows how progressive our hobby can be. Many of these changes have only been possible by the introduction of new materials and manufacturing methods.

We are used to making things ourselves, and also to making things produced by others in the form of kits. A laser-cutting machine gives you the power to produce kits for yourself (and others). Although there is a financial outlay in purchasing the initial machine, the running costs are quite low, and there are no expensive moulds or patterns to make.

The savings (over bought kits) can be even greater for items in the larger scales, or those required in large numbers such as fencing, windows, doors, and even complete houses such as terraced houses. However, it is difficult to justify savings when the outlay on the equipment is so high.

The real benefit lies in the ability to make things it is simply not possible to make by hand, and, through CAD, to alter and amend and refine these items via easily produced prototypes. Once you have the CAD drawing for an item it is relatively easy to alter its size, shape, and other features to produce bespoke items for your model railway.

Laser cutters can cut and/or engrave a wide variety of flat sheet material to an incredible level of accuracy, and can repeat the operation as many times as required.

In this section I hope to explain the basics of how laser cutters work, the materials you can use with them, some hints and tips on operating them, and plenty of examples of items you can make for your model railway.

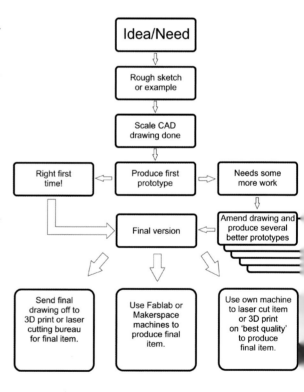

CAD drawings allow refinement of the model via several prototypes, whether for laser cutting or 3-D printing.

8 LASER-CUTTING MACHINES

SIZE

Laser-cutting and engraving machines come in all types and sizes, from those that will accept A4 sheets of 3mm plastic and card, up to huge machines for cutting out sheet metal and 8 x 4ft sheets of plywood.

I am concerned in this book with those machines suited to our hobby of railway modelling. Perfectly adequate are machines accepting A4 (300 x 200mm) size material, such as acrylic sheet up to 3mm thick. Most hobby machines accept material of this size. Usually models can be designed in sections to overcome this limitation in size. Large buildings can have horizontal and vertical features hiding the joins, or materials can be joined in such a way that the join is hidden.

POWER

A more powerful laser will cut thicker materials faster but will cost more to buy and run. Speed is much more important in a commercial environment than it is to the hobbyist. Most laser cutting machines suited to our hobby have 35w or 40w laser tubes: the higher the wattage, the higher the power, just like light bulbs.

This large (over 700mm long), low-relief building in 4mm scale is made up of A4 sections of mount card. The joins are disguised by the rainwater downpipes and other architectural features. All the stonework effect on this building is achieved by laser engraving (see Hints and Tips in the laser chapter) on to black mount card. Not only does this look good from a distance, it also has a texture when viewed close up.

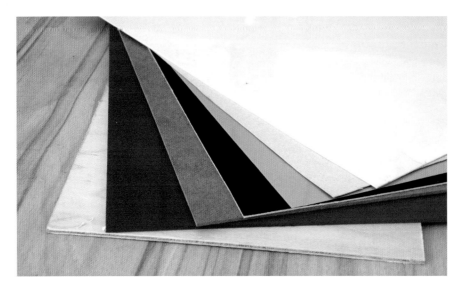

Examples of different materials cut on the laser. From left to right: plywood; acrylic sheet; mdf; black mount board (card); cereal packet; Mylar; and finally Rowmark (Plasticard type sheet).

All laser tubes for this type of machine are CO2 (carbon dioxide) laser tubes and produce a powerful beam of infrared light, which is invisible. You do not need to know how lasers work in order to operate them, and such explanation can be found elsewhere and is outside the scope of this book.

Typically machines of this power output can cut through the following types and thicknesses of materials:

- 3mm acrylic (Perspex) sheet
- 3mm MDF (medium density fibreboard – laserable grade)
- 3mm plywood (laserable type)
- Mount board and most common types of cardboard used in modelling
- 2mm Rowmark (a laserable substitute for styrene/plasticard sheet)
- 1mm Mylar (a thin, tough plastic sheet good for fine detail work)

Note the use of 'laserable' materials. These are sold specifically to be suitable for laser cutting and give good results. Using 'normal' plywood, MDF or plastic will not necessarily give good results and might be a fire or toxic gas risk.

It is possible to cut thicker – up to 5mm – materials, but it is often better to cut out two thinner sheets and glue them together. Thicker materials have to be cut at very slow speeds, and wood, in particular, chars before it is cut right the way through and the charred material makes it even more difficult to cut.

COST

Machines that look suitable are advertised on the internet for £400 or £500. A UK-supplied and supported machine currently costs about £1,400. Before purchasing a machine check the specification carefully against the following checklist:

- Power and type of laser tube: how long should it last, and what is the cost of replacement?
- The size of the material that can be lasered
- The thickness of the material that can be lasered
- Extraction – does it come with a fan and suitable extraction tubing?
- Cooling – does it have a water pump and water tubing?
- Air – does it have a compressor/air pump supplied?
- Pointer – does it have a red laser pointer so you can see the cutting zone?
- Does it come with a UK plug?
- What software is supplied with the machine, and what file types will it accept?
- What version of Windows is needed to run the laser software?

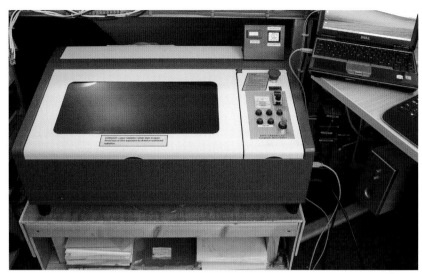

I use a second-hand laptop running Windows XP dedicated to driving the laser via the Newlydraw software supplied with it. This also has a dongle (a device that has to be in one of the USB ports all the time to enable the program to run), so ensure your laptop has at least three USB ports, one each for the dongle, the laser machine itself, and for a memory stick to transfer files from the computer on which CAD is done.

- How does it connect to the computer – is the cable supplied?
- How is initial instruction on the machine obtained? Does it come with manuals? Can I view these on-line prior to purchase?
- Will anyone give me instruction on how to use the machine prior to purchase?
- How is on-going support and maintenance obtained?
- Is the machine set up, calibrated and ready to use?
- What is the warranty – is this on site, or must the machine be returned to base (bearing in mind that machines are heavy and bulky and the laser tube is fragile)?
- Is on-going service and maintenance support available? What is the cost?

If purchasing a machine for home delivery, do think carefully whether you would be capable of installing the laser tube (if it is not fitted), adjusting the mirrors to obtain a focused beam, and generally learning how to operate the laser safely without being shown.

You may have a club member or friend who already has a laser, or it may be worth asking others at your local fab lab or maker/hacker space to see what they have. They may offer to help you set up a new machine, in which case this route might be acceptable.

If you don't have contacts such as those mentioned above, then you need to consider buying a UK-supplied and supported machine from compa-

nies such as HPC Laser (www.hpclaser.co.uk) based in Elland, West Yorkshire, who do have a suitable hobby machine, will ensure it is set up correctly, and will give you instruction prior to you collecting the machine from their premises.

Check on the internet to see whether there are other companies in your area offering a similar service.

The machine illustrated in this book, and which I bought several years ago, is the LS3020 machine from HPC Laser. Apart from an initial problem with the power supply, fixed under warranty, this machine has performed well for several years. It has required two new laser tubes at £250 each, but has been used extensively for projects on my 4mm and G-scale layouts, and to make items for other club members.

The only down side to this machine is the software that comes with it. Somewhat dated by modern standards, it requires Windows XP and will not run on later versions. However, reconditioned computers with Windows XP installed are advertised at reasonable prices on the internet. The software does accept .DXF files for cutting and .BMP for engraving.

If you have an old laptop or computer with Windows XP installed, this may be ideal for running the laser, but it may prove rather slow for running Sketchup Make. CAD programs typically require a reasonable degree of power and memory (see Part 1 for details).

9 THE LASER CUTTER

THE BASICS

Look through any model railway magazine and you will see retailers selling laser-cut items. These range from laser-cut detailing parts, window frames, awning edging, fences, to complete laser-cut buildings.

Laser machines can both cut and engrave, and even the hobbyist machines are powerful enough to cut 3mm thick acrylic sheet (Perspex), plywood and MDF, as well as mount card, cardboard and flexible plastics such as Mylar. Not only can the hobbyist machines cut many of the common materials we use for modelling, but they can do it with nearly the same accuracy as larger professional machines, if somewhat more slowly.

Laser cutters can be used, with some considerations noted later, in the domestic environment, and can make incredibly detailed parts that are easily repeated. Require a row of terraced houses? Do the drawings and make one laser cut example and you can easily make a whole row! If you need different window frames or doors for a few of the terraced houses, then modify those parts of the drawing and simply cut them out on the laser cutter.

The machines themselves are relatively easy to set up and use, but you do need to have a basic working knowledge of a CAD (computer-aided design) program to draw your designs, and to master the printer driver program that comes with the machine.

THE MACHINE

Laser cutter/engraving machines direct the output of a high-powered laser tube through optics to produce a focused beam of energy that will burn through many common materials. It is not necessary to know how the laser tube works (there are several different types), except to note that the tubes used in hobbyist

Cutting Versus Engraving

When cutting, the laser head typically moves slowly along the lines to be cut at high power, burning or vaporizing the material away. A .DXF – Drawing eXchange Format – file is used to determine where to cut.

When engraving, the laser reads a .BMP – BitMaP image format – file, which stores the data required for images. The best images for laser engraving are black and white and made up of tiny dots or pixels. Normal colour photographs have to be converted to black and white and rasterized to achieve this. Rasterizing takes the grey scale of the (now) black and white photograph or image and converts it into tiny dots. The darker the grey, the more dots per mm – black will have 100 per cent dots. The laser then reads each row of dots, firing and vaporizing the material where there is a black dot.

Usually medium power is used for engraving. The laser head moves backwards and forwards like a colour printer printing a photograph, moving down the work a fraction of a millimetre at each pass. The speed of the movement backwards and forwards and the amount moved down the work each time are controlled in the software. Engraving takes a considerable length of time, about 20 to 30 minutes for an A4 sheet.

For details of how to laser-engrave stonework refer to the 'Hints and Tips: Laser' chapter at the end of this section.

Laser-cut examples of fencing, windows' brackets and a signal arm in various materials for 4mm and G-scale.

4mm-scale laser-cut and engraved engine shed in card. Note the stonework has been laser-engraved (see the last chapter in this section, Hints and Tips: Laser) on the mount card. The gate is made up of two layers of mount card. Note the lettering on the gate, which is also laser-cut, as is the cobblestone effect on the floor.

...ced houses in black ...t card. Stonework ...er-engraved on to ...ace of the cardboard ...re cutting out. They ...ser cut as individual ...ings, and glued ...her offset up a slope. ...nd building has been ...fied as a corner shop. ...ownpipes and gutters ...lso mount card. ...model is awaiting ...printed chimney pots! ...group of sloping ...ings slots into a ...ngular housing in ...t scenery.

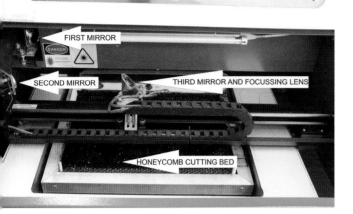

Various parts of a typical hobby laser. The actual laser tube is at the back of the machine and its output is reflected off the first and second mirrors on to the third. Beneath the third mirror is a lens, which focuses the beam on to the work. Maintenance is largely concerned with keeping these mirrors and lens clean.

Honeycomb cutting bed on which the work is placed. I have added an L-shaped stop to the far side of the bed to help locate the sheets to be cut. The square objects are magnets, used to hold thin materials down to the bed.

machines, usually CO_2, will not cut metal. The laser beam is invisible.

The power of the laser tube is expressed in watts, and the higher the number, the more powerful the laser tube. Typically 35w or 40w tubes are used in hobbyist machines and are perfectly adequate for our needs. The machines are kept in a steel cabinet with a viewing panel through which the work can be seen as it is cut. The laser tube is at the rear of the machine, and its output is reflected by mirrors to the laser head, which focuses the beam on to the material to be cut or engraved.

Most hobbyist machines have a removable cutting bed that will accept material up to A4 in size.

The cutting bed is a honeycomb so that the underside of the material is marked less by reflected heat as the laser cuts. The cutting bed can also be raised and lowered to maintain focus on materials of different thicknesses.

FOCUSING

The laser must be correctly focused on the work to achieve the best results. If it is out of focus more power and lower speeds than necessary will be required to cut the material, and engraving will lack resolution and be blurred.

Focusing the laser on the material to be cut or engraved is vital. We've all focused the sun's output on to a piece of paper using a magnifying glass and watched the paper turn brown and burn with the heat. A laser beam is focused in much the same way, by adjusting the height of the laser bed for different thicknesses of material. The laser generally works at its best when it is focused exactly on the top of the material. A simple focusing tool as shown suffices.

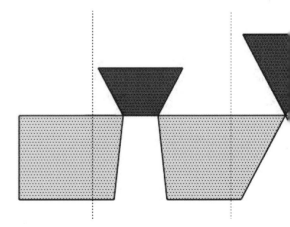

Just as with a magnifying glass and the sun, the laser energy needs to be focused by a lens on to the work to produce the most heat and therefore the most efficient cut. On the left above, an out-of-focus laser will have its power spread over a wider area and be less effective.

The HPC laser focusing tool in action. It is a 62mm square of Perspex, which is placed on top of the current sheet of material to be cut, and the cutting bed is raised and lowered by means of a screw so that the top of the focus tool is level with the top of the lens mount carriage as shown. Thicker materials will require the bed to be raised, thinner materials for it to be lowered.

Here I have laser engraved some stonework on to black mount card. Fast speed lightly engraves the surface, top. Slow speed has over-engraved the centre section, while the optimum speed is shown in the bottom section. Note the difference in the darkness of the engraving. The laser also leaves a beautifully textured finish, not easy to replicate in a photograph! See the Hints and Tips: Laser chapter for more details of preparing a photograph of stonework ready to laser engrave.

SPEED

The laser speed is controlled in the program that comes with the laser. This would normally allow the entry of two speeds, one for *cutting*, typically between 1mm and 50mm per second, and one for *engraving*, normally between 100mm and 300mm per second. Setting the cutting or engraving speed too fast will result in the material not cutting all the way through, or being engraved too lightly. Setting it too high will result in wasting energy on the cut, and a far too deep and 'over-engraved' engraving.

POWER

The power of the laser is determined by a control knob, where each complete turn represents 10 per cent power – thus ten turns equals 100 per cent power. Some of the more expensive machines have power controlled by the software and can set different powers for different operations (for example 80 per cent for cutting, and 40 per cent for engraving).

I have added a counting dial to my power knob, which gives me a numerical readout of 0–100, depending on how many turns are made on the control. I can therefore replicate an exact power more easily.

BELOW LEFT: *Counting dial on the author's machine showing 40.8 per cent power.*

BELOW: *The material used here is a laser engraving plastic, where a thin top layer of one colour is removed by the laser to leave the bottom layer of another showing. The left-hand example shows signs of marking, but insufficient power has resulted in the top layer not being removed sufficiently. The right-hand example shows the result with more power. For this example I have kept the speed constant and raised the power, but lowering the speed with the power constant would have produced similar results – but more slowly.*

ACK PLAN   TRACK PLAN

The type of water pump often supplied with hobby laser-cutting machines. It just sits in a tank of water.

COOLING

The laser tube is water cooled, and a small water pump (think fish-pond pump) is supplied to circulate water from a container (a small water butt is ideal, the larger the better). If the laser is used for long periods at a higher power then the water heats up, and above about 25°C it starts to lose efficiency. Some operators put ice in their water, or change it. Water chillers are available (at about £300) which enable the laser to cut all day without the water overheating. Professional lasers have the water pump and cooler built in.

You have to ensure an adequate supply of water to the laser tube, and that the water is replaced as it evaporates. Use distilled or de-ionized water only – that produced for topping up batteries can be bought for a reasonable price in 5ltr containers at motor accessory shops. Tap water may build up a deposit within the laser tube and affect its efficiency.

A typical small water-chiller unit with temperature readouts. These are only required if you intend laser cutting in a warm room at high (80 per cent or more) power for long periods. They ensure the circulating water is kept at a constant temperature.

VENTILATION

Also supplied with the laser is a fan unit, which usually clips on the back of the laser; it has an output for a 100mm or so diameter flexible pipe which can be stuck out of a window. This is necessary as the cutting process is essentially a burning process and produces smoke and fumes. This requires some thought when siting the laser, as it needs to be near a window or door opening. Although the fan that comes with the laser is adequate, if using the laser in a club environment or extensively at home a hole in the wall/window and a more powerful fan will eliminate any risk of smoke and/or fumes reaching inside the room.

COOLING THE WORKPIECE

A final piece of kit that comes with most hobbyist lasers is a small air compressor. As the laser cuts it produces heat and smoke, both of which are cleared by blowing air directly on the cutting spot. This makes for a much cleaner cut and enables thicker materials to be cut.

The supplied fan unit, which clips on to the rear of the laser. Note how mine has become blackened with soot as a result of the smoke produced by the laser. You do not want this in your lungs! The blue vent pipe can be seen attached to the fan unit.

The small air compressor supplied with the machine.

The compressor simply sits by the laser and is connected by a small bore air tube. The air tube extends to the area where the laser beam is focused, blowing air over the actual cutting/engraving point to produce a cleaner cut.

OTHER CONTROLS

The laser will have an on/off key, buttons to turn on the lighting and air pump, a laser test switch (used when setting up for checking the focus of the laser mirrors), a power knob, and an emergency stop button.

So that you can see where the laser is aimed, the spot where it is about to start cutting is lit by a small red dot.

If all this sounds complicated, it isn't. Typically it takes about thirty minutes to be given instructions on how to use the laser safely.

SITING THE LASER

The laser needs to be on a sturdy table near an opening window or hole in an external wall (for the exhaust tube), with space for the water tank nearby. Space for the compressor (which can be placed on a piece of foam to dampen the noise) behind the laser is useful, and space above for the lid to open!

Fortunately at the time I purchased my laser a hole had already been knocked through an outer

This photograph shows the effect of cutting a material such as MDF with and without the air feed to the laser head. The top fencing, with air, shows a much cleaner cut than the bottom fence without air. Some cheap laser-cutting machines do not have this facility and are therefore more limited in their quality of output.

The control panel on a typical hobby laser (this one is an HPC LS3020 35w machine). The top red button is the emergency stop, the raised box is control for power, the three buttons in the top row are for testing, and the bottom two are for air and light respectively. At bottom right is the key-operated on/off switch. The dial shows the laser output in mA, but is not really necessary.

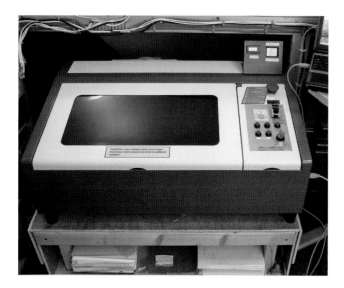

My machine is mounted on a purpose-built low table on sturdy wheels, which enables the machine to be pushed under the layout when it is not in use. Note the materials' store underneath the laser, and the small laptop bought to run the laser driver program. The small red box standing on the laser at top right is my own creation and has a counter for laser hours, and two temperature gauges, one for the room and another for the cooling water.

The additional fan unit installed on my laser vent pipe. The Y piece accommodates the cooker hood extraction for spray painting to the left, and the laser cutter to the right. It is vented out through the wall and is very effective.

wall for a cooker-hood extractor unit vent pipe, which is used for airbrush work and general painting. We have blown air central heating in our house and my railway room was a spare bedroom. Any smell I create is quickly wafted around the house by the heating system, so it is essential I have good extraction, especially for the laser. The addition of a large fan unit and Y piece was all that was needed to accommodate the laser.

HEALTH AND SAFETY

Typically lasers are *much* safer to use than a knife to cut materials! Although the laser runs at several thousand volts it is contained in a steel cabinet with interlocks so that it turns off if the lid is lifted.

Looking directly at the laser beam (it is invisible) is a big no-no, but the acrylic sheet that forms the lid and allows you to look at the laser as it works is made of a material that filters out harmful wave-

lengths, enabling you to check on the progress of your cutting or engraving. Check with your supplier that this is the case, as some suppliers also recommend the wearing of tinted 'laser glasses'.

The biggest risk with a laser is that of fire! For that reason a laser cutting machine *should never be left alone whilst it is working*. Because of the fire risk it is also necessary to have an adequate smoke alarms and a fire extinguisher suitably placed nearby, and also a fire blanket. If in doubt ask your local fire service for advice regarding the type and location of the fire extinguisher.

If cutting out thin materials, card or plastic and you have cut lines very close together, and are using too much power at too low a speed, the thin sliver between the lines will burn or glow. In my experience these nearly always self-extinguish when the machine is stopped and power to the fan and air compressor is turned off. If you notice this happening the solution is to cut with a faster speed and lower power (or to move the lines further apart if you can). Sometimes gluing the material with a glue stick to a thicker material is all that is required.

The type of small pump-up spray I keep handy to put out any cardboard 'glows' or fires. It gives a very fine spray and is useful for misting ballast prior to using PVA glue. It is called a 'Funpump' and is from Ideen (www.ideen.com).

The laser cutting process uses heat to burn or melt through the material, and therefore gives off smoke and fumes; these are removed by the fan. Ensure you have adequate ventilation. I work on the principle that if I can smell it, it is doing me no good. Some materials, such as rubber, PVC and polyethylene, should never be used in a laser cutter as the fumes are very toxic. Check with your supplier and buy materials – especially MDF and plastics – that are sold as 'laserable', and never use materials whose source is in doubt.

Although I have stressed the health and safety aspects of owning and using a laser cutter, in practice I have used mine for six years without major incident. I have it at the side of my computer and work table and leave it working while I get on with general modelling. Often you can be assembling and

---

Health and Safety Checklist

Never leave the laser unattended whilst working, and be sure of the following: that

- you know how to STOP and TURN OFF the laser at the power socket
- you have a suitable FIRE BLANKET handy
- you have an adequate FIRE EXTINGUISHER in place
- you have a working SMOKE ALARM nearby
- you only use approved 'laserable' materials

---

gluing together one set of laser cut parts whilst the laser is cutting the next. This is particularly useful when making something with many repeat parts such as a retaining wall or viaduct.

RUNNING COSTS AND MAINTENANCE

Even quite large professional laser-cutting machines work from a domestic-style three-pin outlet, and a typical hobby machine will take about 150 watts of power to run.

My 35w laser tube costs £250 to replace and lasts about 1,000 hours, so my machine costs about 25p an hour for the tube, plus some electricity as above, to run. The tube gradually deteriorates, and after 200 to 300 hours you will find that given the same material and speed, slightly more power is required to do the same cut; at the end of its life the tube will require full power to cut through even thin materials, and at this point you need a new tube! This is best fitted by an expert as some careful soldering is often required, and after fitting, the mirrors and focus lens need checking and may need adjustment. If they are not set correctly, even by a small amount, the full power of the laser beam will not be focused where you need it to cut correctly.

Distilled water is required for the coolant; 5ltr bottles of de-ionized or distilled water as used for car batteries (I use Halfords) can be purchased at a reasonable cost. The water level should be checked regularly.

Isopropyl alcohol (obtainable from chemists or laser cutter suppliers) and cotton buds are used to clean the mirrors and lens.

The cutting bed and surroundings can be cleaned using baby wipes; these work really well, though just be careful who's around when you buy them! I also occasionally take the honeycomb cutting bed outside and jetwash it.

READY TO LASER!

So, what's involved in cutting a typical railway model? Proceed as follows:

- Switch on the water pump to circulate the cooling water through the laser (this is best run from the same extension lead, so that turning on the laser automatically turns on the water pump and it can't be forgotten). Wait a couple of minutes before turning on the laser to ensure any start-up water bubbles have been driven out of the system
- Turn on the internal light so you can see what you are doing
- Clean the mirrors and focus lens. Use isopropyl alcohol. It takes five minutes about every four or five hours of cutting. The laser head can be moved by hand, gently, whilst the laser is switched off
- Put a sample of your material on the cutting bed (it can be some scrap)
- With the power OFF move the cutting head to different parts of the work surface checking the focus height with the Focus tool
- Run the software that came with your machine (the driver software), and load the laser test piece as shown in the Laser 'How to...' section later in this book
- Estimate an appropriate speed from previous test pieces or experience (30mm/sec for thin material, 5mm/sec for thick). Put this speed into the driver software
- Estimate an appropriate power for the material (20 per cent for thin material, 80 per cent for thick). On hobbyist machines this is often a rotary knob – one turn equals 10 per cent power, ten turns 100 per cent
- Close the lid!
- Turn the power on
- Turn on the air compressor to blow an air jet over the cutting point
- Send the cutting head to the top left corner by clicking on the appropriate button in your software
- Click on cut/engrave and the machine will start cutting or engraving (it cuts .dxf files and engraves .bmp files)
- When finished, wait a few seconds for the smoke/ fumes to clear, open the lid and take out your test piece
- Check the test piece. You are now trying to get the maximum speed and minimum power at which the material will cut. Adjust the speed and power settings accordingly and re-cut your test piece until it just fails to cut successfully. Once this has been determined you can reduce the speed and increase the power by a few per cent to achieve a good, consistent cut over the entire cutting area

Finally, load the design you wish to cut, and using the speed and power determined above, cut it out. Repeat as many times as required.

This looks a daunting list, but after only a few repeats it takes only a few seconds.

NEWLYDRAW LASER PRINTER DRIVER PROGRAM/SOFTWARE

It is outside the scope of this book to provide detailed instructions for every type of software supplied with every type of laser, but these screenshots will give you some idea of the steps necessary in NewlyDraw, the software program supplied with many hobby machines.

First you must import your .dxf file as above, then click on File>Engrave, and the panel as shown in the illustration is displayed.

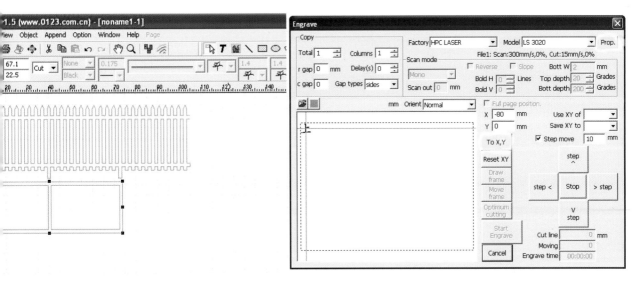

Palisade fence displayed in NewlyDraw.

NewlyDraw laser program showing the main cutting/engraving screen.

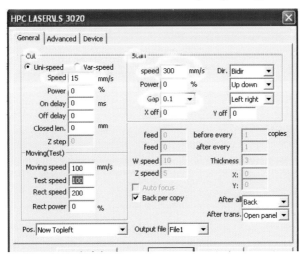

Setting up the cutting and engraving speeds in NewlyDraw.

Most of the default settings can be left. To alter the cut or scan speeds, click on Prop (top right-hand corner) and alter these on the next screen. Once done, click on To XY to send the cutting head to the top left of the cutting area, then Start Engrave to begin.

The screen in the picture above allows you to set the cut and scan (for engraving) speeds, and also the 'Gap'. When engraving, the Gap is the amount the laser moves down the work each time it trav-erses the work, effectively setting the resolution. The smaller the Gap the higher the resolution, but the longer it takes to engrave.

Please don't be put off purchasing or using a laser cutter by the apparent complexity of the above screens. Most of the parameters are pre-set for a particular laser cutter and can be ignored. Given a minimum amount of instruction, laser-cutting machines are an easy and reliable way to cut out many of the materials we use in our hobby.

Use this section as a reference section and for lists and hints and tips when laser cutting/engraving. At the end of this chapter I have included the power and speed settings I use when cutting and/or engraving the different materials, but treat this as a guide only as this will vary with the number of hours your laser tube has run. Increase power and lower speed as your laser tube ages.

It is also worth looking in this section to refresh your memory when cutting a different material. For example, when cutting Mylar for the first time there are several techniques I have found to work which may not be obvious when first working with this material.

CARDBOARD

One of the cheapest and most versatile modelling materials for the smaller scales indoors is cardboard. It cuts relatively quickly on low power, though it does come out of the laser brown and burnt at the edges. Cut at the highest speed/lowest power possible to achieve the cleanest cuts. It does represent something of a fire risk, particularly when doing fine detail with lines close together, so do keep an eye on it whilst it is cutting.

CEREAL PACKETS

Save your old cereal packets, as the (free!) card they are made from cuts really well on the laser, and very fine detail such as that for window frames is possible. It is also very useful for cutting out prototypes quickly to test for size and fit before cutting in the final material.

It is also very useful for prototyping as it cuts very rapidly, at up to 50mm/sec. So before cutting out your expensive 3mm acrylic sheet, make a fast, free cut-out of a cereal packet to test that your shape

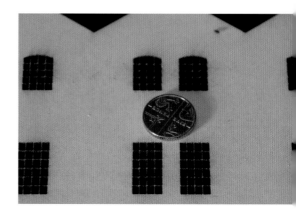

Very fine detail can be cut into free cereal-packet card as shown here, with a 5p coin for scale. These windows are for a 2mm-scale warehouse building. Contrast the appearance of the windows above straight from the laser with those in situ in the building shown next.

2mm-scale warehouse, the cereal-packet windows sprayed white and in situ. The stonework is laser engraved (see the last chapter in this section, Hints and Tips: Laser) on black mount card and built up in layers, just like the terraced house example used in the CAD section of this book.

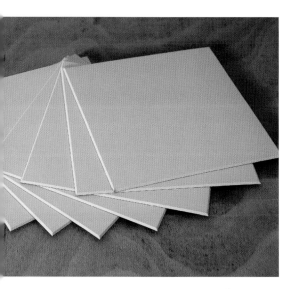

Mount card is available in many sizes. Picture framers often throw away the smaller sizes of card, and these can be a source of free mount card for smaller projects such as window frames. Those above are 140mm square.

2mm-thick acrylic gears, laser cut, form the mechanism for this level crossing. The edges of the acrylic sheet are really smooth when cut with the laser compared with cutting them with a saw. It makes excellent gear wheels for light loads.

is correct. Remember to re-focus when cutting your final material.

MOUNTCARD

This type of card is widely used by the picture-framing industry; it is a high quality card that cuts well on the laser. Normally just over 1mm thick, it is strong enough for quite large structures if suitably braced. Large sheets can be bought relatively cheaply and cut into sizes suitable for the laser, but many picture framers will throw away smaller pieces of mount card, and it could be free!

Large sheets of mount board can be purchased in bulk from various sources. I have found that the board sold by Rapid Electronics (www rapidonline.com), (twenty off A1 size) white one side, black the other, is cost effective and of a consistent quality. Once cut to A4 it works out at about 20p per A4 sheet.

PLASTICS

Many different types of plastic exist and not all are suitable for laser cutting, either because they simply do not cut well (Plasticard), or they give off poisonous,

toxic fumes (PVC). Before cutting any plastics on the laser, therefore, you should ensure that it is suitable.

Acrylic sheets are normally supplied with a protective film on both sides; it is usually best to remove both before laser cutting.

ACRYLIC SHEET (PERSPEX)

This material is either extruded or cast: for hobby use either is suitable. Cutting acrylic sheet with hand tools results in a rough edge and lots of fine particles of plastic dust (usually static-laden), which is difficult to clean off. The edges produced by laser cutting are smooth and clean and dust free.

Acrylic sheet comes in many colours and thicknesses, and it is also possible to purchase sheets that have a thick base colour with a thin top contrasting colour. By engraving away the top colour this type of sheet is excellent for making signs and control-panel facias.

Acrylic sheets up to 3mm thick can be cut on a typical hobby laser with a 35w or 40w tube. If thicker items are required, always consider laminating two or more sheets together to achieve the thickness required. The laser will cut each piece so accurately

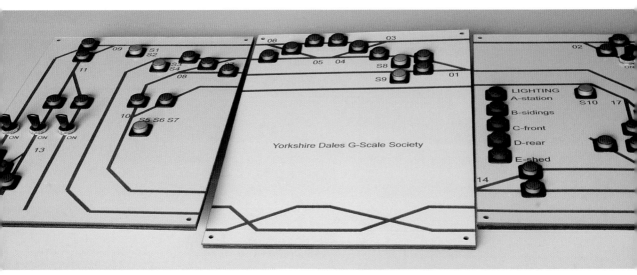

Laser-engraved control panel as A4-sized sheets. The track diagram and lettering are engraved using special engraving laminate, which has a very thin white layer on top of a thicker red layer (other colours are available). By laser engraving to remove the top layer, the red shows, as above. Holes for the control switches are also cut by the laser.

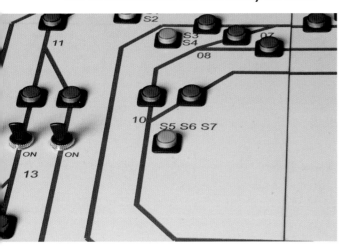

Close-up of the track diagram and lettering with switches on the laser-engraved control panel.

that this technique can be used with plastic, card, plywood and so on.

Acrylic sheets can be welded together, much like styrene sheet, with a suitable product such as plastic weld commonly found in model shops. These products typically dissolve a thin film of the material on each surface, then evaporate to leave the two items joined together permanently.

It is also an excellent material for outdoor use, and in particular as a base for 3-D printed detail such as stonework and roofing.

G-scale signal-box roof tiles, ridge tiles, chimney and finial, all 3-D printed and glued on to a 3mm acrylic sheet underframe.

The roof of the signal box has been laser cut in 3mm-thick acrylic sheet, and 3-D printed roofing tiles bonded to it with a silicon glue designed for PVC facia.

On larger jobs, such as those for the garden railway, some types of gun glues and silicones designed for PVC facia also work well.

STYRENE AND PLASTICARD

Styrene sheet, commonly referred to as Plasticard, is much used in our hobby, but sadly does not laser cut very well at all. The edges melt and become distorted and deformed, and any fine detail is lost completely.

A similar material is available however, which does laser cut well, though it can be difficult to source. It is called 'Rowmark', and is specifically designed for laser cutting. With this material fine detail is retained, and the cut edge does not melt and round as with styrene; it welds together just like styrene with a suitable plastic weld-type solvent.

A cartridge glue gun is ideal for larger jobs such as outdoor buildings and baseboard construction. Just choose a suitable glue/silicon.

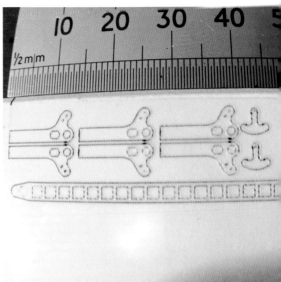

2mm-scale signal arms and ladder in 75 micron-thick Mylar. Mylar is glued to mount card with a glue stick to keep it flat whilst laser cutting. It also helps remove the heat from the cut and reduce distortion.

MYLAR (POLYESTER FILM)

For ultra-fine detail polyester film, brand name Mylar, is an excellent material and available in a wide range of thicknesses from 75 to 500 microns. It is widely used as a stencil material by airbrush artists, and is relatively easy to obtain (www.stencilwarehouse. com do various thicknesses and sizes).

When cutting Mylar use the lowest possible power, and a medium speed when cutting fine detail (because of the weight and inertia of the laser focusing head and slides, faster speeds are slightly less accurate). One problem with the very thin Mylar sheets is that they bend and warp with the heat whilst cutting, taking them out of focus. Use a glue stick to fasten the Mylar sheet to mount card before cutting.

A working G-scale signal laser cut in 'Rowmark' (styrene-type material) for the posts and signal arms, with clear acrylic sheet for the base, which contains the three servo motors and electronics. Used outdoors these proved weather-proof but not fox-proof!

It is an American product, and at the time of writing CSI are the UK distributors (csionline.co.uk). Four thicknesses are available – 0.75, 0.1, 1.5 and 3mm. It is usually available in white. HPC Laser have a similar material available (hpclaser.co.uk).

Now when cutting the Mylar will stay flat but has the added advantage that you can actually see when the Mylar is cut through as the mount card is burnt by the laser and turns brown. With a little experience you will be able to determine the correct power/speed combination from how dark these lines are.

Too much power, too dark, and the Mylar will be very brittle.

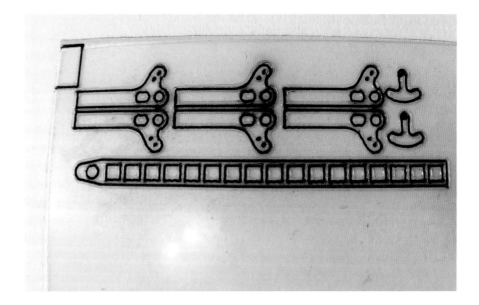

As the laser cuts the Mylar the material melts, leaving a rounded-off edge. This can be minimized by using the lowest power possible – usually around 7 per cent, as below this the laser does not work – a speed of 30mm or 40mm per second, and by repeating the cut two or three times. Do not move the material between cuts. This can produce superbly detailed items, which can be an alternative to etched brass parts for some applications where structural strength is not required. Mylar is also extremely tough, and when bent, will spring back into shape.

Note that if the power is too great, or the speed too low, or the lines too close together, the Mylar will melt and fuse to a brown colour, which is very brittle.

Once cut out, the Mylar can be carefully peeled off the backing card from one corner, often leaving the Mylar parts stuck to the card. The parts can then be prised off the card by careful use of a pointed knife, as shown.

A down side of using Mylar is that it can be difficult to glue together. Two-part epoxy can work, as can superglue, but contact adhesives such as Evo-Stik or Copydex work best.

Mylar peeled off the signal arms and ladder.

Picking a Mylar ladder off a sheet of mount card. In 2mm scale these are very small parts! The entire ladder is just 45mm long and 3mm wide.

Making Self-Adhesive Parts

One technique, which is slightly involved, enables self-adhesive Mylar (and other thin material) parts to be produced on the laser as follows:

- Obtain some A4 double-sided adhesive sheets (available from a number of sources on eBay)
- Peel off the backing paper from one side of the sheet, and carefully glue your Mylar to it. It is probably best to try some smaller pieces until you have the confidence to smooth the Mylar down, from one corner, without bubbles to the adhesive sheet. Bubbles are bad because the two are not bonded at the point of the bubble and will fall apart when laser cut into fine detail

- Finally, before laser cutting, use a glue stick to glue the self-adhesive sheet to mount card/cereal packet so the Mylar is uppermost. This helps keep the Mylar flat during laser cutting
- Cut out the Mylar as a test piece as previously explained, experimenting with speed and power to cut through both the Mylar and the glue on the underside of the adhesive sheet
- Once cut, use a pointed blade in your knife to prise off the Mylar parts produced, and you will find they are self-adhesive

The adhesive is not over-strong, but for items such as fencing posts it is strong enough once the fence has been sprayed with primer and its final colour, as the paint itself holds the items together.

Mylar
Top adhesive layer
Bottom backing sheet
Mount Board or Cereal P

The top backing sheet of double-sided adhesive sheet is removed and the Mylar stuck to it. Both are then glued to mount board or cereal packet with a gluestick to keep them flat whilst cutting. The laser power/speed is adjusted to cut through to the bottom backing sheet.

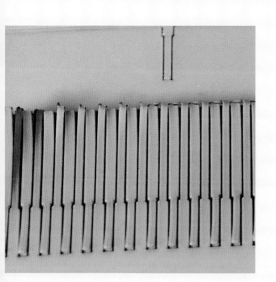

These Mylar fencing posts have been cut glued to one side of a double-sided self-adhesive sheet. When picked off they are self-adhesive, making it easier to position them either side of the lineside fencing posts.

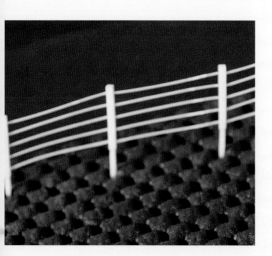

Mylar can be laser cut to incredibly thin structures, as shown here in this fencing. The posts are built up on either side with the 'self-adhesive' Mylar posts as just described.

FRISKET

I discovered this material when considering how to paint some 4mm- and 2mm-scale semaphore signal arms. Supplied on a roll, it is a low-tack masking film, also ideal as a stencil material. By laser cutting a stencil for each of the colours required for the signal arms, I was able to spray paint a batch of ten signal arms each time. Use a glue stick to glue Frisket to card before laser cutting so it stays flat.

Frisket, available from many suppliers on the internet.

MDF – MEDIUM DENSITY FIBREBOARD

MDF cuts well on the laser, provided it is bought as 'laser grade'. Cutting up to 4mm is possible on a hobby laser, but it is often better to cut two or more 2mm-thick shapes and glue them together to make up the required thickness.

The glues and resins used in 'laser-grade' MDF ensure a more consistent cut with fewer toxins in the fumes. It cuts with a black, burnt edge.

2mm MDF is a good material for making 'O-gauge' buildings, viaducts and so on, and can be very effective with laser cut brickwork suitably painted and weathered.

PLYWOOD

For reasons similar to those relevant to MDF, purchase only 'laser-grade' plywood. This should have an even

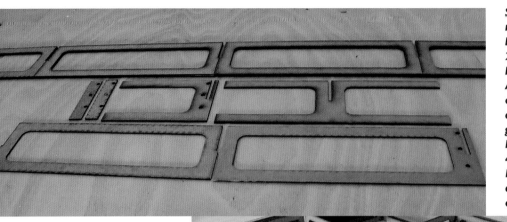

Supports for a modular lightweight baseboard cut in 2mm MDF. Each had to fit on an A4-sized laser cutting bed. They are then overlapped, glued together and laminated into 4mm-thick lengths. Note the blackened edges from the laser cutting.

Underside of lightweight baseboard: 6mm plywood top glued to lightweight 4mm-thick MDF laminated ribs. These sit on existing bench work and are designed to be removable rather than portable for exhibitions.

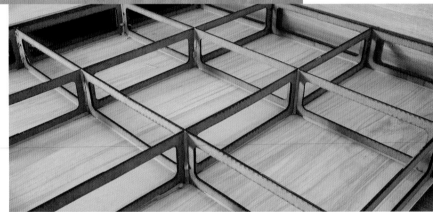

consistency without knots and suchlike in the inner layers. Normal plywood from a DIY outlet is generally not consistent enough to cut well. As with MDF, consider cutting thin plywood and gluing two or more shapes together to achieve your required thickness.

Hobarts (www.hobarts.com) and HPC Laser (www.hpclaser.co.uk) sell a wide range of laserable materials, including a special laser-grade plywood.

LASER CUTTING WITHOUT YOUR OWN LASER

Many companies offer laser cutting of the popular modelling materials. Some, such as Yorkmodelmaking (www.yorkmodelmaking.co.uk), specialize in model railway parts and models. Provided you can draw (or export) your model in one of their supported packages or file types, they can take your design and turn it into a model. Many modellers use these services for specialized parts such as window frames.

If you can provide a drawing in the correct format, usually a .dxf file (check with the company first) of the part you require to be laser cut, you will save yourself considerable expense, as asking a company to do the drawing for you is time-consuming and therefore expensive.

SPEED AND POWER SETTINGS

With a 35w laser tube in a hobby machine, these are some speed and power settings to try for different materials:

3mm Perspex/acrylic sheet = Sp. 12, Pwr. 50 per cent
2mm Perspex/acrylic sheet = Sp. 15, Pwr. 50 per cent
2mm MDF = Sp. 15, Pwr. 43 per cent
Mount card = Sp. 50, Pwr. 30 per cent
.8mm Rowmark = Sp. 40, Pwr. 30 per cent
75 micron Mylar = Sp. 40, Pwr. 8 per cent

11 PROJECTS: LASER CUTTING

INTRODUCTION TO LASER CUTTING

Before trying this section you should be familiar with all the Sketchup tools as outlined in the 2-D CAD Basics chapter in Part I. Where new commands are required I have introduced them in the text.

I have tried to structure the difficulty of the projects, starting with the easier ones, so they are best done in sequence.

SAVING YOUR WORK IN THE CORRECT FORMAT

Throughout I will remind you to save your work at frequent intervals with 'Save As xxxx', where xxxx is the filename and Save As is the Save As in the File drop-down menu. This will always save your entire drawing in Sketchup (.skp) format. Where drawings are best saved as you proceed I will increment the filename with a, b, c and so on – as a fence.skp, b fence.skp, c fence .skp – so that if you make a mistake you can always return to a previous version.

To laser cut the models you will also need to export the drawing as a .DXF file: File >Export DXF. I will remind you with Export as xxxx.dxf, where xxxx is the filename (matching the drawing filename where possible).

You will go wrong from time to time, but by making use of the Undo command and saving your work frequently so that you can return to an earlier stage in your drawing, you can minimize having to start again from scratch.

If your model is made up of more than one part, as are the fencing and terrace house examples outlined later, then select just the part you wish to export (it turns blue) before exporting it. This can then be sent to the laser as a separate file to cut out.

These are just examples. Once you have successfully drawn one window frame or fencing panel and

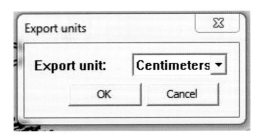

Choose Centimeters as your export units to scale down your drawing by a factor of ten (you will draw everything ten times larger than required to overcome Sketchup's problem with small objects).

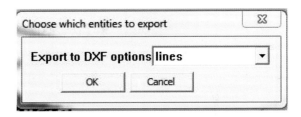

For the laser, choose Lines as the entities to export for cutting out.

have the basic skills, you should be able to design and make ones to suit your own layout and needs.

Have fun!

LASER TEST PIECE

This laser test piece enables you to quickly test your laser speed and power for each new material to ensure you are getting optimum performance from your machine. It is very small, takes only seconds to cut, and you can use up scraps of material from other jobs.

It checks dimensions, the cutting of circles and lines close together, and can be used on all the materials you intend using in your machine.

NOTE: Whenever you enter a number into the Dimensions Box you must tap Enter on your keyboard for the computer to recognize it.

DRAWING THE TEST PIECE

- Use the Rectangle tool to draw a rectangle 500mm square. Because we always draw everything ten times larger in Sketchup to overcome its dislike of small parts, this will cut as a 50mm square
- Use the Tape Measure tool to draw three vertical guidelines 125mm apart, then five horizontal guidelines 100mm apart

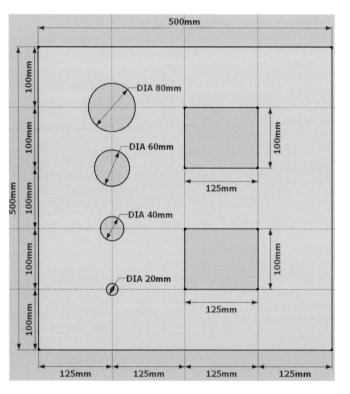

Laser test piece marked out ready for saving and cutting.

- Select the Circle tool and *immediately* enter ninety-six in the Dimensions box (and tap Enter). This will ensure each circle has ninety-six 'sides' rather than the default twenty-four (as circles in Sketchup are made up of straight lines)

- Using the Circle tool, draw circles at the intersection of the guidelines as shown, remembering to halve the diameter since the Dimensions box expects a radius measurement
- Finally use the Rectangle tool to draw the two rectangles using the guidelines. I have removed the blue inside the circles and boxes for clarity

Remember: Use File >Save As a Laser Test Piece.skp (this will save the entire drawing in Sketchup format).

Then for laser cutting, select the whole drawing: File >Export DXF >Centimeters >Lines >a Laser Test Piece.dxf (File menu, then Export as DXF, then choose Centimetres in the box which appears, then choose Lines in the next box, and then a filename – a Laser Test Piece.dxf. It is worth always adding the .dxf extension, as some earlier versions of this plug-in did not automatically add it).

The Export DXF function saves your file in the correct format for the laser.

CUTTING THE TEST PIECE

When cutting the laser test piece always begin with a fast speed, low power, for the material you are cutting. Use the cutting speeds and powers in the previous chapter ('Materials') for guidance.

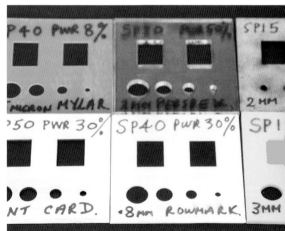

Laser test piece cut in various materials, with the most successful speed and power settings used written on each for future reference.

Note: Before each cut check your focus using the Focus tool supplied with your laser.

You are looking to cut at the fastest speed, lowest power for each of the materials you intend using. The material should fall out of the holes when taken off the laser bed.

Note that as your laser tube ages you may need to cut with higher power/lower speed until you reach the stage where you realize your tube needs changing (after making sure your mirrors and focus lens are clean).

ROOFING TILES

Amongst the simplest items to design and make with the laser cutter are roofing tiles. Cut out of paper, thin cardboard, Rowmark or Mylar, depending on scale and usage, these tiles, when overlapped and glued down, will give your roofs that authentic 3-D look.

Begin by running Sketchup with the Laser3-D template set up as described previously. The dimensions shown are for 4mm tiles.

TIP: Remember to tap Enter after putting numbers in the Dimensions box.

• Draw a rectangle 2,400 x 40mm using the Rectangle tool and Dimensions box (enter 2400,40 in the Dimensions box and tap Enter). This will fit on an A4-sized laser cutting bed. If yours is smaller, then make the rectangle shorter to fit

• Zoom in to the left-hand end (put the pointer on it) using the scroll wheel on your mouse. This does take some getting used to! If your drawing appears to disappear, click on the Zoom Extents icon to display it full screen, and try again

• Using the Tape Measure tool, draw guidelines 15mm down from the top of the rectangle and 30mm in from the left, as shown in the illustration below

• Using the Line tool (pencil shape), draw a line down the lower portion of the vertical guide as shown, leaving the top 15mm without a line

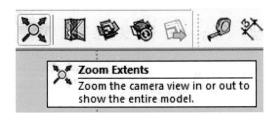

Dimensions | 2400,40

Rectangle drawn with the dimensions entered into the Dimensions box.

Zoom Extents
Zoom the camera view in or out to show the entire model.

At any time you can re-set your drawing to fit the screen by clicking on the Zoom Extents icon shown above.

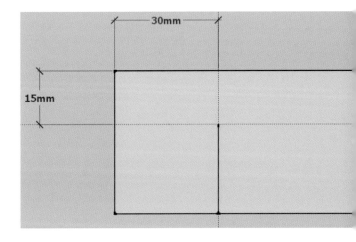

Zoom in to the left-hand end of the rectangle.

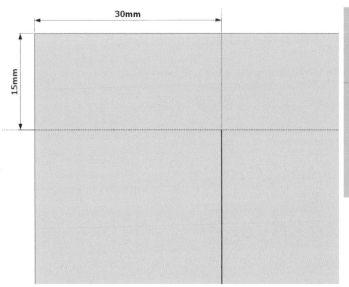

The line selected. It turns blue.

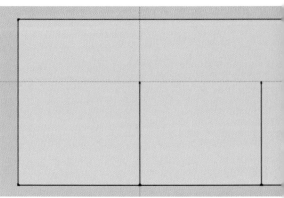

The line copied 30mm to the right of the first line. Each represents a tile in 4mm scale.

Use the Select tool and drag a rectangle around the line. It turns blue to show it is selected.

To copy the line a quite complex series of key presses and mouse movements is required. The sequence is as below (use the Undo tool and try again if you go wrong):

• With the line selected (drag a rectangle around just the line with the Select tool – it turns blue), select the Move tool, then tap the Ctrl key on your keyboard to get a '+' by the cursor (this shows you wish to copy the selected line/object)
• Hover over the bottom of the line with the Move cursor until a small box opens up saying 'endpoint'
• Hold down the right arrow key on your keyboard (this limits movement to the red axis – left/right on your drawing)
• With the Move cursor showing 'endpoint', hold down the left mouse button (with the right arrow key still held down), and begin to drag the line to the right. Once you have moved the line even slightly to the right you can release the mouse button and right arrow key
• Now *immediately* enter '30' into the Dimensions box (at the bottom of the screen) and tap the

Enter key on your keyboard. The line should move to exactly 30mm from the first
• Before touching any other keys, enter *78 into the Dimensions box and tap Enter on your keyboard. This will repeat the line move seventy-eight times!

Finally zoom out using your scroll wheel so you can see the result. If it is not correct use the Undo arrow and try again.

Remember: Save your work with the File >Save As, naming it 'a roofing tiles'. This saves your entire drawing in Sketchup format.

After saving your work, it is worth drawing a second rectangle and repeating the instructions, particularly the copying sequence, until you become familiar with it. You will use it a lot when drawing with Sketchup. Delete this second rectangle before continuing.

You should now have a strip of roofing tiles as shown above. You could now simply save this as a .dxf file for the laser and print it, but it would be very tedious taking them off the laser cutting bed before cutting another, so you are going to repeat the strip and join it to others in such a way that it lifts off the laser bed in one nearly A4-sized sheet.

To enable the lengths to be taken off the laser as an A4 sheet, you must simply remove the end vertical lines:

The line copied seventy-eight times along the length of the rectangle. Each represents a tile.

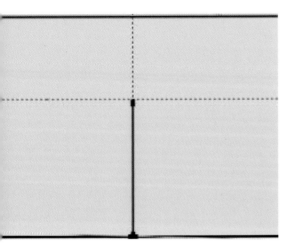

Left-hand vertical line selected.

Left-hand vertical line deleted.

• With the Select tool, click on the line. It should turn blue as in the illustration above. Delete it by tapping the Delete key

Now repeat this process for the right-hand end. To create a sheet of tiles ready for use you must now copy this strip. We do this using the same procedure as copying the lines.

• Use the Select tool to select the entire row of tiles
• Use the Move tool + Ctrl (Ctrl key to add the +) to copy the row 40mm downwards (hold down the left arrow key and the left mouse button) and pull down a little, then enter '40' into the Dimensions box and tap the Enter key
• *Immediately* enter *44 into the Dimensions box to copy the row of tiles forty-four times down the screen. This repeats the tiles so they will fit comfortably on an A4 sheet

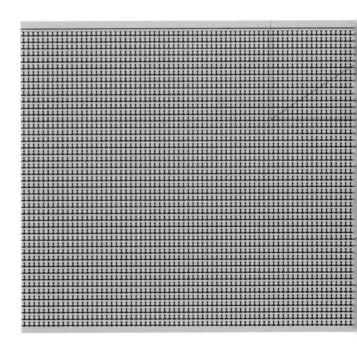

Completed sheet of roofing tiles.

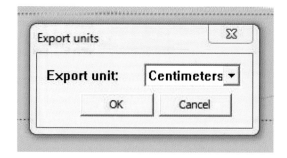

Select Centimeters – this scales down your drawing by a factor of ten so it will cut out at the correct size.

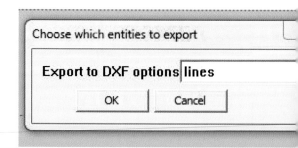

The Export DXF option may be under the Tools menu rather than the Files menu.

Export your file for the laser as Lines.

The uncut ends allow the tiles to be removed as one sheet.

Now use File >Save As 'b roofing Tiles' to save the entire drawing in Sketchup format.

Before you can cut out your tiles on the laser you now have to save the file as a .DXF file via the .DXF plug-in you loaded and installed earlier.

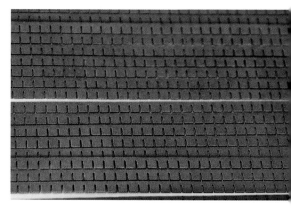

.dxf extension to the filename for laser cutting.

• Use the Select tool to select your entire drawing (it should turn blue)
• Click on the Export DXF option under the File (or Tools) menus.

Selecting Centimeters as the export unit scales down your drawing by a factor of ten. (Remember you have drawn everything ten times larger because Sketchup gets confused by tiny objects.)

The laser will cut along the lines we have drawn, so we export them as lines.

Ensure you add .dxf to the end of your filename if it isn't added automatically, and save as b roofing tiles.dxf. This file can now be loaded into your laser software for cutting out.

A sheet of roofing tile strips laser cut and ready to use.

USING THE ROOFING TILES

The roofing tiles can be cut out of a wide range of materials to suit your scale and purpose.

The Scale icon: use it to scale your drawing up or down.

To scale the drawing you can use the Scale icon and enter your exact figure into the Dimensions box. Remember, if you scale it up it may no longer fit on your laser bed.

The cheapest and quickest material for 4mm scale is cereal packet. In 2mm-scale, 80gsm or 100gsm paper might be appropriate (after scaling the drawing down by 50 per cent). In larger scales mount card can look effective. For outdoor use you need to use Rowmark or thick Mylar.

To use the tiles, proceed as shown, laying the bottom strip first and overlapping subsequent strips by half the width of the tiles (1.5mm in 4mm scale), and to the depth of the cut in the strips. Cut off the ends to match the roof on completion.

To make the tiles self-adhesive, use the technique discussed previously for Mylar in the chapter Materials for Laser Cutting. This does make them easier to use, but you have to be careful to get them in the right position first time.

By shaping the ends of the tiles and repeating this shape along the length, you can achieve a wide variety of styles, as shown.

Finally, paint your tiles to suit.

Start at the bottom of your roof, laying the tiles as shown.

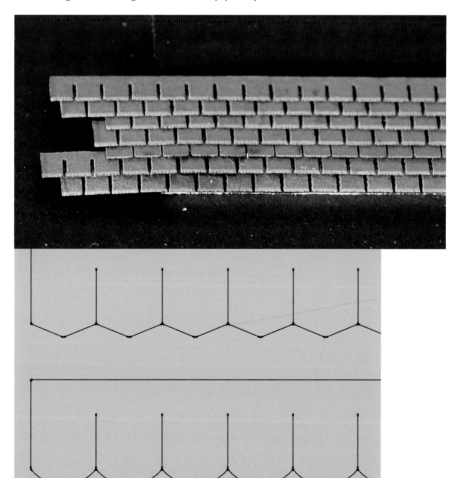

Some example tile shapes to try.

WINDOW FRAMES

Window frames are an ideal item for laser cutting. They are very difficult to cut out by hand and we usually need several of the same shape and design. You can choose a material suited to the scale required from cereal packet for 2mm scale up to 2mm MDF and 3mm acrylic sheet for G-scale. The dimensions are for 4mm scale: adjust them as required, or scale the whole window frame once drawn.

The window frames in this section will cut out as individual window frames to be stuck on the inside of your building window openings in a traditional manner. For laser cut buildings it is often better to incorporate them into a 'Layer' as shown in the advanced CAD section earlier. However, if you are asked to design/make some for others, cutting them as separate window frames with a wide outer frame is probably the best way to do them.

BASIC WINDOW FRAME

Use the Rectangle tool to draw rectangles and the Tape Measure tool to draw your guidelines. You will also need to use the Select tool and the keyboard Delete key to delete unwanted lines.

From left to right:

- 1: Begin by using the Rectangle tool to draw a rectangle the actual size of the window opening in the wall; in the example above it is 150mm wide by 200mm deep (*10 remember!)
- 2: You need to cut the window larger than the opening to allow you to glue it in place behind, so with the Tape Measure tool draw guidelines 20mm outside the rectangle all round
- Draw another rectangle with the Rectangle tool to the guidelines just drawn. This will be 20mm all round larger than the first
- With the Tape Measure tool, measure guidelines for your frames, which will all be 10mm thick
- Begin by drawing guidelines 10mm in from the edges of the original rectangle for the outer frames
- Now add guidelines for the horizontal and vertical centrelines, and add further guidelines 5mm each side of these as shown
- 3: Use the Rectangle tool to draw four rectangles for the window panes using the guidelines

Now use File >Save As >a Basic Window Frame.skp (Sketchup). (This file is used in the next project.)

- 4: Select and delete the four lines which marked the size of the original window opening, you need a wide margin to glue the window into the frame.

Now use File >Save As >b Basic Window Frame.skp (Sketchup); and File >Export DXF >Centimeters >Lines >b Basic Window Frame.dxf (for the laser).

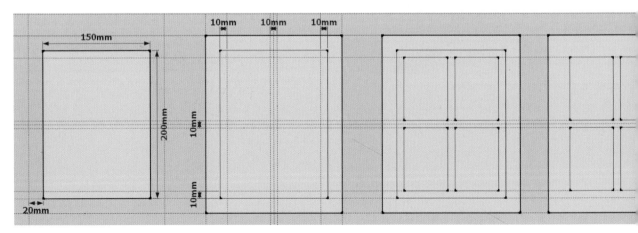

Stages in drawing a basic window frame.

TWO-PART SASH-TYPE WINDOW FRAME

This window frame is in three parts. Load the file >a Basic Window Frame.skp saved above.

From left to right:

- Begin by using the Move +Ctrl tool to copy the window frame twice to the right: Select the entire frame, then Move+ (Move tool plus tap Ctrl key) to the right twice
- 1: On the left-hand frame, remove all the inner panes as shown by selecting and deleting them in turn
- 2: Use the Select and Line tools to remove and add lines on the centre copy to make the top opening the height of the original (left-hand image) and the width of the bottom panes as shown. Remove the three unwanted lines of the original rectangle
- 3: Delete the existing guidelines by selecting the menu Edit>Delete Guides

- On the right-hand copy Select and delete the bottom three lines of the two bottom panes; use the Tape Measure tool to draw guidelines 12mm down from the remaining two lines of the bottom panes and 5mm in from each side. Use the Line tool to complete the bottom of the sliding sash as shown
- Finally Select and remove the two outer rectangles and bottom three lines to leave the top sash as shown

Now use File >Save As >a Sash Window Frame.skp (Sketchup), and

File >Export DXF >Centimeters >Lines >a Sash Window Frame.dxf (for laser).

The techniques employed to make this window frame can be used to make almost any type of rectangular window frame. They can be made in a wide variety of materials to suit scale and usage; for example made in Rowmark or acrylic sheet for outdoor use in the larger scales.

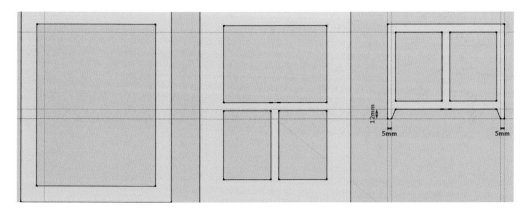

Stages in drawing a sash window frame. The blue background is removed from the panes for clarity. All three drawings are required to laser cut the window frames.

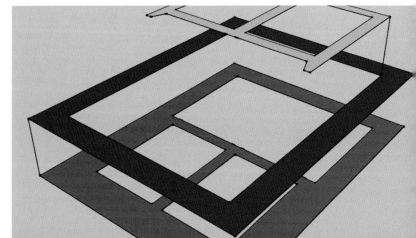

Assembly of the window.

Final window assembled. Use thin glazing behind each set of panes. The upper sash can be glued open if required.

MORE AMBITIOUS WINDOW FRAMES

Whilst it is possible to make straight-sided window frames out of Plasticard strips, it is much more difficult with multi-part and curved windows. Not only can you design and cut curved windows using Sketchup and a laser cutter, but you can cut out as many as required.

- Use the Rectangle tool to draw a rectangle 50 x 80mm, and then the Tape Measure tool to draw guidelines 15mm to the right and beneath it
- Select your first rectangle and copy it to the right 65mm twice (Move tool and tap Ctrl to get +, then sixty-five in the Dimensions box and repeat)
  - Select all three rectangles and copy them down three times by 95mm to get the drawing as above

Now use File >Save As >a Mill Window Frame.skp (Sketchup).

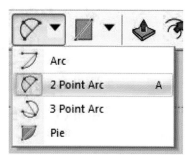

The two-point Arc tool.

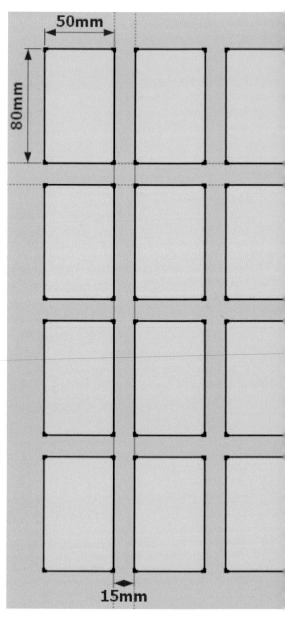

The basic window panes drawn. This would be suitable for a mill or engine shed building just as it is drawn on a Layer (as in the terraced house example).

To use the two-point Arc tool click one side, then the other, and then pull the arc shape and click to complete.

From left to right:

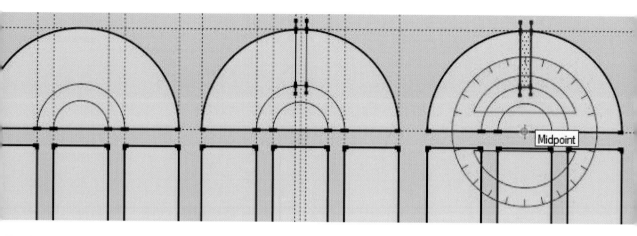

The first three stages of drawing the top windows.

- 1: Click on all the vertical lines of the windows with the Tape Measure tool to create guidelines
- Add a horizontal guideline 15mm above the tops of the windows
- Use the Line tool to draw a horizontal line 15mm above the windows and the width of the windows
- Select the two-point Arc tool and immediately enter 96 in the Dimensions box and tap the Enter key (to ensure smooth half-circles made up of ninety-six lines)
- Use the two-point Arc tool to create three half-circles as shown, each pulled up until you get the 'Half Circle' message box
- 2: Add a centreline guideline, and then two guidelines 5mm each side
- Use the Line tool (pencil) to draw over the two 5mm guidelines, extending the lines beyond the two top half-circles as shown
- Select the two vertical lines just drawn (by dragging a rectangle around them with the Select tool). They should both turn blue along their entire length
- 3: Use the Rotate tool+ (tap the Ctrl key after selecting it to make it copy the rotation), and click on the 'Midpoint' as shown, before clicking again to the right and pulling down to rotate the two lines. Immediately enter 30 into the Dimensions box and tap Enter, followed immediately by *2 in the Dimensions box and tap Enter again

- The two pairs of lines should have been copied twice to the right. Repeat the above two stages, but this time copy the lines to the left
- 4: You should now have the top looking like the left-hand window above
- 5: Delete the portions of the half-circle as shown in the centre window above, and also the two short lines highlighted in yellow. The top curved panes of window should all be separated by the background as shown centre, above

The second three stages of drawing the top windows.

- 6: Finally, draw guidelines 40mm from left, top, right and bottom of the window, and draw a rectangle with the Rectangle tool all around the window
- This will allow the window to be cut out so it can be glued behind the opening in the wall. In practice, however, you would be best making the wall and windows as separate Layers as in the terraced house example earlier, using the shape of the opening in the wall to determine the measurements and shape of the window

By using the techniques above a variety of ornate windows can be designed for various types of building.

PALISADE FENCING

Note: When drawing lines, tap the Escape key to cease drawing.

This fencing is designed to be made from mount card and is in two parts. You might also try it in thin (2mm) MDF, or 1mm-thick Rowmark, or for 4mm and 2mm scales, thin Mylar. (See the earlier chapter in this section 'Materials for Laser Cutting' for more details.)

- Begin by drawing a rectangle 15 x 320mm (Rectangle tool and 15,320 in the Dimensions box)
- Using the Tape Measure tool, mark out the fencing post as shown. The vertical guideline to the right of the fencing is 15mm from it
- Draw the four horizontal lines 30mm long using the Line tool. They begin on the left-hand vertical and extend 15mm out to the guideline
- Use the Line tool to draw the point

Remember to use Undo if you go wrong.

- Delete (Select tool and Delete on the keyboard) the lines of the two triangles at the top of the post to leave the point
- Now Delete two lots of four lines where the horizontal bars meet the vertical post. Delete the vertical lines first. Note the left-hand vertical line of the post should have two 15mm gaps in it, as shown

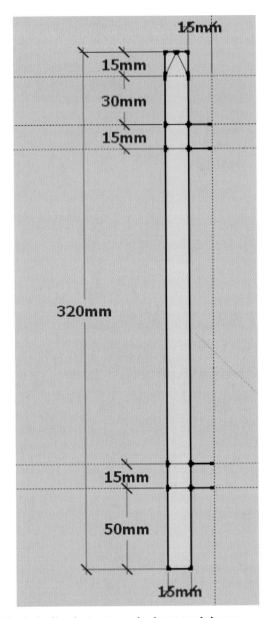

Basic palisade post marked out and drawn.

- Select all the post and copy (Move+ Ctrl key) by dragging it to the right 30mm (Dimensions box 30). It can help to hold down the right arrow key whilst doing this to constrain the move to the red axis. Immediately after the copy enter *10 into the Dimensions box and your copy will be copied ten times, as shown

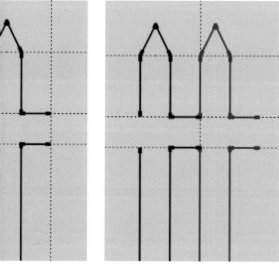

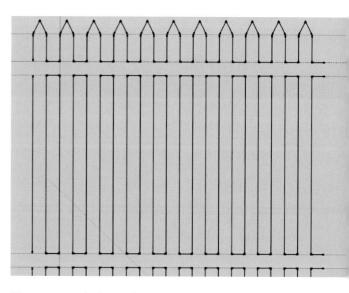

Fence post with point and horizontal rails.

The post copied 30mm to the right of the first.

The post copied ten times using the *10 command in the Dimensions box.

Remember the Undo/Redo tools if you go wrong!
  Save your drawing thus far as File >Save As >a palisade.skp.

• Using the Select tool, select the bottom part of the fence posts, leaving the first outside the selection.

The two circles above show where to begin and end your selection box. The bottom line of all the selected posts will turn blue, as shown

• With the bottom of the posts selected, use the Move tool to move the post bottoms up 35mm

The two circles show where to select with the Select tool (they do not need to be drawn).

BELOW: The bottom of the posts moved upwards.

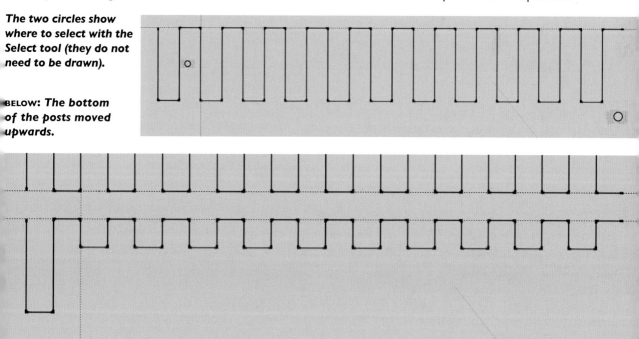

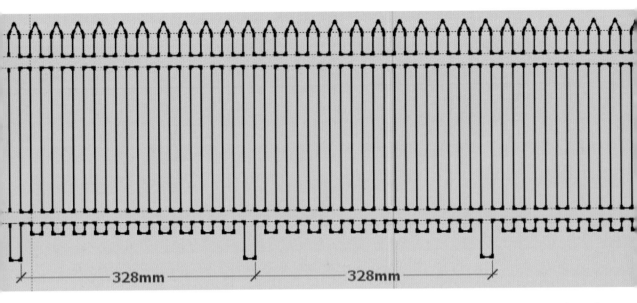

Section of palisade fencing copied twice to the right. By copying more times, you can make a fence to suit the size of your laser cutting bed.

(Dimensions box 35). Holding down the left arrow key whilst doing this will constrain the movement to the vertical

• Now you have your section of fence with post you can copy this by Selecting it all and then using

Move+ (Move tool, tap Ctrl key to get +) to copy it 328mm to the right (Dimensions box 328 and tap Enter), and then immediately enter *2 (Dimensions box *2 and tap Enter). Again, holding down the right arrow key constrains the movement to the red axis (left/right in this example)

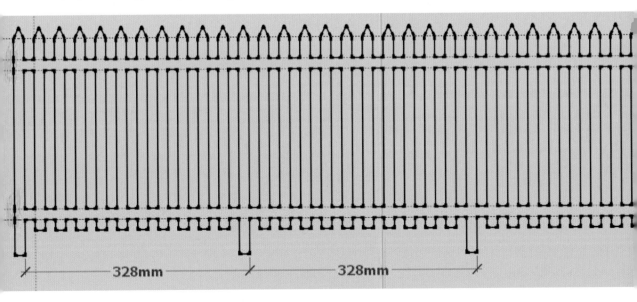

Four lines drawn (highlighted) to complete the fencing.

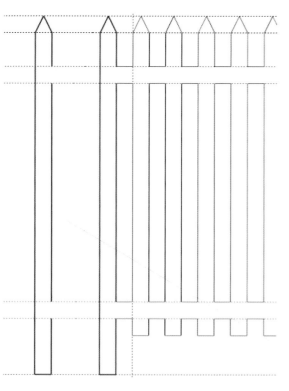

Second layer post copied from the first.

• To complete the basic fencing you just need to fill in the ends as shown using the Line tool to fill in the gaps in the end posts

Save your drawing thus far as File >Save As >b palisade.skp.
  Next we need the second layer.

• Begin by Selecting just the longer left-hand post and copying it (Move tool, tap Ctrl key to get +) 50mm to the left (Dimensions box 50)
• Select your second layer post and copy it 328mm to the left using Move+ (Move tool, tap Ctrl key to get +) and Dimensions box 328
• Immediately enter *3 (Dimensions box *3) to copy it a further three times to get four posts in all
• Use the Line tool to draw the four horizontal lines joining the vertical posts
• To complete the second layer, Delete all the short lines where the rails and posts intersect
• Select the right-hand post and Delete it

Save your drawing as File >Save As >c palisade.skp (this saves the entire Sketchup drawing).

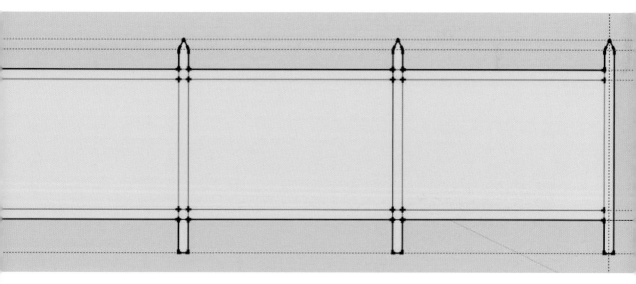

Second layer posts and rails. Note how Sketchup colours these blue as it recognizes them as solid areas.

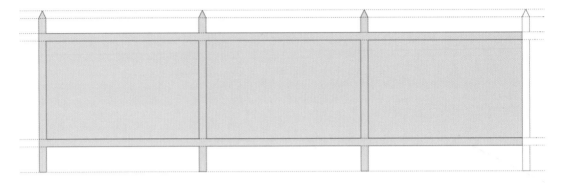

The second layer with the lines removed.

Now export your drawing for the laser cutter using File >Export DXF >Centimeters >Lines >c palisade.dxf (this file can be loaded into your laser cutting software).

By overlapping the second layer as shown before gluing it to the first, any length of fencing can be made. Because the laser cuts so accurately it is often very useful to build up larger models by using overlapping layers, which also makes them stronger.

Once cut, use a sharp knife to cut them free of the sheet.

The example shown is designed for making in mount board. If using Rowmark or Mylar you may be able to make the posts and rails much thinner. Mylar would be suitable for making this fencing in 2mm

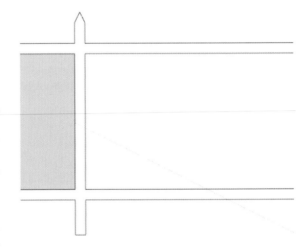

Right-hand post deleted.

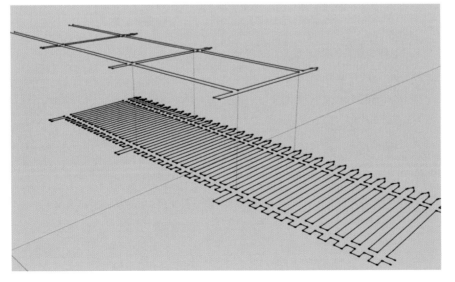

Your drawing will have the two parts of the fence side by side. This is correct. The drawing above shows how the second layer is used to strengthen the fencing.

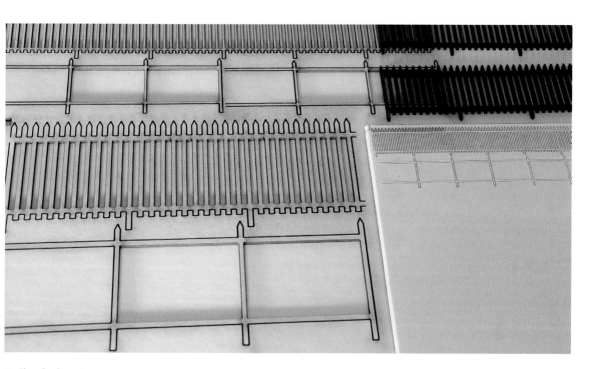

Palisade fencing cut out in different scales/materials: at left in mount card for 4mm and 7mm scales, top right in 2mm-thick MDF for 4mm scale, and middle left in 125 micron-thick Mylar for 2mm scale.

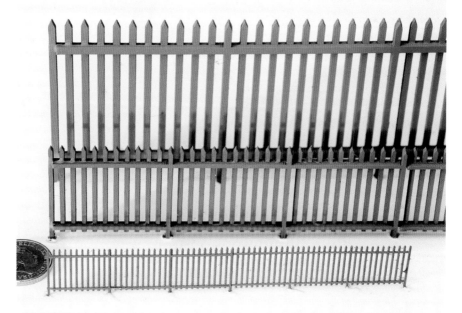

Palisade fencing sprayed matt grey 'in situ': 2mm, 4mm and 7mm scales, with a 5p coin at left. The 2mm fencing is 15mm (7ft 6in to scale) high.

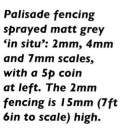

scale using the technique of gluing the Mylar to cardboard as outlined in the earlier chapter 'Materials for Laser Cutting'. This chapter also explains how you can make a self-adhesive layer, which would be useful for the second layer of fencing.

Spray the fencing with grey primer (or other colour of choice) once complete, and use the longer posts to fix the fence in drilled holes.

Try designing and making your own variation of this palisade fencing.

POST AND WIRE LINESIDE FENCING

Using thin Mylar 75 microns thick, it is possible to make realistic post and wire fencing in 4mm scale which is both tough and adaptable.

THE LINESIDE FENCING TEST PIECE

The key to success is in fine tuning the cutting thickness of the 'wire' so that the laser can just cut it to as thin a section as possible, consistently in the Mylar. Some trial and error with a test sample is called for. Once you have achieved the desired result, you can then make a length of fencing together with posts and end bracing.

To determine the thinnest you can cut your Mylar you can use a test piece such as the one in the illustration.

Begin by drawing the test piece as in the illustration.

- Use the Rectangle tool to draw a rectangle 500 × 500mm
- With the Tape Measure tool add three guidelines 20mm in from both sides and down from the top as shown
- Use the Rectangle tool and from the top guide draw a rectangle 460 × 20mm

You are now going to draw a series of rectangles with decreasing gaps between them to test how thinly you can cut the Mylar with consistent results. This is best achieved by copying rectangles down with less and less gap between them.

Remember, to copy a rectangle (or any other part of a drawing) you must first Select it (Select tool), and then with the Move tool chosen, tap the Ctrl key to get a + by the cursor. This indicates to Sketchup that anything chosen is to be copied when moved.

- Select the rectangle just drawn and copy it (see above comment) downwards (hold down the left arrow key to constrain movement to the vertical) 30mm (Dimensions box 30, then Enter key)

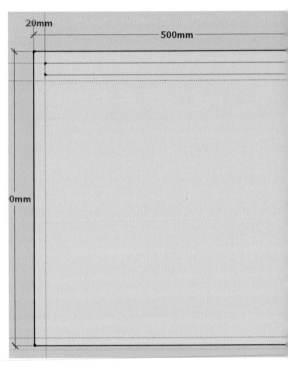

Start of the lineside fencing test piece.

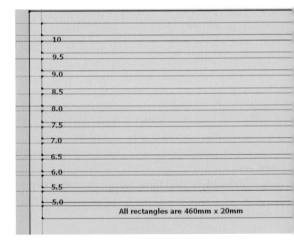

All rectangles are 460mm x 20mm

Your drawing should now look like the one above. Note how each thin bar will cut out between the rectangles.

- Continue to copy the rectangle downwards decreasing the movement by .5mm each time (29.5, 29, 28.5 etc) to achieve the gaps between rectangles as shown in the illustration. Tap the Ctrl key each time to remain in copy mode

Each space between the rectangles is smaller by .5mm. The top gap is actually 1mm and the bottom gap .5mm (scaled down when saving by a factor of 10). The end verticals between rectangles are left solid so that the thin strips remain on the sheet.

Now use File >Save As 'a lineside test piece.skp' in Sketchup format. Save ready for laser cutting, File>Export as DXF >Centimetres >Lines>'a lineside test piece'.dxf.

Using a glue stick, stick your 50mm square of Mylar (I use 125 micron-thick Mylar for fencing wires) down to a sheet of mount card (or cereal packet if flat enough). This prevents the Mylar from bending and warping with the heat of the laser, thus causing it to go out of focus. It also helps draw some heat away from the Mylar, giving a better unburnt edge cut.

NOTE: *Fire risk!* Because you are attempting to leave a very fine thread of Mylar behind when cutting this piece there is an increased risk that the Mylar and/or backing cardboard will flame slightly. Be aware of this and never leave the laser cutter unattended. High speed and low power will help avoid this risk.

Cut out the test piece. Begin by checking the focus, which is critical for this type of fine cutting.

Start with a cutting speed of about 40mm per second, which is quite fast, and a power of ten. Look at the cut: the cardboard should show a brown line if the cut is going through. Too much power, or too slow, and the card will almost cut through and the edges of the Mylar will turn brown, showing they are burnt. Sometimes it is better to cut twice on high speed/low power (don't move the test piece at all between cuts) for a finer cut.

You are trying to achieve the finest thin thread of Mylar consistent with it cutting reliably. Experiment with different speeds and power to achieve the best cut.

Once you have identified the best speed and power, note these, setting them down for future reference (mine were forty speed, 10 per cent power. Note also the thickness of the Mylar used (mine was 125 microns). Use this same thickness when cutting out the final fence.

Here I have altered the power from 10 per cent to 7 per cent and back to 10 per cent as the laser has been cutting. Note how the Mylar has been cut only part-way through on the lower power.

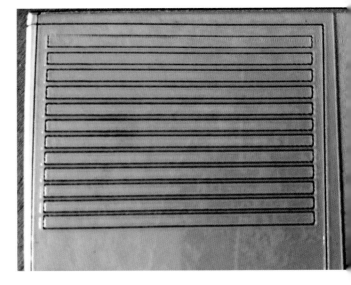

Mylar cut out on cardboard. Note the thin brown lines, which show that the laser has just cut through the Mylar successfully and lightly burnt the surface of the cardboard.

THE LINESIDE FENCING

Before drawing the actual fencing, it is necessary to make some assumptions about size and scale. The measurements are for 4mm scale. In other scales the minimum thickness you can cut remains the same,

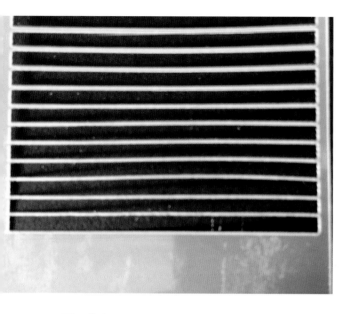

The finished test piece removed from the card. The bottom thread of Mylar is less than .5mm thick. You have to judge which is the best compromise, between appearance and strength.

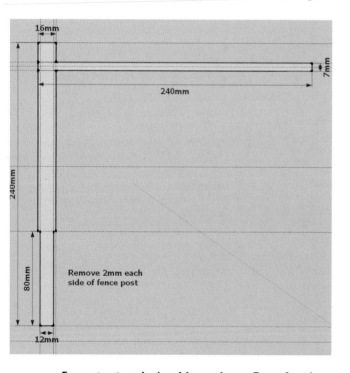

16mm

240mm

7mm

240mm

80mm

Remove 2mm each side of fence post

12mm

Fence post and wire. I have shown 7mm for the wire (.7mm when cut). Adjust yours to suit the best thickness obtained from your test on the material you are using.

but you might like to increase the thickness by .5mm ('5' on the drawing) for larger scales, as the posts will be further apart.

Draw the post and 'wire' as above. The posts are 4ft out of the ground, drawn 6ft here; they will therefore fit in drilled holes in your layout to a depth of 8mm. Remove 2mm from each side of the post bottom up to 80mm. The notches on the posts show 'ground level'.

The fencing shown is five-wire fencing, but three-wire and seven-wire fencing exist and could be drawn and cut out using similar techniques.

To prepare for copying, remove the vertical lines where the posts meet, as shown. Also remove the left-hand vertical line of the post down to the notch for ground level, and the vertical line at the extreme right of the 'wire' as shown.

- Select the two horizontal lines representing the wires, and copy them (Move and tap Ctrl key to get + by the cursor) down 30mm, then immediately enter *4 into the Dimensions box to copy again to make five, as shown
- Select and Delete the vertical lines between the wires on the right-hand side of the fence post. Your drawing should look like that in the illustration

Now use File >Save As>a lineside fence.skp.

Decide on the total length of fencing required (not longer than your laser bed or sheet of Mylar), and copy this 'module' to the right by 240mm and then the number required.

- Select the entire fence drawn so far
- Use Move+ (Move + Ctrl key) to copy the fence 240mm to the right (240 in Dimensions box)
- *Immediately* enter *n into the Dimensions box, where n is the number of times you wish to copy the fence section
- Once copied, Select and Delete the unwanted right-hand wires

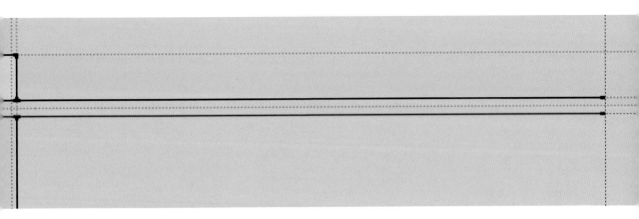

Post and wire with lines removed ready for copying.

'Wire' copied down fencing.

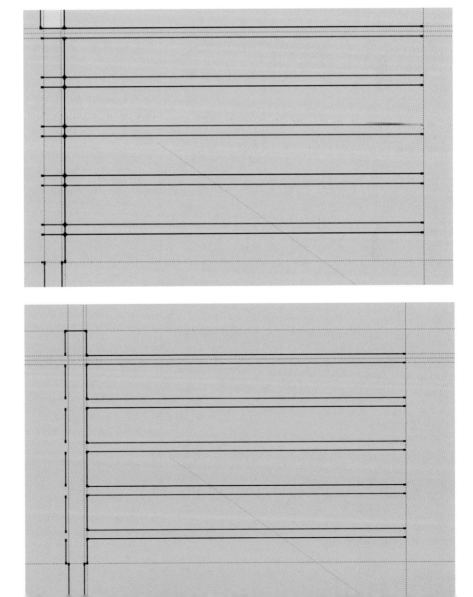

Unwanted lines removed.

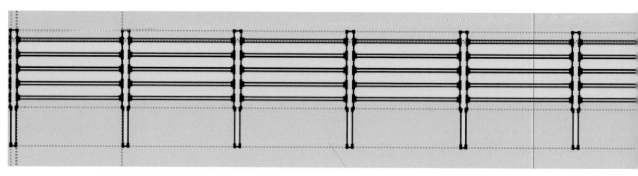

Section of fence copied to the right, 240mm x 6.

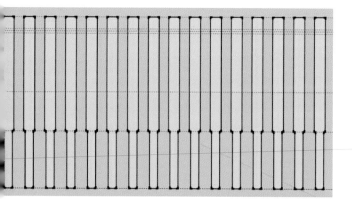

A set of posts ready to be printed. This is best done as self-adhesive, as described.

- Use the Line tool to draw vertical lines over the extreme ends of the left and right posts to close the gaps

Now use File >Save As b lineside fence.skp, and File > Export DXF > b lineside fence.dxf.

You now have a drawing of a section of fence ready for cutting out. Remember, with materials such as Mylar it can be helpful to use a glue stick to glue them to cardboard to keep them flat whilst cutting. This stops the Mylar curling with the heat and going out of focus.

Redraw just one post complete from the dimensions given earlier

- Now copy it (Move tool then Ctrl key to get a + by the cursor) to the right, leaving a reasonable gap between posts, and then *19 to make a set of twenty (or however many are required)

Making Self-Adhesive Parts on the Laser

Double-sided adhesive sheets A4 in size can be purchased at reasonable cost via eBay. These have an extremely thin adhesive film sandwiched between two sheets of paper. Proceed as follows:

- Cut your Mylar (or other material) and your double-sided adhesive sheets to the required size
- Start with small pieces until you are proficient
- Peel off one side of the paper from the double-sided adhesive sheet
- Carefully, press your Mylar to the adhesive making sure you don't trap any air bubbles, starting at one corner and smoothing out as you go
- Mylar side up, use a glue stick to glue the other side of the double-sided adhesive sheet (still with backing paper on it) to cardboard to keep it flat during cutting
- Place in your laser and focus carefully
- Use low power and high(ish) speed to cut through the Mylar and adhesive layers, leaving a brown cut mark on the paper layer under the adhesive
- Repeat cutting if required, but do not move your Mylar between cuts
- Once done, use a pointed craft knife to prise off your fencing posts (or other small objects). You will find they are self-adhesive

This technique does require a little experimentation with laser speed/power but can be very useful with small parts. The glue is not particularly strong, but for tiny items that are to be spray painted, the paint itself helps hold them together.

Now use File >Save As c lineside fence.skp (this saves all your drawing).

Next, select the posts and use File >Export DXF c lineside fence posts.dxf (this saves just these posts).

Again, these will benefit from being cut whilst the Mylar is glued to card.

FINAL ASSEMBLY

All that is required once cut out is an extra post being glued to each side of the posts of the fencing as shown. The fencing can then be spray painted as required, and posts glued into holes pre-drilled into your scenic sections.

To get your fence to conform to the contours of your embankments and hills, simply grasp two adjacent posts, gently pull them apart, and offset them with a sharp tug up/down. The fence will stay in a sloping position as shown.

Paint the wire a greyish/rusty colour and the posts a dark grey, and the fencing disappears into the landscape.

PROBLEMS

The first time I tried printing my fence above the bottom wire broke off at the right-hand side by each post. Eventually I traced this to the extra tiny line as shown. Since this was a mistake on my original post, it got copied to every post/wire. This extra line was sufficient to make the laser cut off the wire at each post! If something unusual happens, then zoom in and check your drawing carefully!

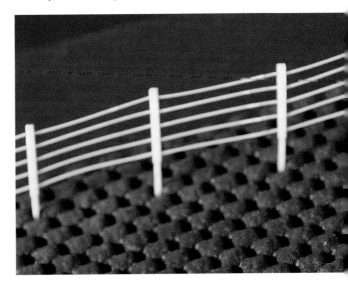

CLOCKWISE FROM TOP LEFT:
Fencing, top, cut out of Mylar glued to mount board. Posts, bottom, cut out of Mylar glued to one side of double-sided sticky sheet with the other glued to mount card. The posts peel off, as self-adhesive, making it easier to glue one on each side of the fence posts.

Wire and post fencing in 4mm scale laser cut from 190 micron-thick Mylar. The fencing posts have an extra layer of Mylar glued on each side.

A tiny bit of extra line caused the bottom wire to be cut off. This could only be seen extremely close up.

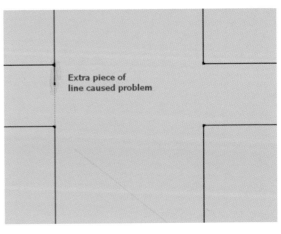

Extra piece of
line caused problem

LASER-CUT BRICKWORK

By lowering the power and increasing the speed of your laser you can effectively 'mark' your work with a shallow cut. This does not penetrate very deeply, and the depth can be easily controlled by altering the power and speed settings until you achieve the depth required.

This technique is ideal for brickwork. Note this is still laser cutting, not engraving. It still uses a .DXF file. It does require a 'registration square' so that your brickwork and the wall are aligned.

It also requires that you are familiar with 'Layers' as outlined in the 'Advanced CAD' chapter of Part I.

Use the drawing of the Terraced House saved in the Advanced CAD chapter: File >Open > e Terraced house.skp

If you have guidelines on the drawing, choose Edit >Delete Guides to delete them.

Remember that you drew the Terraced House using Layers. In the Layers menu add Brickwork as a new Layer. Check you are drawing on Layer0 (round circle checked), and that only the Layer Wall and Layer Brickwork are visible, as shown.

- Use the Select tool and select the whole of Layer Wall
- Double-click on it, or select Edit Group from the drop-down menu
- Use the Rectangle tool to draw a 30mm square at the top left of your Layer Wall
- Click anywhere on the background to close the Group

You have now added the 30mm registration square to your Layer Wall.

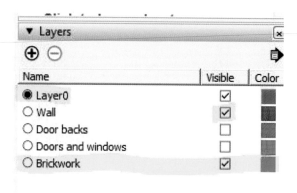

On Layer0, with the wall selected as visible and a brickwork Layer added.

Draw the registration rectangle as highlighted.

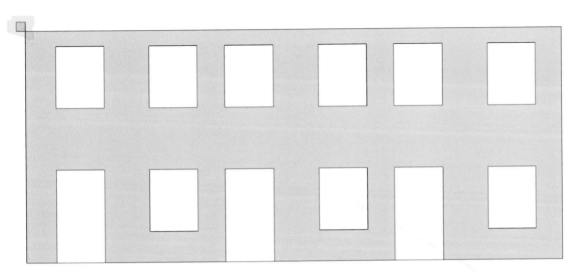

Registration rectangle, top left of Layer Wall.

Now use File >Save As >f Terraced house.skp. Save your file so if your brickwork goes wrong you can re-load and start again.

• Use the Rectangle tool to re-draw over the registration rectangle (this will become part of your brickwork layer)

Brick faces are about 8 x 3in, or about 3 x 1mm in 4mm scale.

• Begin by using the Rectangle tool to draw a rectangle from the top corner of the Layer Wall 30 x 10mm as shown (*10 size).

Registration rectangle and first brick drawn.

The first row of bricks.

Important: Now make your Layer Wall invisible (untick the box in Layers menu). You should have just the one brick on your screen with the registration square.

• Next, select and copy this brick to the right by 30mm (Move + Ctrl key, hold the right arrow key whilst moving, then 30 in the Dimensions box)

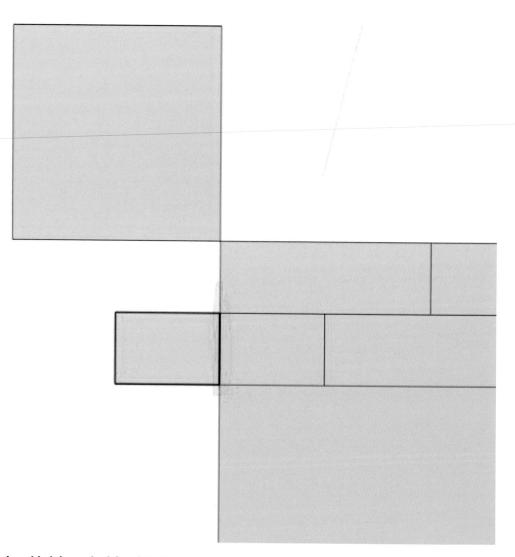

The top left-hand end of the brickwork with two rows offset.

Left-hand brick marked for deletion as it is outside the wall of the building.

- Immediately enter *59 in the Dimensions box to repeat this copy fifty-nine times. The first row of bricks have been copied
- Now, select the whole row of bricks and copy them down 20mm: Move+ Ctrl and holding left arrow key, and then 20 in the Dimensions box (this is not a misprint: you need the rows of brick separate, or when you move them to the left you would also move the bottom line of the top row)
- Now move the bottom row of bricks 15mm to the left (Move – without Ctrl – and right arrow key, then 15 in the Dimensions box). This provides the offset for the bricks
- Finally, move the bottom row of bricks up 10mm (10 in Dimensions box) to join the first row, as

shown. Hold down the left arrow key whilst you move to ensure the correct move direction
- Make the Layer Wall visible and Zoom in on the left-hand end of your brickwork
- The half brick outside the wall boundary needs removing. Use the Line tool to draw a line over the brick on the vertical wall boundary (highlighted yellow above), then select the three other lines of the brick (Select and hold Shift to select all three) and delete them by tapping the Delete key on your keyboard
- Repeat for the right-hand side. There are two pieces of brickwork to remove here. Your brickwork should now be the same width as your Layer Wall
- Make the Layer Wall invisible again

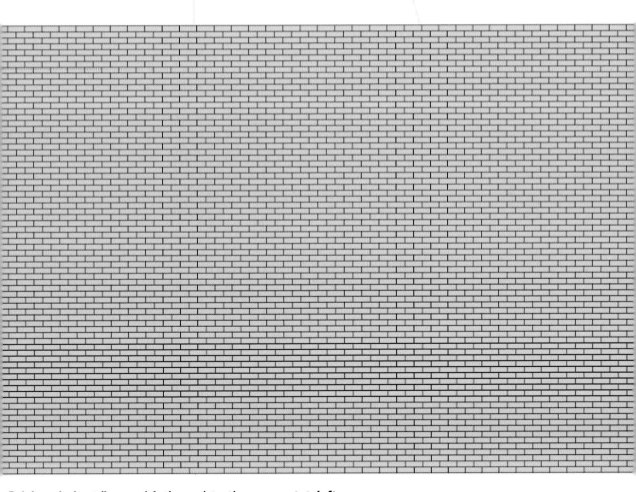

Brickwork sheet/layer with the registration square top left.

Selecting the Brickwork Layer.

- Select both rows of brickwork and copy them (Move+) down 20mm, then immediately repeat that thirty-six times (*36 in the Dimensions box). You will have one extra row of bricks at the bottom of your wall, but it will get cut off when the wall is cut out, so can be left
- With Layer Wall still invisible, select all the new brickwork (it all turns blue)
- Right-click on it and select Make Group from the drop-down menu (or Edit >Make Group), then select Brickwork from the drop-down Layers menu at the top of the screen to make it Layer Brickwork

Turn on and off the visibility of all your layers to check you have them correctly assigned to Layers.

Now use File >Save As> g Terraced House.skp to save your whole drawing in Sketchup format.

You must now save each layer in a format for the laser. To do this make each layer visible in turn, select it all so that it turns blue, and export it as a .DXF file, for example:

File>Export DXF> g Terraced House Wall.dxf

File> Export DXF> g Terraced House Door Backs.dxf

File> Export DXF> g Terraced House Doors and Windows.dxf

File> Export DXF> g Terraced House Brickwork.dxf

CUTTING OUT YOUR MODEL

Before proceeding, find a piece of scrap card similar to the one to be used for the final model (for example, mount card). Load the Brickwork DXF file into your

laser (this may take a long time as there are a lot of lines), and adjust the speed to thirty-five and power to ten (you are aiming to mark the card rather than cut it into several hundred small bricks!).

Cut the file, and you should be able to adjust the power so that your bricks are 'cut' to just the right depth (about a quarter of the way through the card, or less).

Once happy with the result, load your laser with the wall material (it could be red or grey mount card, depending on the brick type). Note carefully the top registration square, which should be *exactly top left* of your laser software screen. Now 'cut' your brickwork on low power to just mark the card. *Do not remove or move your workpiece yet!*

In your laser software, delete the Brickwork file and load your Wall DXF file, carefully moving the registration square to *exactly top left* of your laser software screen. Turn the laser speed down and power up to cut the card (these determined by using a test piece as described earlier). Cut the Wall Layer. You can now remove your wall complete with brickwork.

Laser-cut brickwork on red card. Too much power was used initially at the left-hand corner and some of the 'bricks' have fallen off as the laser cut right through the top red layer of the card.

Load your other two DXF files and cut them out of suitable material. Finally glue your complete wall, windows and doors together ensuring you have them in the right order.

This 'cutting' of brickwork works particularly well on MDF.

SILLS AND LINTELS

For window sills and lintels, simply draw appropriate shapes, copy them as many times as required, and cut them out of a suitable material. If gluing these on to the final model they can be grouped together to cut out the minimum amount of material. Mount card works quite well on card buildings, or even cereal packet which can be cut and then used two thicknesses deep. Paint/colour before gluing on to the building.

STATION AWNING DETAIL

To produce the station awning board valances you will need two Layers, one for marking the join between the boards and another for cutting them out. Add them to the Layers menu now.

The key to making this a success is the small rectangle at top left of the drawing, which allows you to align both drawings on the laser so the vertical lines can be cut on a low power to just mark the material; then the main drawing can be loaded and positioned to cut out the shape.

• Begin by drawing the shape at the bottom of your awning valance as in the very left-hand drawing using the Tape Measure, Line and Two-Point Arc tools

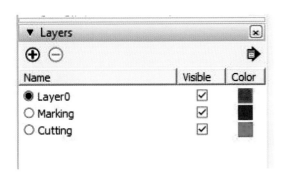

Begin by adding two Layers: Marking and Cutting.

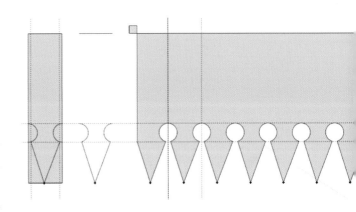

The various stages of drawing the awning valance left to right.

• Select and Delete the unwanted parts, including the vertical lines top to bottom
• Move+ (Copy) the remaining lines to the right by the width of the awning board using the Dimensions box, and then enter *n into the Dimensions box, where n is the number of boards required
• Now with the Line tool, add vertical lines at each end of your valance
• Draw a rectangle with the Rectangle tool at the top left corner (30mm square), as shown
• Select all the valance and small rectangle and right click to Make Group
• Add the valance to the Layer Cutting by clicking on it in the drop-down Layer menu at the top of the screen

Now for the lines separating each board.
• Use the Line tool to draw lines as required between each board, as shown in blue in the illustration
• Move+ (Copy) these lines to suit the length of your awning
• Use the Rectangle tool to draw another 30mm square at top left over the first (remember you are drawing over the Layer Cutting as on tracing paper)
• Make Layer Cutting invisible to leave just the new lines and rectangle as above
• Select all these lines and the rectangle and right-click and Make Group
• Add the lines to the Layer Marking by clicking on it in the drop-down Layer menu at the top of the screen

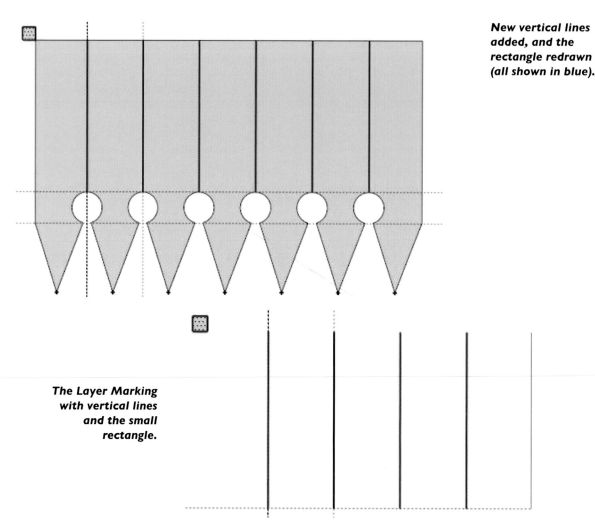

New vertical lines added, and the rectangle redrawn (all shown in blue).

The Layer Marking with vertical lines and the small rectangle.

Untick and re-tick the boxes by the two Layers to check they are correct and that they both have on them the small rectangle.

- Save your drawing as File>Save As>a awning.skp
- Make visible only Layer Cutting and select it all, then save as File>Export DXF>a awning cutting.dxf
- Make visible only Layer Marking and Select it all then save as File>Export DXF>a awning marking. dxf

You now have two drawings to laser. Place your material in the laser and load the a awning marking. dxf file. Carefully align the small rectangle top left with the top left of your laser software drawing area, turn the power down and cut the lines so the material is marked but not cut through.

Do not move your material at the end of the cut.

Delete the first file and now load your second file a awning cutting.dxf. Carefully align the small rectangle again with the top left of your laser software drawing area, but this time turn the power up to cut through the material. Cut out the awning. The key to success is the small rectangle which is used to line up the two drawings so the marking and cutting are in the correct place relative to each other.

I have found that Mylar or Rowmark are good materials for awnings as they are slightly flexible and do not break easily if touched when working on the layout. MDF can look good in the larger scales but is relatively brittle when used for fine detail.

In this chapter I will attempt to pass on some of the materials and techniques I have found useful when laser cutting.

JOINING AT CORNERS

A 'comb' joint is the strongest type of joint for laser cut buildings, and if the 30mm measurement in the illustration is altered to the thickness of your plywood, acrylic sheet or whatever, and the 40mm to the depth of your brickwork, the comb joints can be disguised as brickwork. In the smaller scales the joint may need to be two or three bricks deep/wide or it might not be strong enough.

Begin by drawing just the guidelines and four joint lines with measurements to suit your model as in the illustration right. These can be drawn to one side of the building.

Select the four lines just drawn and copy them down to the height of your building. You may need an additional line or two at the bottom to complete.

Finally, copy these sideways to your building corners, as shown in blue in the illustration right.

BENDING BY PART CUTTING

To bend a material such as acrylic sheet, mount card or plywood, simply draw a number of vertical or horizontal parallel lines on a sheet the size of your laser bed (or your model if smaller). About 5mm apart is usually sufficient, but you will need to experiment with whatever material you are using.

Place a sample of your material in the laser and adjust the power so the laser does not cut right through it, but about half to two thirds. This effectively 'scores' the sheet so it can be bent. This is much easier than doing it by hand with a craft knife!

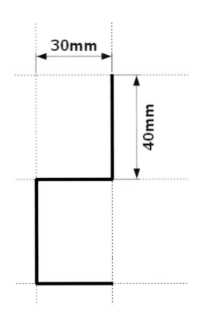

Four lines of comb joint, which can be copied down to the height of your building.

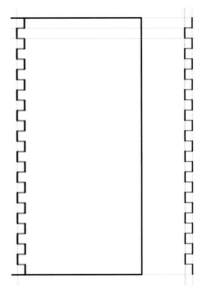

The final joint copied to the building.

LASER-ENGRAVED BRICKWORK

Laser-engraved brickwork/stonework on mount card can look very effective. You will need to adjust the speed and power settings on your laser to achieve the best engraved result. There are a number of stages involved:

- Find or take a suitable photograph of your intended brickwork or stonework (there are copyright-free examples on the internet)
- Process the photograph by making it black and white, high contrast, and 'dithering' it. Dithering converts the grey scales of the black and white photograph to dots – lots of dots where it is nearly black, and few where it is light. The laser 'fires' and marks the card on each black dot
- Save the result as a .bmp (bitmap file) ready for the laser
- Laser engrave on your chosen material

USING COREL PHOTOPAINT

If you have access to Corel PhotoPaint, then load your colour image of the wall, and choose Image>Convert to Black and White. A box opens, as in the illustration below, and you can select the Conversion method (here I have chosen 'Stucki'). Slide the intensity bar to a low number ('1' as shown in the picture) until your image is very high in contrast. Save this as a .bmp file, and try laser engraving it on to the card. Different effects are created when lasering on to white and coloured card. Experiment and adjust the power/speed until you have the laser-engraved stonework effect required.

USING IRFANVIEW

It is possible to create the desired 'dithered' black and white effect using Irfanview, which is free to download from the internet (www.irfanview.com).

Load your original image and select Image>Decrease Colour Depth, and then in the box that opens up choose two colours (black and white),

Converting a colour image of a stone wall to a 'dithered' image (shown on the right) for laser engraving using Corel PhotoPaint.

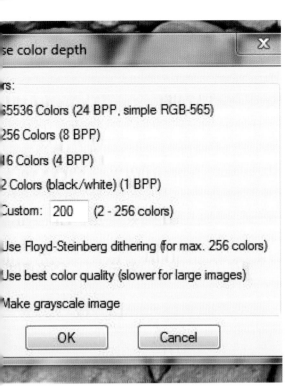

Close-up of laser-engraved stonework using the techniques described, and showing the effect of using different power levels.

A similar process using the free Irfanview program.

and ensure the Floyd-Steinberg dithering option is ticked. Again, some experimentation is required to find the right contrast level for the photograph.

TILING

Most image programs allow you to 'tile' an image to make a repeat pattern. Scale your image and tile it to the required size for laser engraving.

IN USE

Sketchup does not allow you to combine .BMP images with drawings, so the stone 'texture' BitMaP file is best laser engraved on to sheets of A4 (or to suit your laser bed size), and then these are cut out to form your building parts.

If using CorelDraw (or maybe other drawing packages) to do 2-D drawings for the laser, you can make the stonework bitmap image a 'texture' within the program and apply this to your building walls once drawn. This allows your stonework to flow around windows and doors. Do these on separate

Laser-engraved stonework on black mount card, then laser cut and assembled into these terraced houses. Windows are cut on another Layer, and the tiles are simply flat, dark grey card 'laser marked' by cutting at reduced power. I use cheap hairspray to 'fix' the engraving before fitting the window film.

'Layers', saving the stonework Layer as a bitmap (.bmp) file and the line drawing Layer as a .dxf file. Load both files into the laser and select 'all'. It should engrave the bitmap first, then cut out the lines. The actual technique to be used will be dependent on the software available to you, and also the program you use to drive the laser. To align the Layers when laser engraving and cutting I put a small square (3mm or so actual size, 30mm drawn) at the top left-hand corner of *every* Layer. These can then be aligned when loading the files into the laser software.

PART III: 3-D PRINTING

13 ENHANCING YOUR HOBBY WITH 3-D PRINTING

Many of the scenic items we use in our modelling are made of plastic. 3-D printers can, uniquely, make solid objects by building up layers of plastic under computer control, and are potentially able to make these models. From window frames to fencing through to complete buildings, provided you can draw an item a 3-D printer is likely to be able to make it.

Hobbyist machines, from about £300 at present, are limited to printing in plastic, although professional machines can print in a variety of materials including many metals. Plastic filament for 3-D printers is now available at reasonable cost – from about £15 a kilogram – and a kilogram of plastic makes a lot of models!

Once you have a suitable 3-D CAD drawing, the 3-D printer can produce your model in a variety of sizes and materials, and repeat them as often as required. Items either difficult or impossible to make by hand can be 3-D printed.

If the quality of a hobbyist machine's output is less than that required for a finished model, then it is pos-sible to upload the drawing to a 3-D Print Bureau and have them print your design/model on their 'professional' 3-D printer. These use a different technique to print and can produce models of a surprising quality.

Having your own machine is a great advantage as it gives you the ability to develop a final model via several cheap-to-produce prototypes and refinements of the original drawing. Also it reduces the time taken, as you are not having to wait for models to be returned in the post. It is difficult to get a model right first time, especially with complex and multi-part models.

Several models can be rapidly (relatively!) printed in a fast 'draft' (usually .3mm layers) so a model can be checked for fit and finish – for instance, does your window frame actually fit the opening? or does it look correct – for example a chimney pot?

This section of the book describes a variety of 3-D 'hobby' machines and their pros and cons, and generally introduces you to how they might be used to enhance the models you wish to make.

14 3-D PRINTERS – WHAT'S AVAILABLE?

Invented in the 1980s, 3-D printing machines have developed to the stage where they are now a consumer product. The current 'state of play' reminds me of the computer revolution of the 1980s, when many start-up companies were making home computers and names such as Atari, Commodore Pet, Tandy, Sinclair and Amstrad were all trying to produce the machine that everyone would want to own.

Inevitably there were successes and failures, but competition led to innovation and rapid development, and eventually the computer market place settled down to the two big players: Microsoft Windows and Apple. One produces an operating system around which many companies base their hardware, and the other produces both machines and the operating system.

At present it is too early to see this happening in the 3-D printing arena, though there are signs that the smaller, innovative and successful companies are being taken over by the more established larger companies, who then incorporate these innovations in their own products. There are signs also that some of the really big players in the printing machine area, such as HP, are researching how they can produce 3-D printing machines using developments of their existing technologies.

From our railway modelling perspective we almost have too much choice of 3-D printers, and it can be confusing to look at all the different ones on offer. It is inevitable that by the time this book is published further new printers will be on the market and within reach of the model railway club or individual modeller. I can only speculate about what might be available in five or ten years' time, but it will be significantly better than the 3-D printers available today, and at a cheaper price. Whether every home will have one is debatable, but young people today are growing up with these machines in their schools, and a proportion will want to continue this access at home.

Computers (and cameras and telephones and satellite navigation) are currently being superseded by 'smart phones', and as these develop they will become the 3-D scanners we use in the future to capture physical objects in 3-D prior to re-sizing, re-colouring, re-texturing and printing out in a wide range of materials on our domestic 3-D printers.

Currently you have a choice of over a hundred different 3-D printing machines, and several 3-D scanners at a realistic price (say, from £150 up to £2,000). Some of these are available only as kits, but increasingly they are sold as easy to use and ready to print.

In the next chapter I briefly discuss the various technologies used at present by 3-D printing machines, with more in-depth descriptions of those 'hobby' 3-D printers I have owned and had personal experience of using. I hope that by discussing the pros and cons of these machines it will help you understand how they work, but more importantly, whether they would be of use to you in our hobby, and what to look for when considering a purchase.

At present the output from 'hobby' 3-D printers may not be of sufficient quality for models requiring a smooth surface finish or fine detail, but for prototyping prior to sending off your designs to be printed by a 3-D print bureau, they are ideal. Their quality in the larger scales, 'O'-gauge and G-scale, may well be quite sufficient, in which case they have the potential for reducing the cost of models, particularly repeat models, in those scales.

I also discuss machines that are currently outside the 'hobby' price range, but may well be available to us in the future, as well as 3-D scanning.

Unlike the laser cutting machine market place where all the machines are very similar in their technology, differing mainly in the size of material they will take and the power of the laser, 3-D printers are still evolving with creative and innovative solutions being found almost every week. It is a sign of how important 3-D printing is becoming commercially that there are now several international 3-D printing conferences every year, as well as an increasing number of consumer shows and exhibitions.

The spin-off from all this activity is bound to be better and cheaper 3-D printers for consumers in the future.

15 THE 3-D PRINTER

TYPES OF 3-D PRINTER AND HOW THEY WORK

FDM – FUSED DEPOSIT MODELLING – 3-D PRINTERS

Most 'hobby' printers are FDM printers and are available from about £250 upwards. The raw material is always plastic based: it is called filament, and is supplied on spools or reels of about 1kg from about £15 upwards. Filament (basically plastic rod) is supplied in two diameters: 1.75mm and 3mm. Some FDM printers accept both sizes, but most are designed for one size or the other.

The filament is forced by two sprung rollers, one or more serrated, into an 'extruder', which heats the filament to between 190 and 240°C, whereupon it melts. The solid filament being fed into the extruder forces the heated, melted filament out of the tip of the extruder through a small hole, typically .4mm or .5mm in size. Think of it like a very precise hot glue gun.

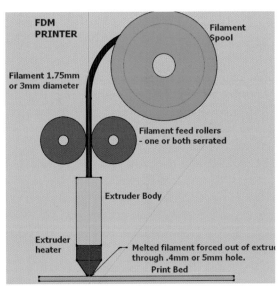

Basics of the FDM printer.

The extruder is moved about the print bed horizontally as the filament is forced out, causing it to be deposited on anything in close proximity to the extruder nozzle. The first layer is deposited on the print bed, and the whole extruder assembly is moved upwards, or the print bed downwards, and the next layer of filament is deposited on the first. This process is repeated, and the model 'grows' upwards by the depth of the filament as each layer is deposited.

The printer will have either a cold or heated print bed. A heated print bed is required for printing certain types of plastic, including ABS. PLA does not require a heated print bed.

The movement of the print bed, extruder assembly and feed rollers are all controlled by the printer electronics, which in turn are determined by the computer software that comes with the printer (or is downloaded from the internet). It is this software that looks at your Sketchup .stl file (your drawing/model) and 'slices' it into a format that can be printed in layers by the printer. Technically this is 'G-code', and is the same system as is used to drive CNC and computerized milling machines and lathes.

You do not need to understand computer programming or anything else about this process, but you do need to be able either to draw or download the model in the correct format (.stl), and have a working knowledge of the software that comes with your printer to enable you to print your model.

Stepper motors and toothed drive belts typically move the feed rollers and print table and require little or no maintenance.

FDM printers, although all using a similar system to print, vary in their actual construction and features, depending on their manufacturer and price. These variations can be illustrated by looking at four different FDM printers.

All the printers here take 'standard' PLA filament on 1kg reels. Some printers that are sold more cheaply take their own proprietary filament, which often costs quite a lot more. Prices are quoted at the time of writing, 2016.

I have direct experience of the FDM printers described below, but there are currently over a hundred different models and manufacturers at all price points. All the printers described have USB connectors and can be driven directly from the computer via a cable.

PRINTRBOT SIMPLE KIT

This printer from Robosavvy (robosavvy.com), about £250 when bought as a kit, has a laser cut plywood body, which is typical of the previous generation of 3-D printers. It took about six hours to assemble. It has a small print area of 100 x 100mm, and the stepper motors drive the platform and extruder via fishing wire wrapped around mini-drill sanding discs. However, it does have a fan for cooling the work as it is printed, and is driven by the same software (Repetier Host and Slic3r) as other larger and more expensive printers.

The results are surprisingly good, and it can print the same .1mm layer height as the other FDM printers here. Updated versions of this printer with a metal body and more traditional toothed belt drive are available (2016).

Printrbot – simple kit-built 3-D printer with laptop (right).

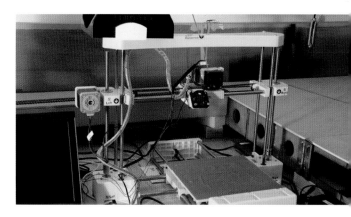

Not the prettiest of printers with all that wiring on show.

PRINT-RITE DIY PRINTER

The Print-Rite DIY printer from Hobbyking (www.hobbyking.co.uk), also available as the Colido DIY 3-D printer, cost around £250 and has a print bed of 200 x 200mm, giving it one of the largest print areas for its price (2016). It is also assembled from a kit, but the kit has only six pre-assembled modules to fit together, and all the wiring harness is done, leaving only a few wires to connect to the printer's circuit board. It took under an hour to assemble.

First results with the supplied filament were encouraging, but less so with my normal filament, and gap bridging was poor with lots of sagging, as the printer does not have a cooling fan for the filament. The addition of a small 12v fan in a housing to direct the air flow on to the work as it printed, transformed this printer. With some experimenting with print temperatures, it now prints excellent quality prints that are almost indistinguishable from its more expensive counterparts.

The fan housing was originally downloaded from www.thingiverse.com and printed on the printer. I later modified the design and added three LED lights underneath to illuminate the work piece. The fan unit was from Rapid Electronics (www.rapidonline.com), and was wired into a separate 12v power supply.

Because it does not have an outside frame it is somewhat more difficult to carry and transport than other printers, and the exposed wiring looks amateurish, but otherwise it is an excellent printer for the price.

Rugged all-metal construction and heated bed on the Renkforce RF1000.

The steel frame and good print area of Makerbot Replicator2.

RENKFORCE RF1000 PRINTER

Also purchased as a kit (but available ready assembled), this printer is sold by Conrad Electronics at £1,099 and £1,299 ready assembled. It has a very sturdy aluminium frame and a 220 x 220mm heated build plate. It took over six hours to build. I found some excellent step-by-step video assembly instructions on-line. Also capable of good prints, the heated print bed enables a wider range of filament plastics to be printed, including ABS, which is more suited to some applications, such as my garden railway.

The printer uses similar software to the previous two printers, Repetier Host and Slic3r. This printer has an LCD screen and SD card reader, and can be run without a computer attached. Also available is an attachment to convert the machine into a milling machine using a rotary mini-drill, and promised is a laser for laser engraving/cutting. A dual extruder version is also produced.

MAKERBOT REPLICATOR 2

The Makerbot Replicator 2 was my first 3-D printer, and is still the one that I find produces the best, most consistent results with least effort. It is no longer available from Makerbot, but at the time of writing Robosavvy (www.robosavvy.com) still have stock. It cost about £1,600 when purchased (and there are some really excellent printers around for this price now). This printer comes in a sturdy metal frame with LCD readout and control buttons; it can also print from SD card, or directly from a USB connection to the computer. It has a useful rectangular print bed of 140 x 260mm. A model also exists with dual extruders for those wishing to experiment with different materials and/or colours.

Makerbot produce their own software, which I find slices drawings more accurately than Slic3r and is easier to use. I have printed over 4,000 hours on this machine and it has been generally reliable. I have had to modify a ribbon cable which shorted due to metal fatigue (it was being bent at an acute angle as the print head moved around), and replaced the thermistor which reads the print-head temperature.

The machine has an SD card reader and LCD screen, making it easy to run print jobs without a computer, but without a heated bed it is limited to PLA and variants.

The printer produces consistent, reliable results, but note that all 3-D printers require some 'tinkering' to get the best results.

SLA – STEREOLITHOGRAPHY – 3-D PRINTERS

Stereolithography printers use a UV-curing resin and a light source, typically a laser, to produce 3-D models. Although there are differences in actual operation, basically the resin is held in a glass container (vat) and the UV light source is focused on the build platform immediately above the container. The light beam is reflected off a fast-moving mirror and draws the first

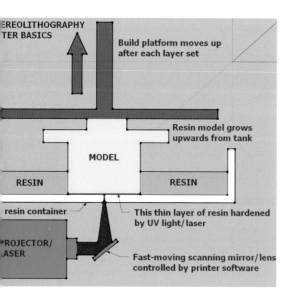

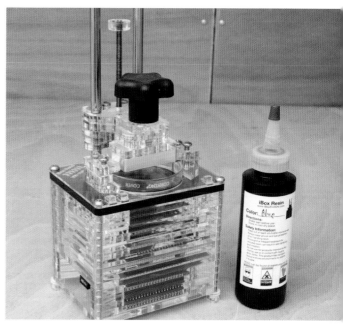

Basics of the SLA printer.

The Ibox Nano 3-D SLA resin printer with the bottle of supplied resin. This is tiny, about 110mm square (no longer available).

layer of the model on the build platform, curing the resin as it does so. The build platform is then raised by a tiny amount, and the process is repeated.

The diagram shows the model after several such cycles as it 'grows' layer by layer out of the resin container. Once complete, the model is removed from the build platform and needs further attention to clean it and then fully harden it, either by exposure to daylight or by UV light box.

Compared to FMD printers, SLA printers are messy and time-consuming to work with. The resin typically has the consistency of honey or treacle, and is not suited to a carpeted home environment.

The advantage of SLA printers is the resolution and detail they can bring to models, with a layer thickness as little as .01mm, or 100 layers per mm. At this layer thickness, however, models of any size take a long, long time to print.

Most SLA printers begin at a price of £1,000 and upwards, though one SLA printer is available at £300, the Ibox Nano.

Currently the cheapest SLA resin printer comes from the USA, priced at $299 (plus shipping). Using LEDs rather than a laser, this printer can only print small models up to a size of 40 x 20 x 90mm. However, the claimed resolution is 39 microns for each layer, compared with FDM printers, which are

typically 100. The smaller the layer the less 'banding' there will be on the final print. At the time of writing I have yet to try out this printer.

SLS – SELECTIVE LASER SINTERING – 3-D PRINTERS

At present SLS printers are too expensive to be regarded as hobby machines. However, as I write several companies are promising releases of SLS machines in 2016 at the £5,000–£8,000 price point aimed at small businesses, so in a few years' time we may have SLS machines at a price that individual modellers or clubs can afford. Whether these will be usable in a domestic environment remains to be seen.

SLS printers use a high-powered laser to fuse together individual grains of powder to make each layer of the model. The laser is directed by a fast-moving mirror as it scans each layer of the model, fusing the powder together as it does so. After each layer has been fused, the print table moves down and a roller pushes the next layer of powder over the print table and the laser then fuses this together, both horizontally and also to the layer underneath.

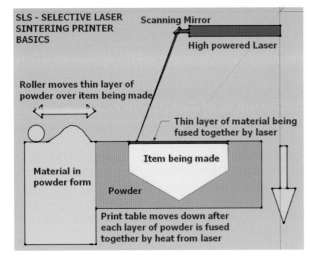

Basics of an SLS printer.

At the end of the process the print table (or more accurately, the print container) will be full of powder, which will have in it the item(s) being printed. These are removed, and usually an air gun is used to blow off unfused powder from the model. The unused powder, after some processing and cleaning, can be reused. Typically several small items are printed at the same time.

Almost any material that can be converted to a fine talcum-like powder can be used in the SLS process, including plastics and almost all metals. SLS printers are now being used in the production process for the manufacture of aircraft parts in aluminium and titanium, as well as by jewellery makers in gold and silver. Some of these objects could not be made by any other method.

The huge advantage of SLS printers is that the items being made are self-supported by the powder in the print table/container. Overhangs and complex shapes can be printed, though hollow shapes must have holes to allow for the unfused powder to be removed. SLS printers are often used by print bureaus such as Shapeways (www.shapeways.com).

OTHER EMERGING 3-D PRINTER TECHNOLOGIES

The 3-D printing technologies discussed so far have a single point of 'manufacture': the extruder print head or laser beam. HP (and no doubt others) are working on 'multi-jet' technologies that will work in a similar way to colour printers, laying down a whole layer of 3-D print at a time. HP have announced they are about to release such a machine (well outside a

hobby budget!) and claim it is at least ten times faster than the fastest existing 3-D printer.

Other, specialized printers are aimed at dentists and dental technicians, food manufacturers, jewellery makers, builders, aerospace, medical and so on. Who knows, one day we may have a 3-D railway modelling printer complete with pre-programmed viaducts and bridges, or even complete layouts!

In the future, as with all technologies, 3-D printers and 3-D scanners will get faster, incorporate colour, and maybe also textures and at cheaper prices.

THE BASICS

The basics of 3-D printing are as follows:

- CAD drawing is complete
- After saving your work in Sketchup format, the selected item in the drawing is exported as an .STL file
- The drawing (project) is opened in Netfabb and 'repaired' to ensure it will 3-D print correctly
- The .STL file of the drawing, now repaired, is loaded into the 3-D printer software
- The 3-D printer software 'slices' the drawing into printable G-code
- The 3-D printer prints your drawing/model

3-D PRINTER DRIVER SOFTWARE

When you purchase a colour printer you have to install a printer driver program on

CAD Drawing

⬇

Export as .STL file

⬇

Repair in Netfabb

⬇

Load into 3D printer

⬇

Slice into G-Code

⬇

Model printed

Stages in 3-D design and print.

your computer which enables the computer to 'talk' to your printer and use any special features. 3-D printers are similar and also need a printer driver program. Some of these are proprietary, such as the Makerware program described below, but many of the cheaper machines use 'generic' free open or closed source software, which may or may not have been tailored for their specific machine.

When you purchase a machine it will come with a CD or a USB stick, or will simply download instructions to a suitable program on the internet. It is likely to have been set up by the manufacturer with the basic printing parameters required for the 3-D printer just bought.

Because the instructions for setting up and using these programs will come with, and be specific to the printer bought, I am giving only an overview here.

MAKERWARE

This program is downloaded from Makerbot's web site and is designed specifically for their range of printers. It has pre-programmed parameters for high, medium and low quality prints, and this makes it extremely easy to use.

See www.makerbot.com for further details and downloads.

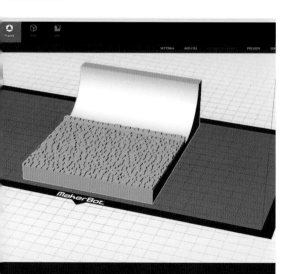

Makerbot Makerware with the model loaded and ready to print – in this case half a 4mm-scale viaduct pier.

Large structures can be made up of several smaller parts to overcome the limitation of print-bed size. This curved viaduct in 4mm scale is over a metre long.

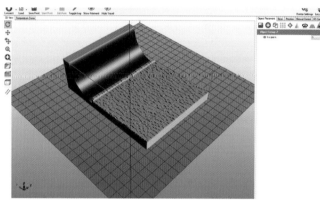

Repetier Host with model loaded and ready to print.

REPETIER HOST

This program is the one you are most likely to encounter if purchasing a cheaper 3-D printer; it will be supplied ready to use as a branded product with the printer, or you will have to download it from the internet and input specific figures into specific boxes in order to set it up. See www.repetier.com for further details and downloads.

SLICING SOFTWARE

WHAT IT DOES

The slicing software is run from within your printer driver, such as Makerware or Repetier Host (as

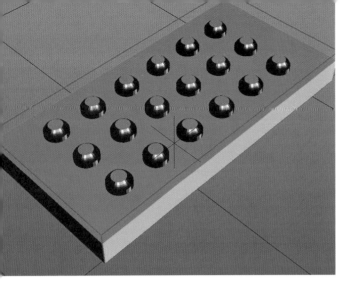

Rivet plate design as seen placed on the printer table.

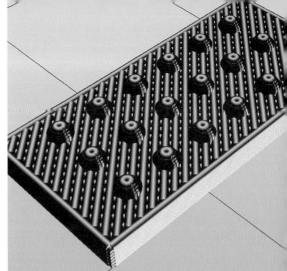

'Sliced' at .1mm per layer, high resolution. Each rivet is made up of five layers and the top surface is also denser, but will take longer to print.

SLIC3R

Slic3r is one of the most popular slicing programs. More can be found at www.slic3r.org.

CURA ENGINE

Cura Engine is another popular choice. See https://ultimaker.com/en/products/cura-software

USING AN FDM 3-D PRINTER

Note: This is essentially a reference section, and can be bookmarked and referred to if you experience problems when 3-D printing.

LEVELLING THE PRINT TABLE

If the gap between the extruder nozzle and the print table is not correct and the same over the entire print surface, then it is likely the first layer will not stick to the print table properly and your print will fail.

TIP: The first 3-D project enables you to produce two test pieces, one of which is designed to test if your print table is levelled correctly. This ought to be called 'gapping the print table', as it is not the 'spirit level'-type levelling of the print table which is critical, but the gap:

If the gap is too small there is insufficient space for the filament to flow out of the extruder head, the filament gets squashed to the print table, and the extruder may become blocked or partially blocked.

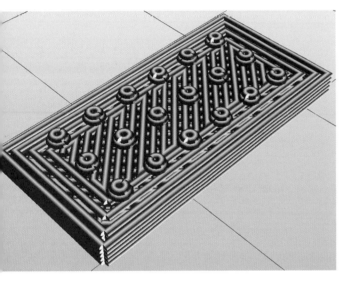

'Sliced' at .3mm per Layer, low resolution. This preview shows the individual layers and threads of filament that will make up the model. At this resolution each actual rivet is made up of just two layers of plastic.

described above). It looks at your model and creates horizontal G-code 'slices' of it as a toolpath that your printer can then print as layers to build up the model. You can choose what thickness these slices are – typically .1mm to .3mm thick. The thinner the slices, the more there are, and the longer it takes to produce your model, but this way it will usually be of better quality.

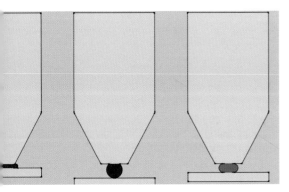

Gap between the extruder nozzle and the print bed: at left is too small; at centre is too large; at right is correct.

If the gap is too large there is insufficient pressure to force the filament to stick to the table (or more likely the blue painter's tape) and it will simply flop onto the surface, get picked up when printing the next layer, and create a blob on the end of the extruder head.

If the gap is just right then the filament will be partly squashed on to the print table and stick so that subsequent layers can be printed correctly on top of it.

If small holes don't stick and your gap is correct, then it may be you have to use a 'stickier' material for the print bed; blue tape is normal, but I have used double-sided adhesive tape on top of the blue painter's tape to get very delicate and complex prints to stick correctly.

Note that the bottom layer of any print, because it is squashed on to the print table, will stick out a little further than subsequent layers. This is most noticeable on small vertical holes where the side of the hole printed on the print bed will be smaller than the rest of the hole.

LOADING AND CHANGING THE FILAMENT

Eventually your filament will run out. *You always need the extruder pre-heated when loading and unloading filament.* I always choose load and make sure the filament is flowing out of the extruder before immediately selecting unload and removing it. This ensures the filament in the extruder is hot and melted.

Blue painter's tape and ordinary masking tape used to cover the print bed. Both are available in rolls 50mm wide.

Don't let your filament run out whilst printing as your print will fail and you may be left with a 'plug' of unmelted filament between the feed roller and the extruder. You can sometimes push it through with the new filament, but often it requires disassembly to get at it and pull it out with pliers (after pre-heating the extruder).

Check that you have enough filament left on the spool before each print job.

PRINTING THE MODEL

Blue painter's tape (a type of masking tape) is used to coat the print bed and helps the first layer to stick. I find that for models with a large surface area on the print bed and no detail (such as the viaduct piers), blue painter's tape grips too tightly, and I have found that 'normal' masking tape is adequate. There is room for you to experiment here as the internet is awash with hints and tips for 3-D printing.

Once the first couple of layers have been successfully printed, most print jobs will run through to completion without further intervention. 3-D printer manufacturers always suggest you do not leave 3-D printers unattended, but with prints taking up to ten hours or more to process, this is often not practical. Not only do I have two smoke

Troubleshooting Your FDM 3-D Printing

The following problems may be encountered, and below each one I have suggested the possible causes/solutions, and how to deal with them.

Not sticking to the print table:
When prints don't stick to the print table, the filament sticks to itself and forms a mass at the end of the extruder. This condition is most likely when the first layer contains detail, such as small holes. If caught early and the print stopped it can be removed whilst still hot with a paper towel or similar (always with the extruder hot). If not caught early, some or all of it will have solidified, and it may then need heating with a hot air gun or similar to remove it. Check that the first layer has been laid down successfully before leaving the printer, and this problem is easily sorted.

- Print table is not the correct distance from the extruder end all over the entire print table. Check and re-calibrate as per your printer instructions
- Filament is not hot enough – increase the print temperature
- Print bed is not hot enough (when printing ABS and other filaments requiring a heated print bed)
- Print table surface is not the correct type – usually blue painter's tape works best for PLA, and Kapton tape for ABS; you may need to experiment. Renew as appropriate. Try wiping with isopropyl alcohol
- The extruder hole is partially blocked. With the extruder hot, try clearing it with a short length of piano wire
- In extreme cases, for tiny objects, try double-sided sticky sheet over the blue painter's tape. Stick it to the blue painter's tape, then remove the backing sheet to print on a sticky surface. You may only need to treat a small corner. Remove the final prints carefully, and it can be re-used several times

Sticking to the print bed too well:
- Make the gap between the print bed and extruder slightly larger
- Lower the print temperature
- Lower the print-bed temperature (if using a heated bed)
- On objects with a large surface area and little detail on the first layer, try using 'normal' masking tape, which holds the print less firmly

Layers not bonding to each other:
- Filament is too cool – increase the print temperature
- Extruder hole is partially jammed – clean it out (use fine piano wire of a size just under your extruder hole size – usually .3mm or .4mm is good)
- Filament is not consistent in diameter – check it at several points over a 1m length

Not printing the complete model:
- Printing direct from the computer using USB cable – computer 'sleep mode' – will stop print, or sometimes using other applications whilst printing will also upset the printing, or the USB connection is unreliable. Use the SD card or the USB stick directly in the printer if possible
- Filament jam – the printer will carry on printing in 'thin air', with no filament from the extruder. This is usually a filament diameter problem, as above
- Filament has run out

Extruder jams:
- Print temperature is too low
- Filament roller feed jams – this is often accompanied by a 'clicking' sound. Check feed roller cleanliness and spring pressure. Also check the diameter of your filament in several places over a metre or two of its length to check it is a consistent size and round. Check the print temperature
- Filament has run out. This can leave a 'plug' of unmelted filament in the extruder which must be dismantled

and cleaned out; some-
times a drill is needed

Sagging over gaps:
• Print temperature is
  too high
• Insufficient cooling on
  the printed filament –
  make sure your cooling
  fan (if fitted) is switched
  on
• The gap is too wide!
  Anything over 10mm is
  asking for trouble. Build
  supports (see the 1mm
  columns in the Test
  Piece in the Projects'
  section) so the gap is
  less, and remove the
  supports after printing
• Wrong settings in the
  printer driver software
– check your manual for instructions on altering these
so the printer moves faster and extrudes less over
the gaps, thus 'stretching' the softened filament across
the gap

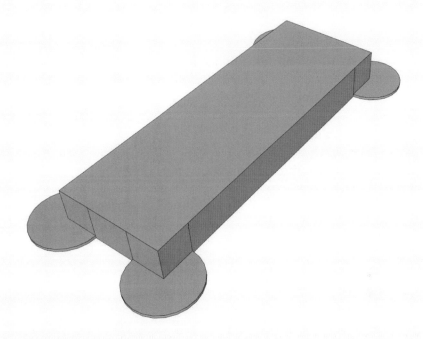

'Pads' added to the corners can help keep the print flat on the bed and prevent warping. Cut them off when the print is finished. They are best designed in from the start and can easily be removed if not required. They need not be more than 1mm thick, so take little time to print.

Model not printing/slicing – error message:
• Error message model not 'manifold' or watertight.
  This is a common problem. Use Netfabb to repair the
  model (described in the CAD section), and try again

Blobs on the top surface:
• Usually over-extruding (too much filament is being
  produced). Measure the filament, and adjust the size
  to suit in the printer software

Poor or sagging top surface:
• Lower the print temperature

• Make three or four 'shells' (outer surfaces – the
  default is normally two) in your printer software to
  add more outer layers

Warping of the bottom layer away from the print table:

• Add 'pads' to the corners of the object, as shown in
  the illustration
• Increase the print temperature for the first layer, and
  lower it for the rest (this can be done via your printer
  software)
• Increase the temperature of the print table (or add a
  heated bed – about 70°C – if printing PLA)

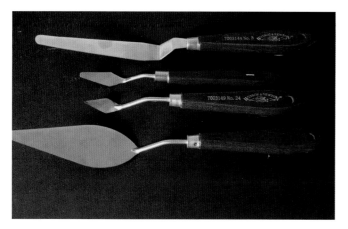

A selection of palette knives used to remove prints once they are complete.

alarms in my room, I have also set up a webcam on my 3-D printers so I can use my Smartphone to keep an eye on things. Some of the more sophisticated printers are Wi-Fi enabled, and not only can you view the print as it takes place, but they will send you alerts as to problems, and tell you when the print is finished.

REMOVING THE PRINTED MODEL

Well stuck models, particularly those with a large surface area on their bases, can be difficult to remove from the print bed. I use a range of artist's palette knives as shown. The very thin pointed one is most useful for attacking a corner of the print and lifting it off the print bed, so a more robust tool can then be used to prise it upwards. Do be careful not to damage your print bed whilst doing this – though inevitably you will damage and need to replace the painter's tape or other covering from time to time.

3-D PRINTER RESOLUTION

This is the smallest thickness, diameter or hole that the 3-D printer can 'resolve' and make in a particular material. Most 'hobby' 3-D printers will print a post or hole down to 1mm, as in the Test Piece outlined in the 3-D Projects section. If your printer cannot print a .5mm thick wall, then there is no point in designing one! You do need to design to your printer's capabilities.

When using a 3-D print bureau, check first to see what their limits are for wall and post thickness and so on, in their different materials, before you begin your design.

THE PROS AND CONS OF 3-D PRINTING METHODS

FDM PRINTERS

Pros:
• Relatively cheap to buy and use
• Can be used in a domestic environment

Cons:
• The banding effect caused by their printing in layers of .1 to .3mm. They cannot print a perfectly smooth

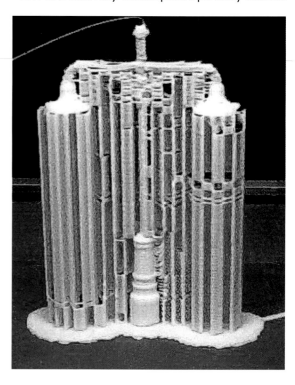

This is what you get trying to print a station lamp upright! Because of the overhangs you need supports, and whilst the software will add these for you, it makes for an awful lot of printing, which in turn takes a long time and uses a lot of material. It is also difficult to remove the supports without damaging the model.

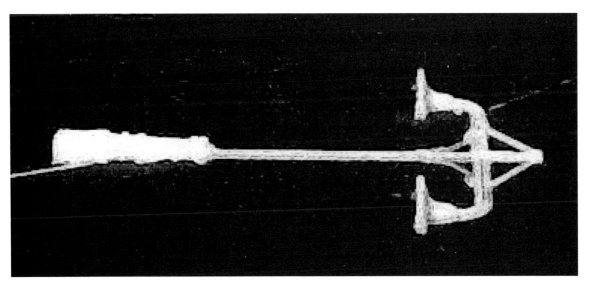

Printing the station lamp in two halves and gluing them together is not only quicker and cheaper, but wires for the LED can be placed inside the lamp before the two halves are glued.

surface. This makes their mode of operation better suited to prototyping in the smaller scales rather than producing the final object, which may have to be done by a print bureau. A sprayed coat of high-build grey primer can mitigate the banding appearance, but at risk of losing some of the fine detail

• Their inability to print an overhang or span a large empty space without supports; this can be overcome by printing supports, but on small delicate objects removing the supports can damage the model. Printers with two extruders can print water-dissolvable supports with their second print head. By splitting the model into different pieces and printing them flat on the print bed this limitation can often be overcome

• Their slow speed: they are slow to produce large models. Used for our hobby, this is less important as we can often be getting on with other modelling whilst they print

SLA PRINTERS

Cons:
• Generally more expensive than FDM printers

• Resin is expensive!
• Resin is messy to use – this may be a problem in a domestic environment
• Models need post-processing to finish them (cleaning and exposing to UV light)
• Their slow speed (but they can produce very high quality prints)
• The size of the models they can produce (in hobby machines) is limited

SLS PRINTERS

Cons:
• The process is not suited to the domestic environment
• Cost, though 'desktop' machines at less than £6,000 are promised!

Pros:
• Results are of excellent quality
• Almost any material can be printed, including most metals
• Powder supports the printing of objects with overhangs; any shape can be printed.

16 THE 3-D SCANNER

3-D scanning (or digitizing) is a method of creating a drawing of an object by laser-scanning it. A number of different types of scanner are available, from 'turntable'-based systems to hand-held devices, and professional scanners mounted on tripods.

3-D scanning as a technique is now used by model manufacturers such as Hornby and Bachmann to produce digital images of actual railway locomotives and other large items. They use professional scanning bureaus, which use professional equipment costing thousands of pounds.

Companies such as Modelu (www.modelu3-D. co.uk/) are using hand-held scanners at model railway shows to scan people dressed in 'railway attire', and then producing a model of them on an SLA resin printer in virtually any scale required.

My experience is with a Makerbot Digitizer currently costing about £500. This is a turntable-based digitizer where the object to be digitized is placed on a turntable and rotated in front of two lasers and a camera to capture it to a digital file.

Once the digitizer has been calibrated, a process that takes about fifteen minutes, the object to be scanned is placed on the turntable and software run. The turntable revolves in a number of small steps, and each time it stops a camera takes a picture of the two laser lines that are projected on to the object. Once scanned, the software stitches all these images together to produce a 3-D drawing. The object can then be moved to expose hidden parts to the lasers and camera – for example, it can be tilted to expose its underside, and then scanned again. This process

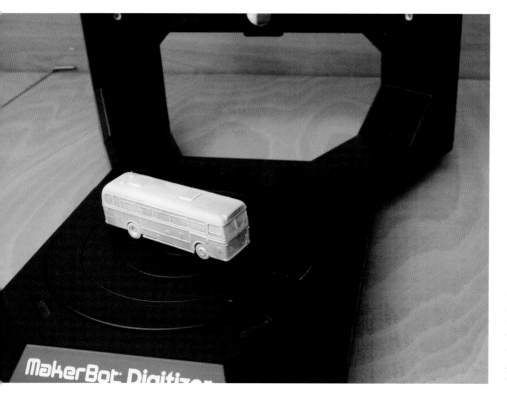

Single-deck bus on Makerbot Digitizer turntable. At top you can just see the two lasers on either side of the camera filter (centre).

can be repeated a couple or more times. Each scan takes about twelve minutes.

In the illustration the bus has been sprayed with dry shampoo hair spray, which dries matt white. This is to produce a better scan, as the laser responds better to light colours and is confused by reflections from shiny surfaces.

I have a Faller Road System and hoped to make my own vehicles by scanning them in and then printing them in plastic to make them lighter, as die-cast vehicles would not cope with the road gradients on my layout. However, I found the resolution of the Makerbot Scanner (quoted as .5mm) was insufficient to reproduce the vehicles with any acceptable detail remaining, so it has had very little use.

3-D scanning is likely to be built into smartphones in the next year or two. It will then be possible to 3-D scan a person or an object and either print it yourself on your own 'hobby' printer, or upload it from your phone to a 3-D print bureau for printing in your required material and size. Whether it will be possible to successfully scan items such as locomotives remains to be seen, but smaller railway items, such as platform furniture, are likely to succumb to this technique.

Dry shampoo hair spray.

At the time of writing there are two types of 'hobby' 3-D printers in use: the FDM ('fused deposit modelling') printer, which is the most common; and SLA (stereolithography) printers, which focus an ultraviolet (UV) laser on to a vat of photopolymer resin to set it.

Most of this section is about the most common materials for the most common printer: FDM.

FILAMENT FOR
FDM 3-D PRINTERS

All FDM printers use a filament (thread) from a spool. These are usually nominally 1.75mm or 3.0mm in diameter and on 1kg spools. It can be important to know the exact size. A cheap (around £10) digital vernier as shown is useful not only for this task, but for accurate measuring of other items and models.

TIP: Try not to buy any quantity of filament which is not on a spool. It tangles and breaks easily, and once broken or tangled cannot be used even for relatively small print jobs.

If your filament varies by more than plus or minus .2mm, or if it is not perfectly round, then this can cause your printer to misfeed or jam. It can be useful to know the exact diameter of the filament you are using so that you can set this in the printer's software program. If you are getting inconsistent results then it may be worth checking your filament dimensions.

It is worth purchasing and using a cheap (under £10 on eBay) digital vernier caliper.

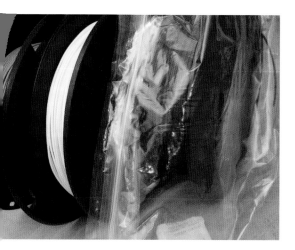

Filament spools. Note the front spool is in a resealable plastic bag with a packet of silica gel desiccant to absorb any moisture. It is vital that you keep filaments dry as they all attempt to absorb moisture, which will adversely affect how they print.

There are two main materials used for filament for FDM 3-D printers: PLA and ABS. Both are available in a wide range of colours.

PLA FILAMENT

PLA (polylactic acid) is the most common type of filament used in FDM 3-D printers. It is a biodegradable polyester derived from renewable resources such as corn starch. It sticks well to an unheated print bed on to blue painter's tape. It also shrinks less than ABS filament as it cools.

PLA prints at between 200 and 230°C. You should always check the print temperature recommended by the PLA manufacturer, and use this to print the Test Piece (see the Projects section later).

Initially, when filament was £60 per kilogram, I shopped around for the cheapest, but this was not always of a consistent quality. Eventually I found a company that supplied consistent quality filament at good prices, and have been using 3-D Filaprint (www.3dfilaprint.com) for my supplies for the last couple of years or so. Their website also has some useful information and hints and tips on filaments generally. At the time of writing they are also able to supply what they refer to as 'wraps' – small lengths

can be squeezed out for small jobs, and even small bottles last a good length of time. I know others use Superglues and/or contact adhesives such as Evostik and Copydex.

ABS FILAMENT

ABS (acrylonitrile butadiene styrene) is a tough chemical-based filament (like Lego bricks). It is not biodegradable and is therefore more suited to outdoor use than PLA (see ASA under 'Other Specialist Filaments' below). ABS requires a heated print bed and can be more difficult to get to stick to this, even heated. Also, note the following:

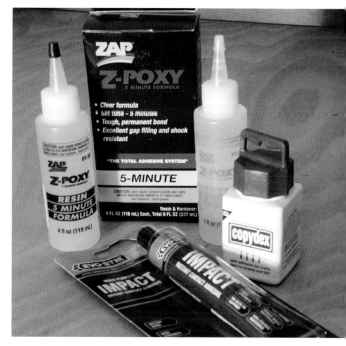

Two-part 'five-minute' epoxy and contact adhesives can be useful for PLA.

of filament that they sell at low cost so you can try them. There is a plethora of companies selling filament via the internet.

PLA prints almost without any smell, though a well ventilated room is recommended.

Note that PLA filament does not weld or melt together with plastic weld and other 'melting' glues. I use five-minute two-pack epoxy in plastic bottles bought off eBay. Tiny amounts of hardener and resin

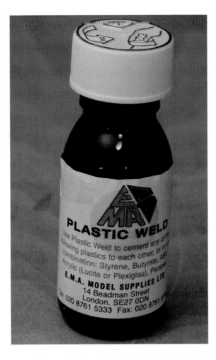

Plastic weld or similar styrene glues can be used to 'melt' and glue together ABS plastics but will not work on PLA.

- It prints hotter than PLA, up to about 270°C
- ABS smells of 'plastic' when printing, and some sort of extraction is suggested if in a small domestic room
- ABS does melt/weld together using plastic weld and other glues for styrene

SPECIALIST FILAMENTS

Various specialist filaments are now being produced which all have particular properties. All are more expensive than standard filament. Here are a few, but an internet search of companies producing/selling filament will no doubt produce many more. It is often possible to get free or low-priced samples to try.

Laywood: As its name suggests, it prints to look like wood. Different print temperatures produce different effects. It is not good for fine detail.
Laybrick: As above, but it looks like grey stone.

Flexible: It prints rubber-like objects for stoppers, belts, springs and so on. I have used it successfully for LGB coupler springs.

Conductive: It prints a conductive thread. At present it is high resistance, so it is only suitable for certain applications and is best used with a dual head printer so it can be printed with 'normal' PLA.

Strong: PET and nylon are strong and can be bought as filaments for 3-D printing.

Metal effect: PLA combined with metal powders can be polished to give a metallic effect.

Glow in the dark: It is charged by exposure to light, and then glows in the dark. It may have modelling applications for street/station lights and suchlike.

Colour changing: This filament changes colour when it is exposed to light.

ASA: UV stable, and designed for outdoor use. It may be good for garden railways. It probably needs a heated print bed to print.

RESIN FOR SLA PRINTERS

Resins for SLA 3-D printers tend to be relatively expensive, between £50 and £100 per litre. However, SLA printers are best at producing small, detailed models, so the amount of resin used per model will be relatively small. Unused resin can be re-used.

The SLA printer manufacturer will recommend which type of resin to use, and some resins are available in several colours.

SLA 'prints' always require some post-print processing: usually they have to be cleaned using isopropyl alcohol or similar, and must then be 'cured' or hardened off under a UV lamp (or exposed to sunlight for a few days).

18 PROJECTS: 3-D PRINTING

INTRODUCTION TO 3-D PRINTING

Before trying this section you should be familiar with all the Sketchup tools as outlined in the CAD Basics and 3-D CAD Basics sections of the book. Where new commands are required I have introduced them in the text.

SAVING YOUR WORK IN THE CORRECT FORMAT

Throughout I will remind you to save your work at frequent intervals with the Save As>xxxx, where xxxx is the filename and Save As is the Save As in the File drop-down menu. This will always save your entire drawing in Sketchup (.skp) format. Where drawings are best saved as you proceed I will increment the filename with a, b, c and so on – a table. skp, b table.skp, c table .skp – so that you can always return to a previous version.

Remember: To print your model you will also need to export the drawing as an .stl file. I will remind you with File >Export STL >xxxx.stl, where xxxx is the filename.

Note that saving in Centimetres will scale the drawing down by ten to its correct size for printing (always draw ten times larger than required to over-

come any problem Sketchup has with tiny objects). Ensure the ASCII File Format is selected. If the Export selected geometry only is ticked then only those parts/items of your drawing selected (they turn blue) will be selected. If you forget to select at least something of your drawing then your printer will give you an error message when trying to load the file, as it will be of zero length.

Remember to run your model through Netfabb as described in the CAD section to ensure that it will 3-D print.

You can load your .STL file into your printer software to print the object, or you can send it off (upload it) to be printed by a 3-D print bureau and receive your printed model back by post. If sending it off, then be sure to check the 3-D print bureau's maximum build size and minimum sizes and thickness for walls and so on, *before* you start your drawing.

I have tried throughout to show you physically small projects that will print relatively quickly, whilst still covering the various Sketchup drawing techniques required to devise and design your own models.

Your drawings will go wrong from time to time, but by making use of the Undo command and saving your work frequently so that you can return to an earlier stage in your drawing, you can minimize the chances of having to start again from scratch.

Have fun!

3-D PRINTER TEST PIECES

There are thousands of settings that can be changed when 3-D printing, and each one can affect the quality of the prints. You must manage these settings to produce consistent results each time you print in a new material (filament). The temperature and humidity of the room, and the type and age of your filament can also affect the consistency and quality

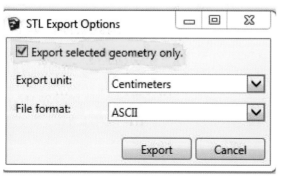

Export .STL box.

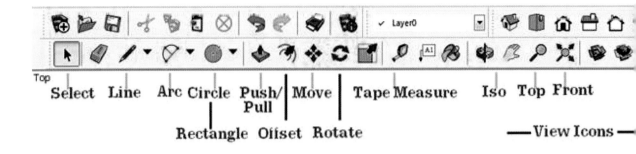

Basic icons used for Test Piece drawings. Refer to the 'Icon and Keyboard Guide' in the CAD Basics chapter for information on how to use them.

of you prints. This is particularly true if the printer is kept in an outhouse, garage, or a badly insulated/ heated club room.

So where do you start? In general, most of the software settings recommended by the printer manufacturer can be left alone. You will need to try different settings for layer thickness (usually .1mm, .2mm or .3mm for best, normal and draft) and for temperature of printing (usually between 200 and 230°C). In particular, each time you change filament you should print a test piece in your desired quality setting to determine if your temperature setting is optimal.

The test piece should check the following:

• Whether prints are sticking to the print bed adequately
• The quality of the top surface
• The quality of fine detail, vertical and horizontal
• Sloping surfaces, the angle at which prints will build outwards successfully
• The ability to bridge a gap without sagging
• The resolution and size of small holes (does a 2mm hole print as 2mm?)

I have found the following two test pieces useful in checking the quality of prints with a wide variety of filaments and different printers. I always produce my prototypes in white as it is easier to see the fine detail in this colour, but clearly you should print the test pieces in whichever colour/type of filament you want to test.

The test pieces take between four and eight minutes to print on most 3-D printers, but then a successful print means you have a good chance of further prints printing well in that filament and at that temperature. It is also useful to write on the back of Test Piece 2 the settings used, for future reference.

If you are new to Sketchup or are yet to install it on your computer, then work through the 'Sketchup Basics' section in Part 1. Run Sketchup and load your 3-D drawing template, which begins with the Top-Down view. Note that 'Top' is displayed at top left when in Top-Down view, *and we draw everything x10 size.*

TEST PIECE 1: PRINTING THE FIRST LAYER

This Test Piece checks that your printer bed is set up correctly. To be able to print this Test Piece:

• your print bed must be correctly 'levelled' (the gap between extruder and print table is correct over the whole of your print table)
• your print bed must have a suitable surface for the filament you are using (usually blue painter's tape for PLA filament and Kapton tape for ABS and a heated bed)
• your filament must be printing at the correct temperature to stick to the print bed

If when printing the Test Piece the printing pulls away from the print bed (it is not sticking) and the corners are not forming well, then the gap between your extruder and print bed is probably too large, or the filament temperature is too low. If this happens in only one or two corners, then the gap between your print bed and extruder is not even all round. The ideal print is one that has printed in the correct shape, lifts from the print bed in one piece, and is an even thickness all round. For further help with printing problems, see the end of 'The 3-D Printer' chapter.

To draw the Test Piece, proceed as follows:

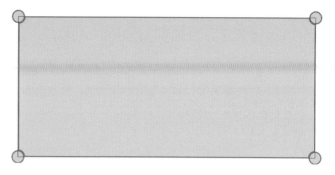

Test Piece rectangle and circles drawn with 5mm 'offset' inner line forming a frame.

- Measure the size of your print bed and take off 40mm from the length and width. Note down this size
- Use the Rectangle tool to draw a rectangle of the size noted above x 10 (for example, a print bed 100 x 200mm would have a rectangle 600 x 1600mm = 10 x 60 x 160mm). Remember to draw everything ten times the size required
- Using the Circle tool, draw two circles of 50mm and 45mm radius at each corner of the rectangle, as shown
- Use the Offset tool to draw an inner line 5mm inside the rectangle (this will also draw a line inside the rounded corners). Remember to enter 5 into the Dimensions box to get this offset
- Zoom in to each corner in turn
- Select and Delete the inner curved line and the two short straight lines at each corner, as shown in the illustration

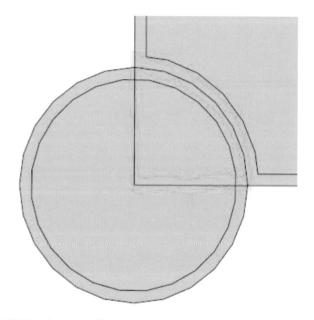

Highlighted are the lines to delete at each corner.

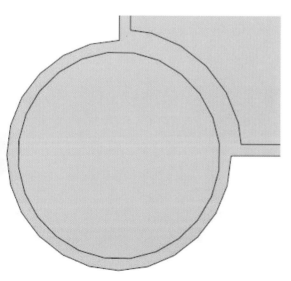

Corner after the deletion of unwanted lines.

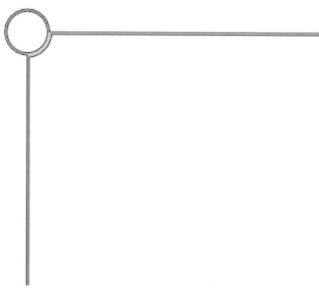

Blue background deleted to leave the final 'frame'.

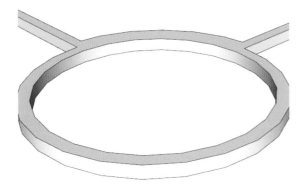

Corner showing the 'frame' pulled up 5mm.

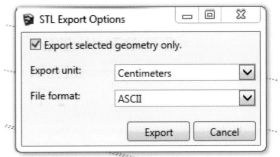

Export STL dialogue box.

- Also Delete the two straight lines within the circle
- Click on and Delete the inner blue backgrounds within each corner circle and the main rectangle to leave your drawing looking as in the illustration
- Select the Iso view icon to get a 'perspective' view of your drawing
- Zoom in to a corner
- Using the Push/Pull tool, hover over the top of the frame until it turns to blue dots, hold down the left mouse button, and pull the frame up 5mm (5 in the Dimensions box) as shown. If all the lines have been deleted correctly, this should result in the entire 'frame' being pulled up 5mm

You now need to save your file as a Sketchup file which can be loaded and amended later, as well as an .stl file which is used by your printer to print the drawing.

Save this in Sketchup format File >Save As 'a Test Piece Bed Level.skp'.

- Use the Select tool to select the entire object by dragging top left to bottom right (the object should turn blue with dots)

Now save it in .stl format for the 3-D printer: File > Export STL >Centimeters >Export>Filename 'a Test Piece Bed Level.stl'.

Choosing Centimeters automatically scales down your drawing by a factor of ten. Always use ASCII as the file format.

Note the tick box 'Export selected geometry only'. When ticked, only those parts of your drawing you have selected by dragging around them (they turn blue) will be saved as an .STL file for printing. This is useful if you have several components of a drawing on the screen but only wish to save and print one of them. If you fail to select part of your drawing you will get an error message when you try to load the file into Netfabb or your printer.

Now print the Test Piece to check your printer.

TEST PIECE 2: QUALITY OF THE PRINT

Each time you load a different filament into your printer, or alter any of the print settings, you will need to know if your printer is printing at its best. This Test Piece will allow you to do that in the shortest possible time.

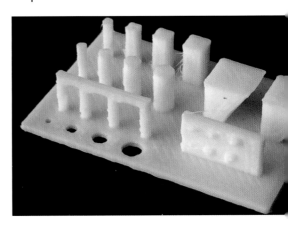

The finished Test Piece.

Rectangle drawn with dimensions in the Dimensions box.

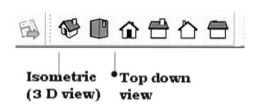

Viewpoint icons.

At only 5.8mm tall, this Test Piece prints quickly but is a 3-D printer torture print, testing your printer to the limit by having vertical columns, small holes, overhangs and thin details. If the Test Piece does not print correctly, then neither will your other designs.

- Begin by using the Rectangle tool to draw a rectangle 300,200mm. Remember you set the size by immediately adding the dimensions to the Dimensions box at bottom right, and then pressing Enter
- Use the scroll wheel on your mouse to Zoom in and out, and to position the rectangle

Throughout this process if you make a mistake you can use the Undo/Redo icons to go back. Next, you need to give your rectangle a thickness.

- Click on the Isometric icon (3-D view) – the icons below are the viewpoint icons
- Select the Push/Pull tool, and hover over the rectangle. It should change to small dots to show that you have it selected
- Hold down the left mouse button and pull the surface upwards 8mm: start the pull up and enter 8 into the Dimensions box. Your rectangle should now be an 8mm thick solid object, as shown in the picture

At this stage it is a good idea to save your drawing so that you can return to it if the next stage goes wrong; save it as File>Save As>a Test Piece2.

Rectangle in Iso view pulled up to a solid 8mm thick.

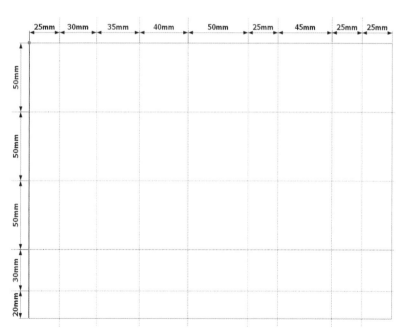

Top surface of the rectangle marked out with guidelines.

Having drawn your base, you now need to mark it out for the next stage. This is easiest in Top-Down view. Do this as follows:

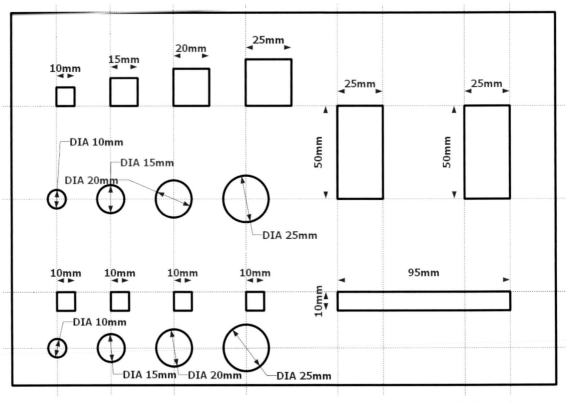

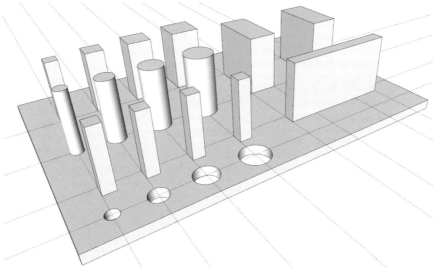

Circles and rectangles drawn using guidelines. Once printed, you can refer back to this diagram to compare what has actually been produced with the drawing of it.

Four circles as holes at the front, and other rectangles and circles pulled up 50mm.

- Select the Top-Down view icon to change your viewpoint. 'Top' should be displayed at top left of your workspace
- Hold down and rotate the scroll wheel to Zoom in to make your rectangle nearly full screen

- Select the Tape Measure tool and mark out the top surface of your Test Piece with guidelines, as in the diagram. (Using the Tape Measure tool is explained in detail in Part I.) The easiest way is to start a new guideline in the direction required from an existing line or guideline, and then enter the exact distance required in the Dimensions box (and tap Enter)

Save your drawing again, starting with a 'b', as File>Save As>b Test Piece2.

Draw some rectangles and circles, as in the diagram, using the Rectangle tool and Circle tool and the guidelines already drawn. Remember that the Dimensions box determines the *radius of the circle*, so halve the diameters shown. You can put decimal points in the Dimensions box – for example 7.5 – to give a 15mm diameter.

Use the guidelines for the corners of the rectangles and squares, adding the exact dimensions into the Dimensions box each time. Ensure your circles start from where the guidelines cross.

Once you have drawn the circles and squares as described, make your drawing clearer, ready for the next stages, by deleting *all* your guidelines: do this by selecting from the menus Edit> Delete Guides.

Save your drawing again starting with a 'c' as File>Save As>c Test Piece2.

You are now going to punch four holes in Test Piece 2 and then pull up all the other circles and rectangles to 50mm:

- Select Iso view and Zoom in to the four front circles
- Select the Push/Pull tool, and push down the first circle to 8mm to create a hole. Use the Dimensions box to input the exact depth. Double-click on the other three circles to repeat this. Look under the Test Piece to check you have created four holes
- Select inside the first 10mm square and use the Push/Pull tool to pull it up 50mm (remember to use the Dimensions box)
- Now double-click inside each of the other squares, rectangles and circles. They will all 'pull up' to 50mm (you could pull each individually to a different height if required, but since we need them all 50mm high, this method is quicker)

Save your drawing again starting with a 'd': File>Save As>d Test Piece2.

Next we are going to join the tops of the 10mm posts with a 10mm square beam (this tests if your

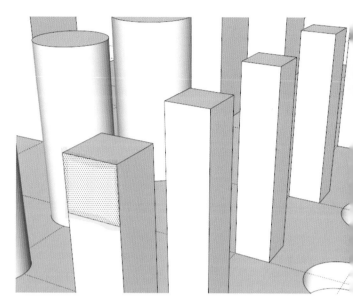

10mm square drawn on the end of a post.

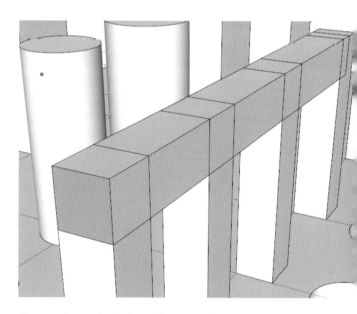

Rectangle pushed along the tops of the posts with the Push/Pull tool.

printer can print across gaps without too much sagging).

- Use the Rectangle tool to draw a 10mm square on the side of the first post at the top, as shown in the diagram

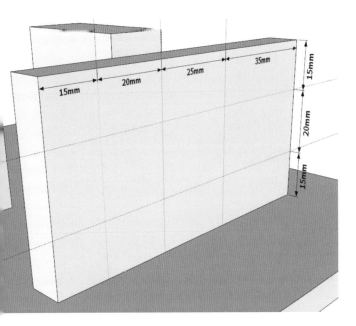

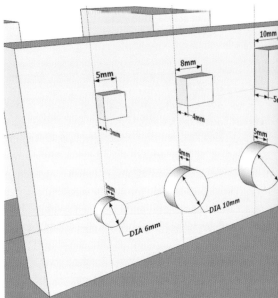

Guidelines drawn on the vertical block.

- Select the Push/Pull tool and tap the Ctrl key to get a + symbol by the Push/Pull cursor. This tells the Push/Pull tool to start a new face, rather than push/pulling the existing one. Now push the rectangle horizontally through the two centre posts and into the fourth (far) post, as shown

Next you are going to add some detail to the side of the thin rectangle to see how the printer copes with small overhangs and lines (as in rivets and linear detail on coaches).

- Use the Tape Measure tool and the Dimensions box to mark out guidelines on the rectangle as shown in the diagram
- Use the Rectangle tool and the Circle tool to draw the rectangles and circles as shown in the illustration
- Use the Push/Pull tool to pull out the rectangles to 3mm, 4mm and 5mm

We now need a different view of the Test Piece, as in the picture.

- Hold down the scroll wheel on your mouse and move it around the screen to rotate the Test Piece

Circles and rectangles pulled out from the vertical block to test the resolution of the printer on things such as rivets. From left to right, pull out the shapes 3mm, 4mm and 5mm.

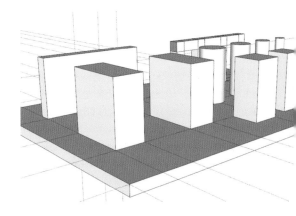

View rotated to see behind the Test Piece.

to get the view as shown. Some practice is required. If you get hopelessly lost, press the Isometric icon (3-D view) to get the 'standard' 3-D view, and try again.

Our next test is that of overhangs. How far can your printer print out from the layer below before needing supports?

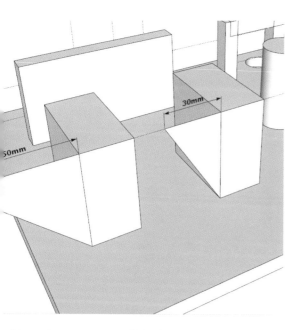

Lines drawn out parallel with the sides of the blocks as shown.

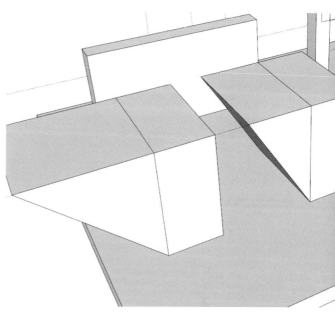

Triangles pushed to the depth of the block with the Push/Pull tool.

- Using the Tape Measure tool, double-click on the nearest top line of one of the blocks to make a guideline between the two blocks
- With the Line tool (pencil), draw lines out from the top of the two blocks along this guideline 30mm and 50mm as shown, then draw lines from the ends of these to the base of the blocks to make triangles. (Escape stops the Line tool from drawing lines)
- Use the Push/Pull tool to push the triangles 50mm along the sides of the blocks as shown to make the overhangs

We now have our final Test Piece, looking as in the illustration. Save this in Sketchup format with an 'e' in front, as File >Save As>e Test Piece.skp.

Next, use the Select tool to select the entire object by dragging from top left to bottom right (the object should turn blue with dots). Now save it in .stl format for the 3-D printer as File > Export STL >Centimeters >Filename e Test Piece.stl.

Choosing Centimeters automatically scales down your drawing by a factor of ten. Always use ASCII as the file format.

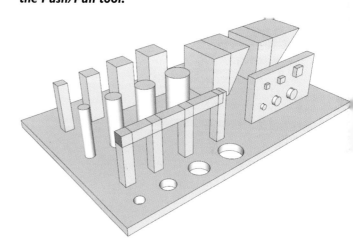

Final Test Piece ready for printing.

STL Export Options box.

3-D PRINTING PROBLEMS

For a list of common problems and possible solutions, see the end of the '3-D Printer' chapter.

The photographs below indicate how important temperature is to the 3-D printing process. Note that different colours of filament, even from the same supplier, can require a different printing temperature to achieve optimal results.

Test Piece printed at 205°C temperature on the Makerbot Replicator 2. There is little stringing and the columns and 'rivet heads' are quite well defined.

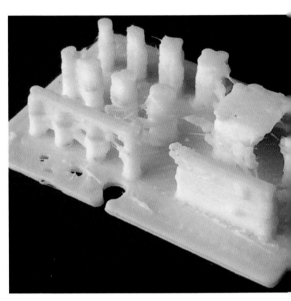

The same Test Piece printed at 230°C. Note the stringing has nearly filled the gaps between the columns, and the left-hand edge of the vertical wall is ill defined, as are the 'rivet heads'.

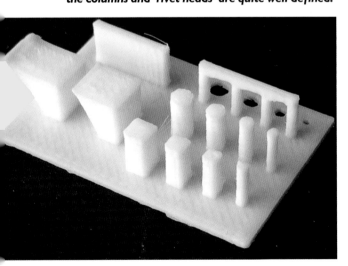

Printed at 205°C temperature. The right-hand column is only 1mm square, and the columns have printed with little stringing between them. Once you have this quality of Test Piece you can go on to print your models with confidence.

Printed at 230°C the stringing is severe, so printed at this temperature with this particular spool of filament, your models would not look very good.

FURNITURE

Creating these drawings will enable you to practise and consolidate the skills covered so far. Detailing buildings with furniture is often something done in 4mm scale, particularly if they have internal lighting, and is nearly always required in larger scales. Throughout this furniture section all the drawings will be done in 4mm scale, but you have the choice of halving my dimensions for 2mm scale (although some items such as chair and table legs may not print well at this scale), or multiplying by seven and dividing by four to get 7mm scale.

Perhaps the easiest way of scaling is to draw using my dimensions, export your .stl file as suggested, and then scale once you have your item on the 3-D printer print bed (by 158 per cent for 7mm scale). The driver software of most 3-D printers will allow this type of scaling. I have kept the furniture 'modular' so even the larger pieces should be able to fit your print bed when scaled up to 7mm (or most even scaled up to G scale). You may like to add more detail for the larger scales.

The internet is a good source of tables of scale factors for converting from one scale to another, so I am not going to repeat them here.

RECTANGULAR TABLE

This rectangular shape is very simple to draw and print, but it must be printed upside down. To avoid having to rotate it later, it will be drawn upside down.

A 6 x 3ft table in 4mm scale is 24 x 12mm – drawn ten times larger it becomes 240 x 120mm.

- Use the Rectangle tool to draw a rectangle 240 x 120mm (Dimensions box 240,120)
- Zoom in to make it a reasonable size on your screen
- Select the Iso view (left-hand house icon)
- With the Push/Pull tool, pull this rectangle up 8mm to form the table top
- On the top surface of the rectangle use the Rectangle tool to draw a rectangle in each corner 12mm square (Dimensions box 12,12)

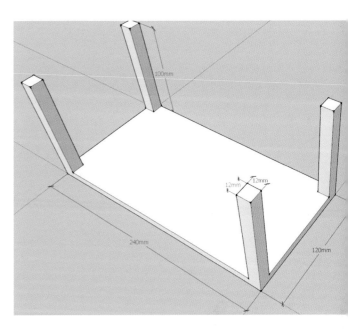

The finished table drawing ready to 3-D print.

A typical table is about 2.5ft high, therefore 10mm in 4mm scale.

- Use the Push/Pull tool to pull up each corner leg 100mm (Dimensions box 100)

Then use Save As >a table.skp: this saves the entire drawing in Sketchup format). Now select the entire table (it turns blue) and use Export as >a table. stl: this saves selected parts of the drawing in 3-D printer format).

If you find the legs of the table do not print well on your printer, I suggest you make them larger, say 15mm or 20mm square, until they do. You can alter the size of the table easily to suit your needs by selecting half of the table (two legs will turn blue) with the Select Tool and then moving them up/down, left/right as required using the Move Tool.

If you would like tables of different sizes for future projects, then as you alter the table add the size into the filename, for example b table 6 x 4 (where 6 x 4 would be the actual scale size of 6ft by 4ft).

The .stl file is ready to print on your 3-D printer. The table is printed upside down to avoid overhangs.

CIRCULAR TABLE

This project is for a three-legged circular table. It uses the Circle tool, Tape Measure tool, the Push/Pull tool, and the Rotate and Copy (Move+) tools.

- Re-run the program, or click on File>New and begin by selecting the Circle tool and changing to ninety-six sides by *immediately* entering 96 to replace the twenty-four in the Dimensions box. Your circle will now have ninety-six sides and be much smoother
- Draw your circle centred on the red, blue and green axis shown on your screen. Draw it 120mm diameter, or 3ft diameter in 4mm scale (remember drawn x10 size). Do this by starting the circle and entering 60 into the Dimensions box (remember this is the radius)
- Select the Iso icon and pull the circle up 8mm using the Push/Pull tool
- Using the Tape Measure tool, click on the centre and the outside of the circle (anywhere) to create a guideline
- With the Select tool, click on the guideline to select it. It should turn blue

You are going to Rotate+ (rotate and copy) the guideline so you know where to draw the three legs.

- Select the Rotate tool, tap the Ctrl key to get the + by the side of the cursor (indicating copy), and centre the protractor by clicking on the centre of the circle
- Move your cursor to the right and on the line as shown. Click to fix it there. Now pull the cursor down slightly to begin rotating the blue guideline. Enter 120 into the Dimensions box (and tap Enter) to rotate the guideline 120 degrees. Immediately enter *2 into the Dimensions box (and tap Enter) to copy the line twice

You should see the guideline copies as above.
    Our three legs are going to be 16mm in diameter and 10mm in from the edge of the table, so we need a guide mark 18mm (10mm in from the edge + 8mm radius).

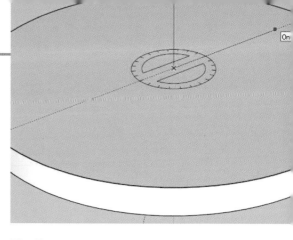

The Rotate tool protractor centred on the table circle and the cursor now at the red square on the line ready to rotate.

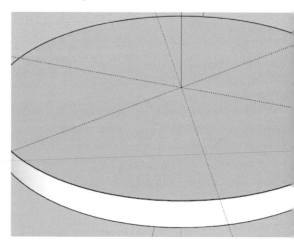

The guideline rotated 120 degrees twice to give six equally spaced segments to the circle.

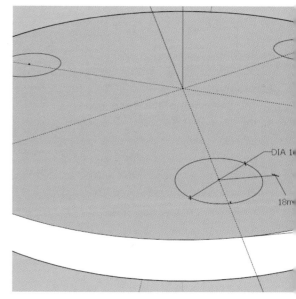

Leg circles drawn using guidelines and crosses.

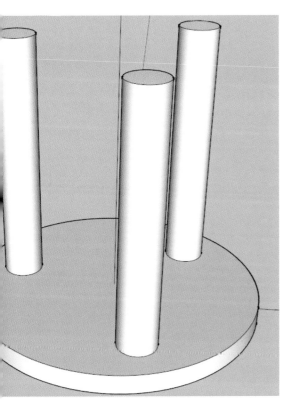

The final table drawn and ready for 3-D printing (upside down).

- Using the Tape Measure tool, measure 18mm up three of the guidelines as shown by clicking on the end of the line and moving the Tape Measure tool up the guideline and entering 18 into the Dimensions box (and tap Enter). A small cross should appear on the guideline 18mm in from the edge of the circle. Repeat for the other two guidelines as shown, to give you the centre of the three legs
- Use the Circle tool to draw three 16mm diameter (8mm radius) circles on the three crosses just made. Your drawing should look as the one illustrated
- With the Push/Pull tool, pull each circle up 100mm to make the final legs (100 in the Dimensions box). You should have the final drawing as shown.

Now save as follows: Save As >a round table.skp (Sketchup format); and then use Export as >a round table.stl (for printing).

Try printing the table.

Working with Circles

When working with circles remember that circles are made up of straight lines in Sketchup – even if they are too small for you to see them. This has implications when drawing lines to the edges of circles. Sketchup will only 'snap' these lines to where two lines join on the circle edge as shown.

By extending the line required to beyond the circle, this snapping action does not take place and so the line remains where you want it. Simply delete the unwanted part of the line outside the circle to tidy up your drawing.

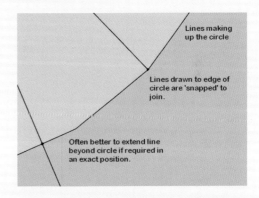

Showing the line extended to beyond the circle so it does not 'snap' to the join of the lines making up the circle.

You will need this technique in the next adaptation of the circular table, but you need to extend inside the circle to follow your guidelines.

You can now try variations of the tables as in the drawings. I will leave you to do these to your own measurements. Use the Tape Measure tool to draw the guidelines parallel to guidelines drawn between the circle centres, and then the Line tool to draw the lines before selecting the areas and pulling them up using the Push/Pull tool. Finally pull the legs up to 100mm as before.

Use Save As >b round table with supports.skp, then Export as >b round table with supports.stl. I have found it useful to keep the Sketchup files and the .STL 3-D printer files the same name.

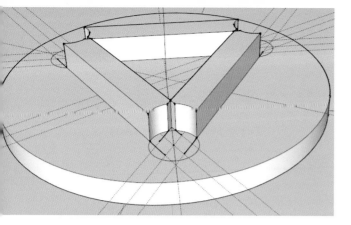

Outside supports.

If modelling in 7mm or G-scale then I advise you to draw them in that scale, rather than scaling them up or down later. In 7mm you will be able to print even the legs of furniture to scale size.

BED

Beds are drawn and printed upside down to avoid overhangs. Two examples are shown in the picture: you can draw these following the techniques used for the chair.

Then use Save As >a bed.skp – this saves all the drawing in Sketchup format – then select the right-hand bed (Top Down view) and use Export as >a bed solid.stl, and finally select the left-hand bed and use Export as >a bed open.stl.

WARDROBE

Start with a rectangle 160 x 60mm, and pull it up 240mm (4mm/00 scale measurements). Mark out

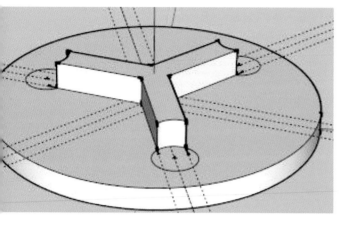

Two variations of leg support. Draw and pull these up before the legs.

BELOW: *Two styles of double bed.*

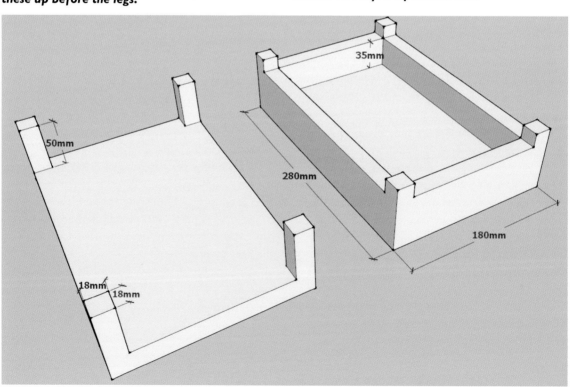

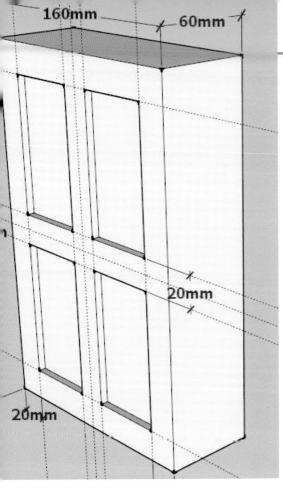

A simple wardrobe.

20mm wide borders and centres, and draw the four rectangular door panels. Push these back 5mm.

Use Save As >a wardrobe.skp, and Export as >a wardrobe.stl.

Try a similar style but with the door panels pulled out 5mm. Save as b wardrobe.

DRESSING TABLE

Using the techniques learned so far you can create a dressing table, as shown below. Adapt the measurements as required. Note how this is drawn and printed in two parts to avoid overhangs. Glue together once printed.

Remember to save it.

KITCHEN CABINETS

Draw the basic shape: two rectangles and a joining piece 8mm wide in Top-Down view. Change to Iso view and pull up 50mm. Use the Offset tool to draw the inner line 6mm in all round on the fronts, and push the cabinet fronts in 5mm.

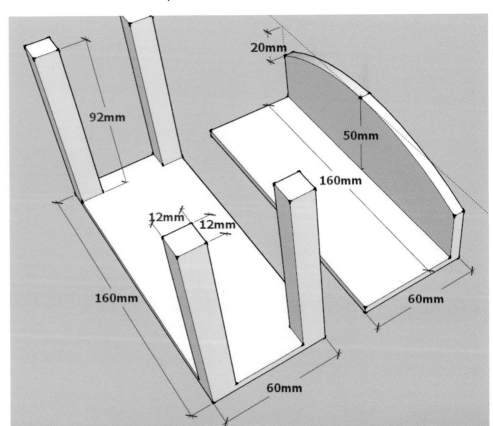

A simple dressing table.

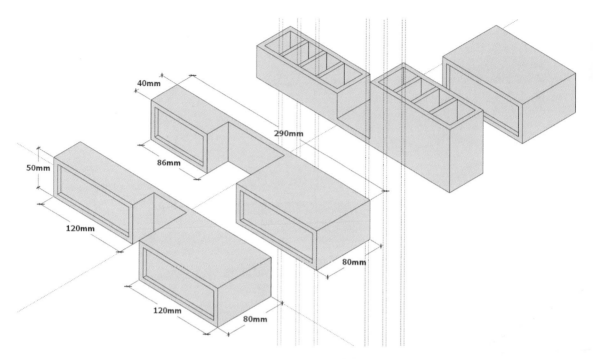

Kitchen cabinets dimensioned for 4mm 00 scale.

The use Save As >a kitchen cabinet.skp, and Export as >a kitchen cabinet.stl.

Copy this basic cabinet and modify it into different units. I have shown some examples to give you ideas. Note that the unit with shelves has to be printed on its back in order to avoid overhangs.

With the finished units as shown, you can easily make the cabinets double width by selecting each in turn and moving a copy (Move+) 50mm upwards (or to the side in the case of the shelving units). Use the Rotate tool to turn the shelving unit by 90 degrees, then the copy to the left to make it double.

For a different appearance, use the Push/Pull tool to pull the doors out 10mm so they are 5mm proud. Remember to re-save these with a different filename (+double width) both as Sketchup and .STL formats. For instance use Save As >a kitchen cabinet double

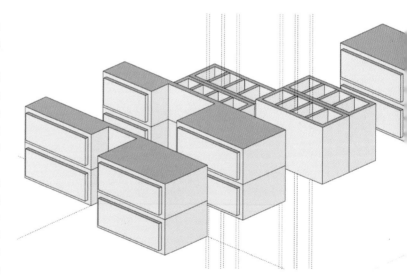

Kitchen cabinets modified to double width, with the doors sticking out instead of indented.

width.skp, and Export as >a kitchen cabinet double width.stl.

Mix and match these units in your kitchen. You can then print, in a different colour, a 'worktop' matching the length of the units used.

Printing More than One Item At Once: Caution!

Sometimes when printing several items at once, one or more item does not stick to the print bed, causing the whole print to fail. It is important that they all lie flat on the print bed. If you add single items to the print bed they will either lie flat on it, or your printer software will give a message asking you if you would like to place them on the print bed. However, when printing several items from the same drawing they may not all be on the same vertical plane in your drawing.

You can check this by selecting the menu Camera >Parallel Projection as above, and then Front or Side views (small house icons).

Note in the picture that the second unit from the left is not in line (flat) with the others (exaggerated), and would not therefore print correctly if all were saved and printed together. If one item is raised by even a fraction of a millimetre it can stop the first print layer sticking to the print bed, leading to a failed print.

This mode can also be useful for lining things up accurately.

Ensure you return to Perspective view straightaway as Sketchup does not always display drawings correctly in Parallel Projection mode.

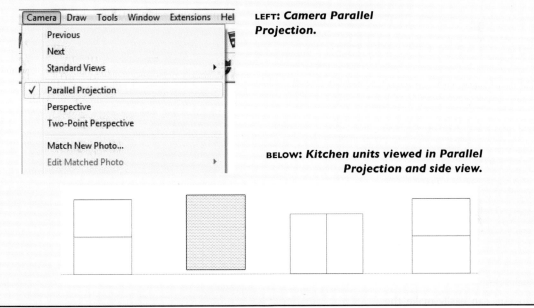

LEFT: *Camera Parallel Projection.*

BELOW: *Kitchen units viewed in Parallel Projection and side view.*

THREE-PIECE SUITE

This project uses the two-point Arc tool to make the curved surfaces required for drawing our three-piece suite.

In order that we can print the suite from the ground up and add arms on it later, we are going to start drawing in Front view – so begin by clicking on the Front view icon, as shown.

Begin with two rectangles as shown, then use the 2-point Arc tool to draw curves, as shown. Click

on either end of the curve, then 'pull' the arc into a curve by holding down the left mouse key and dragging the arc. The amount of curve can be determined in the Dimensions box if required. I have not put dimensions on the curves – just keep adding and deleting arcs (use Undo) until you have a shape you are happy with.

Once you have your shape, delete all the unwanted lines to leave your suite end shape, as shown overleaf.

Copy the final shape two or three times. Change to Iso view, and pull the final shape required for each

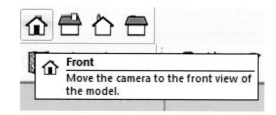

Use the Front view icon to start your drawing so your chairs and settees will print easily later.

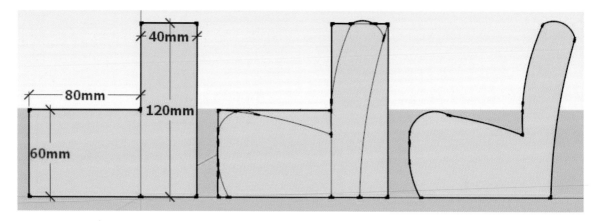

Stages in drawing the settee. I have copied the drawing to show the stages – you would have only one shape.

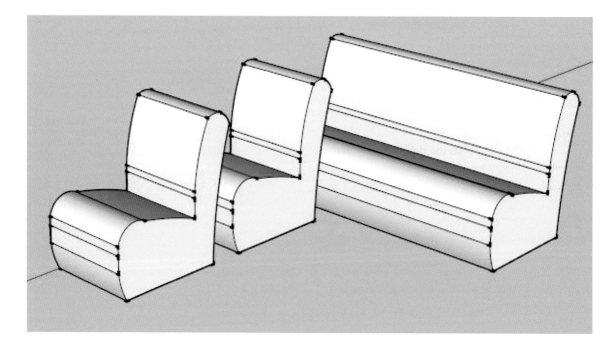

The final suite viewed in Iso view and 'pulled out' to any length required.

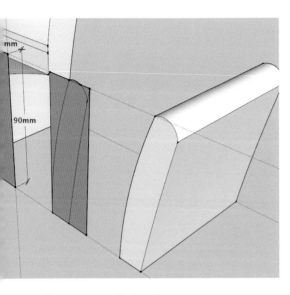

ABOVE: *A settee arm being drawn.*

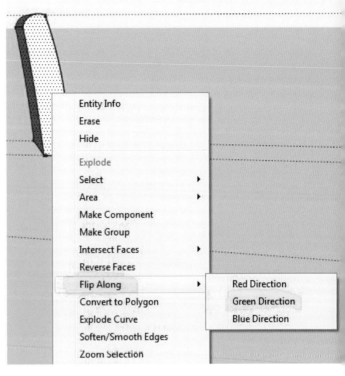

RIGHT: *Flipping turns the object round in the chosen axis.*

using the Push/Pull tool. Here I have pulled the shape into two chairs and a settee by copying it and then pulling them 80mm and 240mm.

Then use Save As >a 3 piece suite.skp.

To draw your settee/chair arm, begin by drawing vertical guidelines and a rectangle, as shown – use the Tape Measure tool to draw a vertical line 90mm high from the front base guideline; your rectangle should then 'snap' to it to draw a vertical rectangle. Then using the Arc tool, form the curve of the arm before pulling it with the Push/Pull tool to the depth of your settee (this will be different on your drawing from mine).

Begin by selecting and copying (Move+) the arm to the right, then right click on the arm and select Flip >Green Direction from the menu.

You should now have two arms, as shown.

Use Save As >b 3 piece suite.skp to save it.

Make copies of both the seat and the arms and move them to the side as shown. Hold down the left arrow key as you do so to constrain the movement to the green axis. Now that you have copies, if you go wrong simply use the Undo tool and make fresh copies to work on.

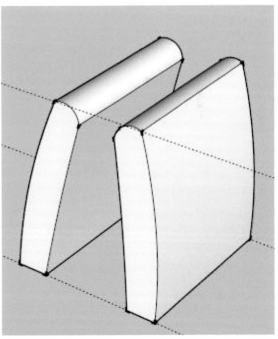

The two arms of the settee/chairs.

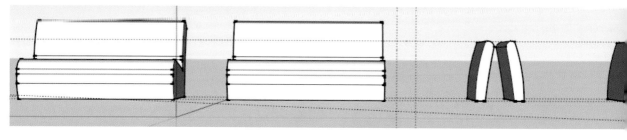

Copies made of the settee and arms.

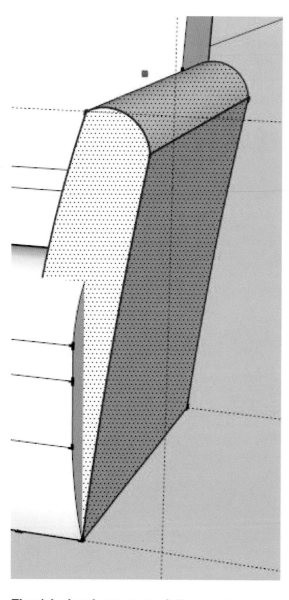

The right-hand arm successfully moved into position.

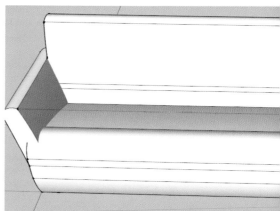

The final settee.

Select the right-hand arm, being careful not to select any part of the left-hand arm. The Move tool has a useful feature here. We wish to move the arm to a specific location, so select the Move tool and click on the right-hand bottom corner of the right-hand arm, and then the right-hand bottom corner of the seating. The arm will move to the exact spot.

Remember to use the Undo tool if it goes wrong.

Now repeat the process for the left-hand arm: select it, then click on the left-hand bottom corner with the Move tool and the bottom left-hand corner of the seating block.

Finally save it as Save As >c 3 piece suite.skp.

The final settee should now look as the one in the picture above.

We need two chairs, but remember we can print as many as we require, so we only need one drawing of it!

Here we are going to use another trick of the Move tool. By selecting just the right-hand end of the settee, we can move it to make the settee wider or narrower. By making it narrower we have our chair, wider and we have station platform or waiting room seating. Proceed as follows:

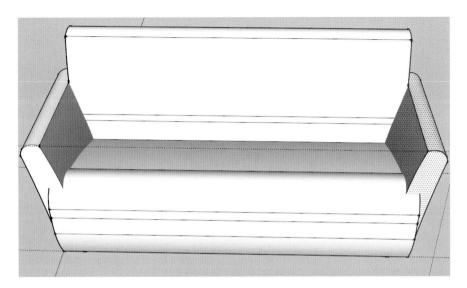

The right-hand half of the copied settee is selected with the Select tool.

- Make a copy of your settee
- On the copy, using the Select tool, select just the right-hand half of the settee by drawing the select box around it. Those areas entirely within the selected area will turn blue. Note that the horizontal lines of the settee, although partly selected, remain black
- With the Move tool selected, hold down the left arrow key on your keyboard. This restricts the move to the green axis – along the settee. Now simply hold the left mouse button down and slide the settee narrower to make a chair

By modifying the chairs and settees shown, and with the skills acquired, you can make almost any type of seating s required for carriages, stations, houses, playgrounds and so on.

I estimate that each seat will use less than 2p worth of plastic in 4mm scale.

Now save as Save As >d 3 piece suite.skp: this saves all your drawing in Sketchup format.

Export the settee and chair separately so you can print them separately in any quantity required. First select the settee – it should turn blue – then use Export as >d settee.stl. Then select just the chair and use Export as >d armchair.stl.

Now you have separate files for the settee and the armchair for 3-D printing. The letter 'd' prefix to your filenames allows you to associate the Sketchup

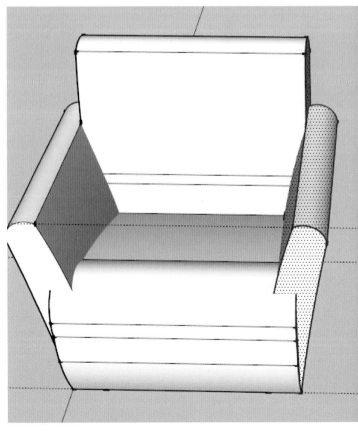

The finished chair with arms.

drawing version with the .stl files produced from it and required for printing.

CHAIRS

Chairs come in all shapes and sizes. This first example is simple to produce in two parts: a base with four legs, essentially a small, low table but tapered front to back, with a separate back. These are best printed in specific orientations on the 3-D printer, and introduce the concepts of breaking down items into smaller parts, and of always trying to print upwards without overhangs and supports.

Note: This chair pushes your printer to the limit. If your printer cannot print the smallest 1mm columns on Test Piece 2, then it probably won't be able to print the back and legs of this chair.

Now draw the base of the chair:

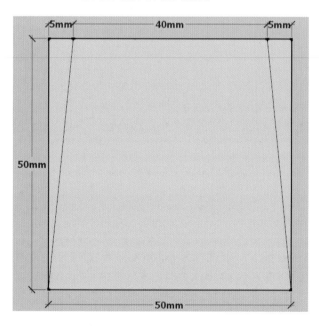

Chair base drawn in Top-Down view.

• Use the Rectangle tool to draw a rectangle 50 x 50mm
• Use the Tape Measure tool to mark guide points 5mm in from the rearmost edge, as shown
• With the Line tool connect these marks to the front corners
• Delete the two triangles to leave a trapezoid shape: this will make our chair base wider at the front than the back

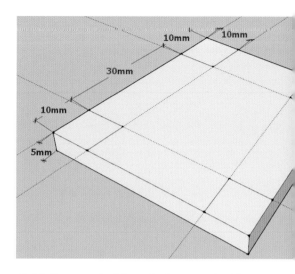

Guidelines made 10mm in from each side.

• Switch to Iso view
• Use the Push/Pull tool to pull your base up 5mm. Since the base is no longer rectangular, neither will the legs be
• With the Tape Measure tool, draw guidelines 10mm in from each side, and complete with two lines at each corner, making (nearly) rectangles for the legs

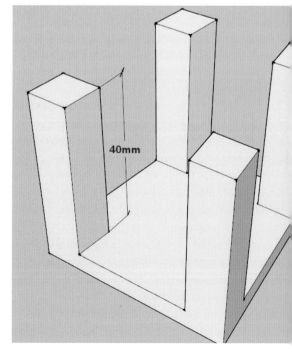

Chair legs pulled up 40mm to form the chair base.

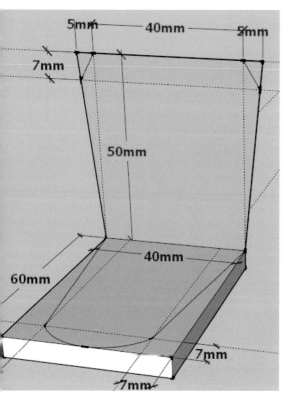

The chair cushion and back marked out with tapered lines front to back. The back is flat, the seat 'cushion' is here being drawn vertical.

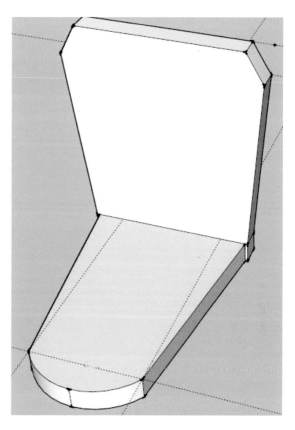

The chair back with the cushion pulled to 5mm, and the back shaped.

• Next, use the Push/Pull tool to pull each leg up 40mm

The size of the legs is determined by the smallest size your 3-D printer can print reliably. This model as drawn assumes your printer can print a 10mm square, the smallest on Test Piece 2, as described elsewhere.

Use Save As >a chair.skp to save it.

• Select Top Down view
• Use the Rectangle tool to draw a rectangle 40 x 60mm. This is the chair back
• Change to Iso view
• With the Push/Pull tool, pull the back up to 5mm thickness
• Use the Tape Measure tool to draw guidelines upright (it should 'snap' to the blue vertical axis) 50mm long from each rear corner

• Join the two vertical guidelines with a horizontal one
• On the horizontal guideline, mark points 5mm out from either side: hover over the top of the vertical lines, hold down the left mouse button and slide along the horizontal line. Enter 5 into the Dimensions box and tap Enter
• Draw a further guideline 7mm down from the top of the chair base
• Use the Line tool to draw a line to connect the corner of the back to the outer 5mm markers. Draw a further line to cut off the corner as shown. Repeat for the other side. This shape matches that of the base to be drawn later

Now for the chair back:

• Use the Tape Measure tool to draw guidelines 7mm in from three sides of the chair back

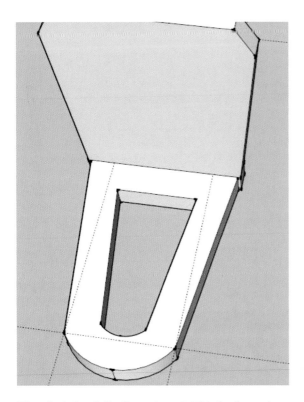

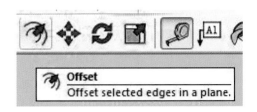

Offset tool.

The chair back 'hollowed out'. This looks rather chunky, but remember how small the chair is: the back is only .8mm thick and near the limits of how small the printer can go!

Furniture as printed in white PLA 4mm scale.

- With the Line tool, connect the outer bottom of the back with the points where the guidelines intersect, as shown
- Use the two-point Arc tool to make a rounded top, as shown
- Use Select and Delete to select and remove the two triangles at the front of the seat cushion by deleting the two lines forming the corner
- Use the Push/Pull tool to pull the cushion towards you to a depth of 5mm
- With the Push/Pull tool, push the outer portions of the seat back down 5mm (Dimensions box 5). The outside portion of the back should disappear, as shown
- Select the Offset tool, and then the outside of the chair back. Drag the Offset tool 8mm inwards (Dimension box 8): this should draw a parallel line 8mm inwards from the outer line of the chair back. Push the centre down 5mm with the Push/Pull tool: it should disappear, leaving the chair back as above.

4mm-scale pub interior with furniture painted and figures added.

Now use Save As >b chair.skp, and Export as >b chair. stl (in Centimetres to scale it down) to save it.

MORE SEATING

By adapting the simple techniques above you can draw many different types of seating for both indoor and outdoor use, as well as for inside coaches.

Note the orientation of the seat base and back. To produce the seat in one part would have involved overhangs. These are bad as they require supports on FDM printers, and in removing the supports you risk damaging the model, especially smaller models.

By breaking the model down into two or more parts you can avoid overhangs. The chair back shown is placed such that openings in the back are printed flat on the print bed, not upright. You can get quite good detail with a properly set up 3-D printer in this way.

FIREPLACE AND SURROUND

This design uses the Offset tool to draw the lines for the raised areas around the fireplace, but you could just use guidelines to measure them instead. I will leave you to determine the measurements and method of drawing for the fireplace project. You have the skills, it is just using them in the right order and place!

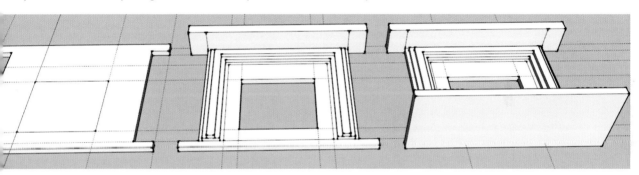

A fireplace surround showing the stages of drawing.

FURTHER PROJECTS

I hope that once you have produced the above items 'from the ground up', you will be able to design and produce your own items.

IDEAS FOR FURNITURE AND FITTINGS

Four-poster bed
Bedside cabinets
Central heating radiators
Bath
Sink
Cooker
Microwave
Washing machine/drier
Picnic tables
Television
Picture frames
Poster frames (station platforms/waiting rooms?)

3-D STATION NAME BOARD

This project uses the 3-D Text function of Sketchup to draw a station name board. The size of the board will be determined by your chosen modelling scale and the actual text for your board. After doing this project you should be able to make your own boards as required. The resolution of your printer will determine whether these are viable in 4mm scale, but for larger scales they can be made to look very real indeed.

Proceed as follows:

- Begin by drawing a rectangle with the Rectangle tool 5,000 x 350mm. This is deliberately longer than most station names (unless you are modelling the very famous one in Wales, in which case make your board longer!)
- Switch to Iso view (3-D view – the first 'house' icon)
- Pull the rectangle up 15mm using the Push/Pull tool
- Use the Offset tool to create a line 25mm in all round from the rectangle

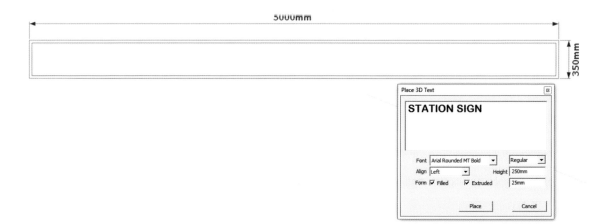

Station name board and parameters for the 3-D text.

• Do not pull this border up at this stage
• Switch to Top-Down view (the second 'house' icon)
• Select Tools>3-D Text from the menus
• Enter your station name text into the box, as shown above. Choose your font: Arial Rounded MT Bold gives a good approximation of BR and railway fonts
• Make it 100mm less in Height than your rectangle: 250mm
• Alter the Extruded height to check it will be extruded 25mm (the same as your surround)
• Click on Place and place the text into the rectangle with a suitable space at the left-hand side, as in the diagram. When placing your lettering ensure you get a tiny box saying 'on face' before left-clicking to place it. This ensures that your lettering is actually placed on the face of the background with no space between the two
• Select the right-hand end of your board, and with the Move tool slide it towards the lettering until the gap on the right equals the gap on the left
• Finally, select Iso view and using the Push/Pull tool to pull the 25mm surround of the name board up 25mm

Adjust the size of the board and text to suit, and you can very easily add supporting legs and so on, for platform mounting.

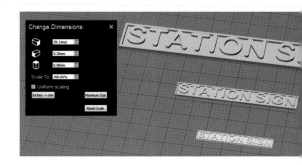

Station name boards copied and re-sized on Makerbot Replicator2 print bed.

The 3-D Printer software usually allows you to copy and alter sizes on the print bed before printing. This can allow for easy conversion to other scales, though as you make items smaller the resolution of your printer may make them unprintable.

Completed station name board with border and 3-D text.

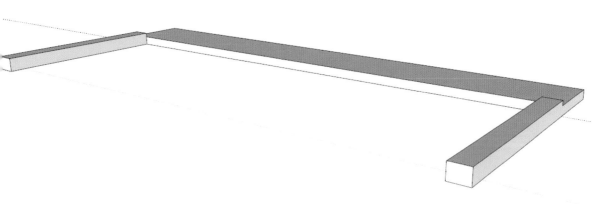

The posts for the sign.

A simple way to create posts for the sign is to print a separate item to the size of your board when lettered, as shown. Note how the posts 'step down' 25mm in order to accommodate the board. Doing the name board in two parts allows the printing of the text to be vertical in the smaller scales. Glue them together once they are printed.

To complete the sign, spray with grey primer, then the background colour, and finally pick out the tops of the lettering in the appropriate colour.

BARREL

For any industrial scene, particularly period industrial scenes, crates, barrels and milk churns were commonplace objects. These are easily drawn and made using Sketchup Make and a 3-D printer.

This is an easy-to-draw, basic barrel shape:

- Select Iso view to give perspective to your drawing
- Select the Circle tool and immediately enter 96 into the Dimensions box and tap Enter. This makes for smoother circles
- With the Circle tool, draw a circle of 65mm radius centred on where the three axis guidelines meet (65 in the Dimensions box)
- Zoom in to make the circle larger
- Use the Tape Measure tool to mark points: 200 up the blue axis and also 120 along the red axis. Tiny crosses mark the spots
- With the Rectangle tool, draw a 120 x 200mm rectangle by clicking on the first marked point up the blue axis, and then clicking on the second on the

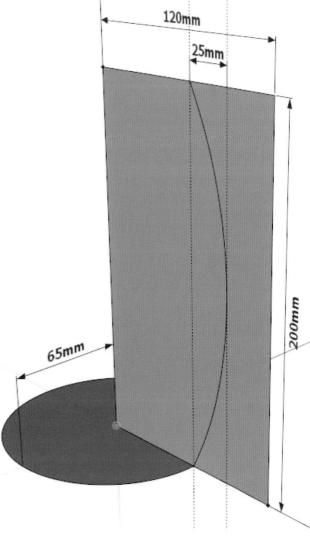

Circle and rectangle with guidelines and arc drawn on the face of the rectangle.

red axis. The rectangle should line up with these points vertically as shown. This rectangle gives us a surface 'plane' on which to draw the outline shape of the barrel

- Use the Tape Measure tool to draw two vertical guidelines as shown, 25mm apart, the inner one in line with the outer edge of the circle
- Select the two-point Arc tool and enter 96 into the Dimensions box to make smoother arcs
- With the Arc tool draw an arc as shown to touch the outer guideline
- Use the Tape Measure tool to draw guidelines 15mm down from the top of the rectangle and 15mm upwards from the bottom
- Zoom in to the top of the rectangle
- With the Circle tool, draw a circle of 5mm radius on the intersection of the arc and the guideline (when zoomed in sufficiently the intersection will show as a red cross: start the circle on it), just drawn 15mm down from the top of the rectangle
- Do similar at the bottom of the rectangle
- Select and Delete the inner half of the two small circles and those parts of the arc that lie inside circles, and then the outer part of the rectangle, as shown above. You may have to zoom in and/or change your viewpoint to enable this without also selecting other lines in the drawing

You now have the outline of the barrel shape drawn on a circle. You could easily have drawn the outer shape of a chimney or a road bollard using the same techniques. Now for the magic!

This drawing would not 3-D print as the walls have no thickness.

- Using the Select tool, click on the outside of the circle: the outer ring of the circle should turn blue. (Note only the outer ring should turn blue, not the area of the circle)
- From the menu, select Tools>Follow Me and click on the vertical surface (area) of the barrel shape (the blue on the outside of the circle disappears when you click on Follow me but it is still selected)

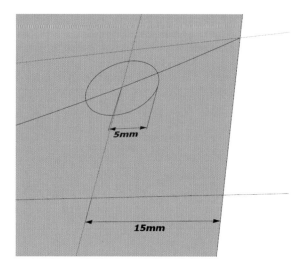

The top of the rectangle showing the guideline and circle.

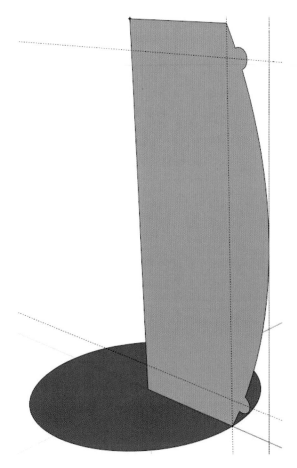

Lines deleted to leave two 'bulges' on the arc. The remainder of the rectangle is also deleted.

Barrel drawn with the Follow Me command. The underside is not solid at this stage.

Once you have clicked on the barrel shape: wait! The computer is doing loads of calculations and it takes some time to draw the barrel.

If you have managed the correct sequence as above you should now have the barrel shape.

- Rotate the barrel. Hold down the scroll wheel and move the mouse until you can see underneath it. It is hollow
- Use the Line tool to draw a line from one side of the underneath of the barrel to the other. A surface should appear on the bottom of the barrel
- Delete the line just drawn: the surface should remain. The underside of the barrel should now look solid
- Rotate the barrel so you can see on top of it
- Use the Circle tool to draw a circle of 58mm radius inside the outer top circle of the barrel
- Use the Push/Pull tool to push the inner top surface down 8mm as shown

Save your work as File>Save As>a barrel.skp.

Final barrel.

SCALING YOUR BARREL

To scale your barrel you could use the Scale icon and drag it smaller, but there is an easier way. Currently your barrel is 200mm high, which when printed would be 20mm. Proceed as follows:

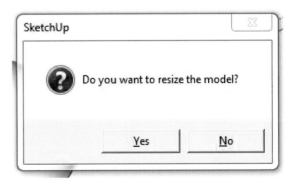

Resize box.

- Use the Line tool to draw a line 200mm long alongside the barrel, but not touching it. Use the Dimensions box to fix the length

- Use the Tape Measure tool to measure the length of the line – the measurement appears in the Dimensions box
- Immediately enter into the Dimensions box the height you wish the barrel to be, say, 150
- An input box as shown in the picture will appear. Click on Yes to re-size your model

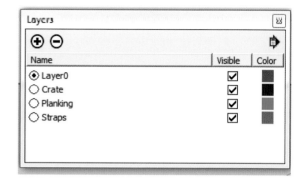

Crate, planking and strap layers defined.

Save your work again, but this time include the new size of your barrel: File>Save As>a barrel 15mm.skp.

This scaling technique can be used on any model, and is particularly useful if you wish to produce the same model in, say, 4mm and 7mm scales. Be aware, though, that scaling up or down can have consequences for both appearance and printing resolution, so it is always best to design for the scale you wish to print at.

PACKING CRATE

This packing crate shows how a complex object can be drawn relatively quickly by using some of the more advanced features of Sketchup Make. You need to have become familiar with the 2D and 3-D Advanced CAD chapter – the last chapter in Part I – before attempting this project.

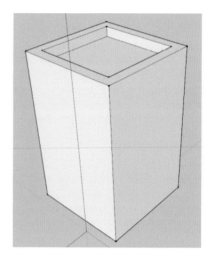

Basics of the packing crate.

- Begin by loading Sketchup with the Laser3-D template selected
- Add the Crate, Planking and Straps to the Layer menu at right of the screen
- Use the Rectangle tool to draw a square 100 x 100mm
- Push/Pull the rectangle to 160mm in height
- Use the Offset tool to draw a line 10mm inside the top of the crate
- Push/Pull the inside top surface down 10mm as shown above

Remember always to draw on Layer 0 (indicated by the dot in front of Layer 0) in the Layers menu.

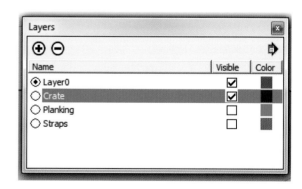

Use the ticks against Layers to control the visibility of Layers.

- Now Select the crate (drag round it holding down the left mouse button – the crate should turn blue)
- Right-click on the crate and select Make Group from the menu that appears

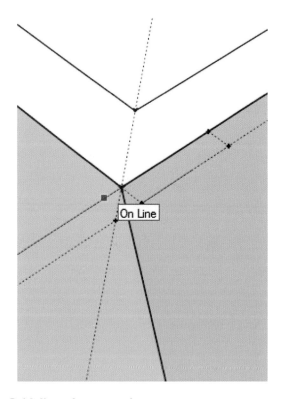

Guidelines drawn on the top corner.

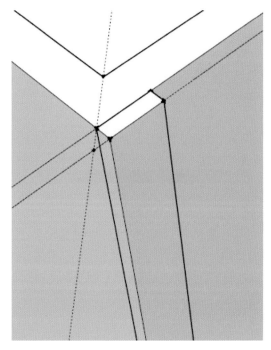

Top of the plank drawn and pushed down 160mm to the bottom of the crate.

• From the drop-down Layers menu (at the top of the screen) select Crate to assign the drawing to the Layer Crate

Whenever you click on or select a Group, the drop-down Layers menu at the top of the screen shows you the current Layer.

Now save your work thus far as File>Save as>a crate with crate layer.skp. Objects that are Groups can only be edited if they are first made editable by double-clicking on them. Once edited, click anywhere on the background to return them to uneditable.

Now add some planking down one of the sides. Make sure your crate object is still a Group by making it invisible, then visible again.

• Select the Tape Measure tool
• Double-click about halfway along each top corner line to produce a guideline stretching beyond them
• Click in turn on each of the four top corners to produce two guidelines, which cross in the centre of the crate top
• On one side, pull a guideline 3mm out from the corner
• Create another guideline 15mm along the plank top, as shown
• Use the Rectangle tool to draw the rectangle (3 x 15)
• With the Push/Pull tool, push the rectangle shape 160mm downwards to the bottom of the crate. This is the first plank
• Make the Layer Crate invisible (untick the box next to Layer Crate in the Layers menu; you should see just the plank)
• Select the plank just drawn – it should turn dotted and blue
• Make the Layer Crate visible again
• Now using the View icons, select the view of the crate with the plank to the left, as shown. Only the plank should still be blue

Plank selected, as shown by the blue colour.

Planks copied to one side.

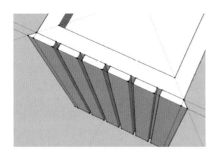

Corners drawn and pushed down to the bottom of the crate.

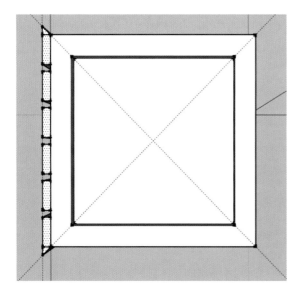

Planks selected...

You are now going to copy the plank along the face of the crate.

• Select Move and tap Ctrl: a + sign appears by the Move cursor. This enables Move to copy an item. Carefully select the plank and move the copy to the right of the crate body
• Enter 85 into the Dimensions box to move the copy exactly by this amount. It should move to the opposite corner of the crate
• Immediately enter /5 into the Dimensions box, and five more planks will be drawn equally spaced between the first two. (Use Undo to go back and try again if needed)

Next you do the corners:

• Zoom in to the top of one end plank
• Use the Line tool to draw over the two guidelines to make a triangle at the corner of the plank, as shown
• With the Push/Pull tool, push this triangle down the crate by 160mm (160 in the Dimensions box), as above
• Now repeat for the other end plank

Now save your work, File>Save As>b crate with planking.skp, so you can return to it if things go wrong!
    You could repeat this process for the other three sides, or you can use more Sketchup techniques to copy and rotate this one side on to the other three. You do this as follows:

• Select Top-Down view
• Make the Layer Crate invisible
• Select all the planking – it turns blue
• Make the Layer Crate visible

You are now going to rotate and copy the planking to the other three sides.

• Select the Rotate tool and tap Ctrl to get a + by the cursor: this indicates you wish to rotate a copy of the object

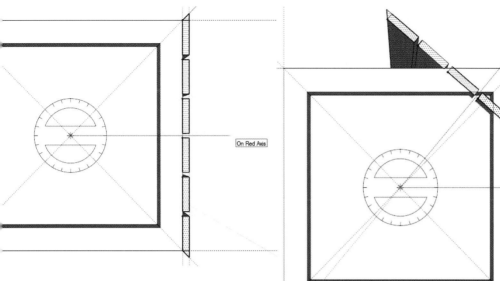

...and about to rotate to the other sides.

Planking being rotated.

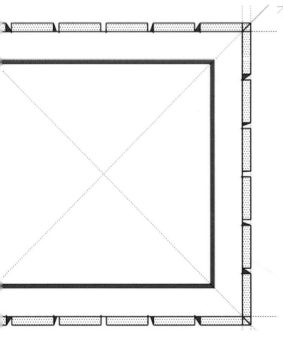

Planking copied to all sides.

- Click on the centre of the crate and then to the right. Move your cursor upwards a little, and type 90 into the Dimensions box, and then Enter
- *Immediately* type *3 into the Dimensions box and tap Enter. The planking should be copied to the other three sides
- Make the Layer Crate invisible

- Select all your planking and then use right-click, Make Group, and add them to the Planking Layer (click on Planking in the drop-down Layers menu at the top of the screen)

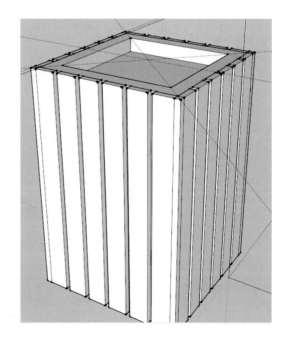

Planking on the sides of the crate.

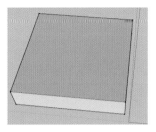

Rectangle pushed down to 20mm thickness.

• Make the Layer Crate visible, and you should see your crate with planking, as in the illustration

Now save your work as File>Save As>c crate with planking.skp so you can return to it if things go wrong!
    Next you need to add two straps round the crate. Rather than drawing these round the crate, we will simply draw two cubes in the right place, as follows:

• Change to Top-Down view
• Use the Rectangle tool to draw a rectangle from the outside corners of the planking
• Make the Layer Crate and Layer Planking invisible (untick the boxes in the Layers menu)
• Use the Offset tool to draw another rectangle 3mm outside the one just drawn
• Select and Delete the original rectangle, leaving just the larger one
• Use the Push/Pull tool to push the rectangle down 20mm
• Select a Front view
• Select all the strap just drawn (it should turn blue dotted)
• Make the Layer Crate visible

Now we need to do some calculations. The strap is 20mm deep, the crate is 160mm deep, and we want the straps 25mm from each end. The first move is therefore 25mm down:

• Select the Move tool and begin moving the strap down the crate. Holding down the up arrow key whilst making this move will 'lock' the move to the blue (up-and-down) axis
• Enter 25 into the Dimensions box to complete the move

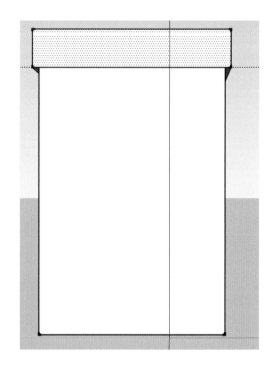

Front view of the strap with it selected ready to move.

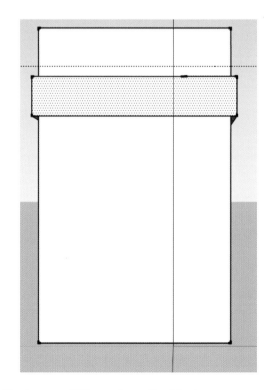

Strap moved 25mm down the plank.

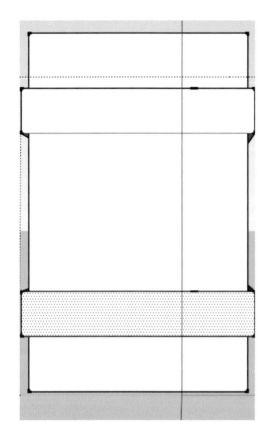

Strap copied down the crate.

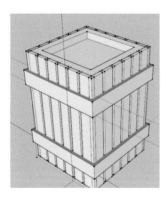

Complete crate with planking and strapping.

The next move/copy is 160–25 (already moved) –25 (up from the bottom) –20 (the width of the strap) = 90.

• With the Move tool still selected, tap the Ctrl key to get a + by the cursor. This indicates you wish to copy the move

• Pull the strap down again slightly and then enter 90 into the Dimensions box

This should copy the strap and place the copy in the correct position on the crate. Now we have our straps.

• Make the Layer Crate invisible
• Select both straps and right-click
• Select Make Group from the menu
• Click on Straps in the drop-down Layers menu at the top of the screen
• Make everything visible

Now save your work as File>Save As>d crate with planking.skp

Ensure all your object is selected (turned blue) before saving it as STL. Ensure Centimeters is selected when saving, as this scales down your drawing by ten, which is exactly what we require.

Export your file as an .stl file for 3-D printing File>Export STL>d crate with planking.stl

Load your crate into Netfabb, repair and re-save it repaired ready for 3-D printing.

The techniques of planking the crate can be applied wherever planking is required, such as for workmen's huts and so on.

GUTTERING AND DOWNPIPES

Almost every building has guttering and downpipes: these are just printable in 4mm scale, and look even better in 7mm.

This project uses Layers, and remember there are two Layers menus: a Layers menu at right of the screen, where you can add Layers by giving them a name, and a drop-down Layers menu at the top of the screen where you assign parts of your drawing to the Layers names already created.

Also remember that wherever I suggest entering a number into the Dimensions box you should tap 'Enter' on your keyboard afterwards. This box also changes name depending on which tool you are using.

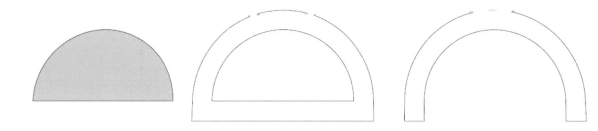

Stages in drawing the guttering: 1, 2 and 3 from left to right.

GUTTERING

- 1: Change to Front view (the third 'house' icon from the left): this enables you to print the guttering upside-down on your printer
- Use the Line tool to draw a horizontal line 36mm long
- Zoom in to make the line larger
- Select the Arc tool and enter 96 into the Dimensions box (to give a smoother arc)
- Click on either end of the line and pull the Arc up into a half-circle (18 in the Dimensions box)
- 2: Use the Offset tool and add a line outside the shape to 5mm larger, as shown
- 3: Use the Line tool to draw two vertical lines on the ends of the inner arc, and delete the horizontal lines between to leave the guttering end shape, as shown
- Switch to Iso view

- Use the Push/Pull tool to push the end shape to 500mm (you would choose this length to suit your building)
- Switch to Front view (notice how you get a perspective view of the guttering)
- Add the titles 'Guttering' and 'Guttering Brackets' to the Layers menu, as shown
- Select the guttering, right-click and use Make Group
- Click on Guttering in the drop-down Layers menu at the top of the screen to add the Guttering to the Layer Guttering
- Check that when you untick the box by 'Guttering' in the Layers menu on the right of the screen the Guttering is hidden. Re-tick the box so it is not hidden
- There are two lines on the inside of the guttering. Use the Tape Measure tool to draw a guideline along the front of the guttering at the level of the

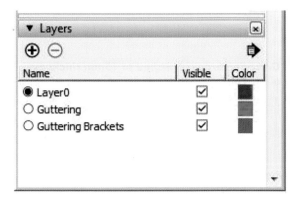

Guttering and guttering brackets added to the Layers menu.

Guttering Push/Pulled to length.

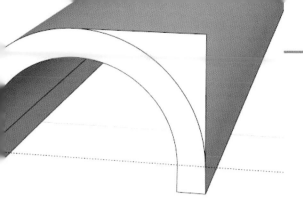

Guttering end with bracket outline...

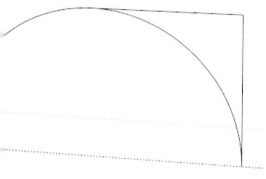

...and how it looks with the 'Guttering' Layer hidden.

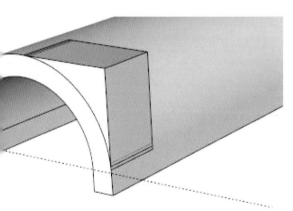

Guttering bracket pushed to 15mm thickness along the Layer Guttering.

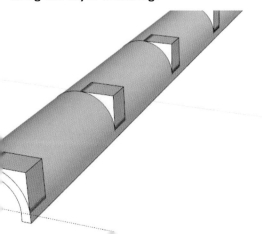

lines on the inside (which marks where the curve begins)

• Use the Arc tool to draw the outer end arc again over the top of the existing line, from the guide-line just drawn (remember the tracing paper idea, where you draw over a Layer but do not become part of it)

• Now use the Line tool to draw a line vertically (on the blue axis) from the right-hand edge. Draw this slowly by holding down the left-hand mouse key. When this line reaches the height of the arc, Sketchup should add an 'inference' line to show you when this height has been reached. Click to finish the line

• Add a horizontal line to the top of the guttering

• Hide the Layer Guttering to check your drawing against the above

• Select Iso view

• Use the Push/Pull tool to push the bracket to 15mm thickness

• Hide the Layer Guttering by unticking the box next to it in the Layers menu

• Select the bracket, right-click and select Make Group

• From the drop-down Layers menu at the top of the screen select 'Guttering Bracket'. Make the Guttering visible again (tick the box in the Layers menu at left of the screen)

• Hide the Guttering Layer by unticking the box next to it in the Layers menu

• Select the bracket (and as little of the rest of the arc as possible)

• Make the Guttering visible by ticking the box next to it in the Layers menu

• Use Move + (Move + Ctrl key) to copy the bracket to the other end of the guttering, then hold down the left arrow key and begin the move, then put 485 (the length of the guttering minus the width of the bracket) in the Dimensions box, then *immediately...*

• ...enter /5 into the Dimensions box and Sketchup will add five more evenly spaced brackets to the guttering as shown! Alter this to suit the length of the guttering being drawn (note the forward slash, not a back slash)

LEFT: *Guttering with brackets ready to print.*

Now use File>Save As>a Guttering.skp.

By drawing the guttering upside down it should print reasonably well on most printers. The top of the inside surface will fall away, but this can usually be cleaned out easily.

In larger scales you may need a thin 'rib' across the inside every few millimetres. These can be drawn just like the bracket on the inside of the guttering, and then repeated more frequently. Cut them out after printing.

Square guttering could be printed the other (correct) way up as it has a flat surface from which to print.

DOWNPIPES

These can be useful for hiding joints in brickwork and stonework in larger models.

Round objects are often better printed in two halves and glued together once printed, as this ensures that they can be printed flat on the print bed. The join can easily be cleaned up afterwards, and only one half need be drawn as you can use the copy and flip commands to create the other.

These downpipes are perhaps a little chunky for 4mm, but they work really well in the larger scales when more detail can be added. They do not need to be hollow.

15mm

End of the downpipe drawn, then Push/Pulled to 500mm.

- Change to Front view (the third 'house' icon from the left): this enables you to print the guttering upside-down on your printer
- With the Line tool, draw a horizontal line 15mm long. You will need to zoom into it to see it!

- Select the Arc tool and enter 96 into the Dimensions box (to give a smoother arc)
- Click on either end of the line and pull the Arc up into a half-circle (put 7.5 in the Dimensions box)
- Select Iso view
- Use the Push/Pull tool to push the downpipe to 500mm in length (or as determined by the height of your building)
- Select Front view
- Add 'Downpipe' and 'Downpipe Brackets' to the Layers menu at right of the screen
- Select the 'Extruded' downpipe and right-click>Make Group (select Make Group from the menu); a blue frame appears around your downpipe to indicate it is a Group
- Use the drop-down Layers menu at the top of the screen and click on 'Downpipe'
- Check the downpipe is now a Layer by unticking and re-ticking the box opposite it in the Layers menu at right of the screen. The downpipe should disappear when it is unticked
- With the downpipe visible, select the Tape Measure tool and double-click on the bottom line to produce a guideline. Remember you are now drawing over the Layer Downpipe, not on it
- Using the Tape Measure tool, place a marker 2mm each side of the bottom line (click on the bottom corner and drag the Tape Measure tool along the line, then enter 2 in the Dimensions box; a small cross should appear on the guideline)
- Use the Line tool to draw a line between the markers just made (that is, 2mm wider each side than the bottom of the downpipe)
- Use the Arc tool to draw a new arc from each end of the new line. Entering 9.5 in the Dimensions box will fix the height
- Use the Push/Pull tool to push the shape just drawn back 15mm: this represents the strap around the downpipe
- Use the Line tool to draw a vertical line (on the blue axis) 9.5mm high from the right-hand bottom corner of the shape just drawn
- With the Line tool, draw a line from the one just drawn to the top of the arc

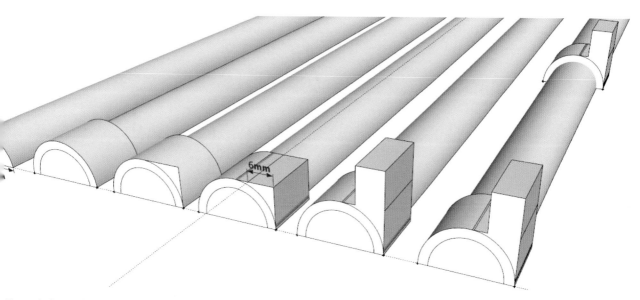

From left to right, the stages in drawing the downpipe.

- Use the Push/Pull tool to push this shape back 15mm as shown
- Select Iso view so you can see on top of the shape just drawn
- Use the Measuring tool to draw a guideline 6mm in from the edge of the bracket
- Use the Line tool to draw a line over the guideline just drawn
- You should have a rectangle 15 x 6mm on the top of the bracket, which you can now pull up 8mm using the Push/Pull tool

This completes the first bracket, which now needs copying down the length of the downpipe.

- Make the Layer Downpipe invisible (untick the box in Layers menu)
- Select all the bracket (it should all turn blue)
- Make the Layer Downpipe visible again
- Select Move + Ctrl key and hold down the left arrow key. Move the bracket slightly in the direction of the other end of the downpipe, and enter 485 into the Dimensions box; this copies the bracket to the other end of the downpipe
- *Immediately* enter /4 into the Dimensions box. This will make four more copies evenly spaced along the downpipe

- Make the Layer Downpipe invisible
- Select all the brackets
- Right-click on the brackets and select Make Group
- Now click on 'Downpipe Brackets' from the top drop-down Layers Menu (at the top of the screen)
- Make the Layer Downpipe visible again

You now need to draw the other half of the downpipe by copying and 'flipping' the downpipe to make the shape of the other half.

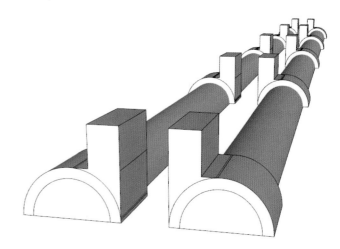

Downpipe copied and flipped to make the other half. When glued together after printing, these will form the final downpipe with wall brackets.

- Select the entire completed downpipe and brackets
- Use Move+ (copy) to copy it to the right of the existing downpipe
- Right-click on the copy and select Flip Along>Red Direction axis from the drop-down menu. The brackets on the copy will appear to move to the downpipe, as shown

Save your drawing as a Sketchup file File>Save As>a downpipe.skp

- Select the entire drawing, which means both down-pipes: they should both be in 'cages' and turn blue

Export your drawing as an .stl file: File>Export STL>a downpipe.stl

'Repair' in Netfabb and print using the highest res-olution setting of your printer, usually .1mm layers.

Using the above you can now re-draw using your own dimensions and lengths, depending on how the drawing appears from your own printer and the dimensions of the buildings you are making.

The techniques shown above can readily be adapted for more 'industrial' guttering and downpipes with larger dimensions, or to square downpipes. Just ensure you are not trying to print into 'thin air' any-where in your drawing.

USING 'FOLLOW ME'

Downpipes are rarely just straight, but how do you bend them? Sketchup has a 'Follow Me' option that allows you to draw complex shapes.

To use the Follow Me command, draw a curved line freehand or using the Line and Arc tools. Then draw the 'section' (circle, rectangle, square, polygon) of the object touching the line and at 90 degrees to the end. Highlight the line by clicking on it with the Select tool to turn it blue. If the line is made up of several sections then hold the shift key down whilst selecting them all.

Once all the lines are selected and blue, go to Tools>Follow Me and then click inside the 'section' (rectangle, or whatever shape) you have drawn at the end of your line. The shape should follow the

Bottom of the downpipe drawn with the Arc tool. The half circle is at 90 degrees to the line and represents the bottom of the downpipe.

The half circle now follows the contours of the line using the Follow Me option.

The Follow Me command is under the Tools menu.

line. It is a quirk of this command that once you click on Follow Me your lines turn back to black and you will think they are no longer selected – but they are

This command does require some practice but is very useful for drawing complex shapes.

RIVET HEADS, FINIALS AND CHIMNEY POTS

RIVET HEADS

This project will enable you to see how to place and copy rivets on to your drawing. You can also use this as a test piece to determine the best size of rivet to suit your modelling scale and printer resolution.

The project uses the 'Follow Me' command to create the dome of the rivet head, introduces a method of scaling your rivet head, and then makes it into a Group, which can be reloaded into future drawings requiring rivet heads.

If you can draw just one rivet head you can re-size and copy it easily to where it is required. The 'Follow Me' command used to draw the rivet head seems to struggle if used on tiny objects, so the rivet head is best drawn large and then shrunk to the size required for printing.

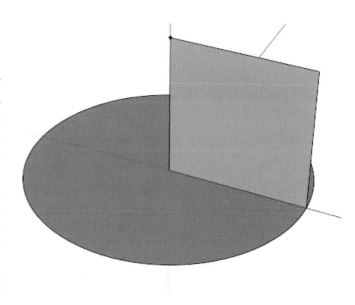

Basic circle and rectangle.

- Begin by selecting Iso view (3-D perspective view)
- Select the Circle tool and enter 96 (and Return) into the Dimensions box to give smoother circles
- Draw a circle with a 200mm radius, with its centre on the intersection of the axis guides (blue, green and red lines)
- Select the Tape Measure tool and click on the centre of the circle, then slide it up the vertical (blue) axis to 200mm (enter 200 in the Dimensions box)
- Use the Rectangle tool to draw a rectangle as shown on the red axis and up the blue axis to the guide mark just made
- Select the two-point Arc tool and enter 96 in the Dimensions box to make the arc smoother
- Draw an arc on the rectangle
- Use the Undo tool if required and re-draw the arc until it looks right
- Use the Select tool to highlight and the Delete key to remove the unwanted parts of the rectangle
- Use the Select tool to click on the outer edge of the circle and turn it blue
- From the Tools menu select Follow Me and click inside the arc shape (note there could be quite a

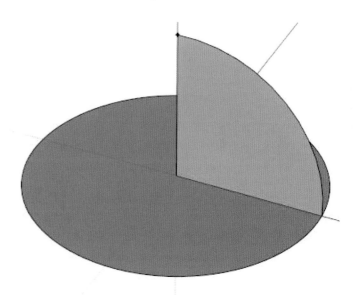

Arc drawn on the rectangle.

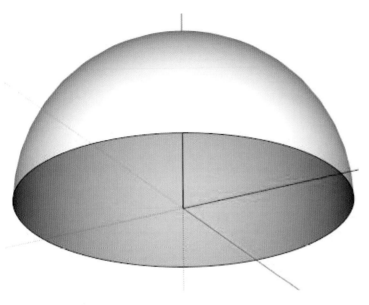

Rivet head from underneath.

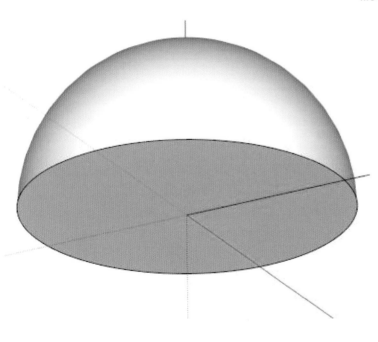

Final rivet head.

delay between clicking and anything happening whilst your computer calculates the dome shape)

The arc shape should revolve 360 degrees to form a dome shape.

The illustration shows the rivet head after using the Follow Me command. It is hollow underneath.

• Orbit your model to view underneath it (hold down the mouse scroll wheel and move the mouse away from you)
• Use the Line tool to draw a line across the bottom of the rivet head. This should result in the bottom being filled in
• Use the Select tool and click on the line to turn it blue. Delete it

The illustration shows the final rivet head, which is now a 'watertight' shape and 3-D printable. Save it as File>Save As> a Master Rivet Head.skp – and now any time you need a rivet head you can reload this file and rescale it.

SCALING THE RIVET HEAD

Scaling the rivet head is easy, and the technique applies to any of your drawings.

• Use the Line tool to draw a line (anywhere, but not on your rivet head!) 100mm long. Enter 100 in the Dimensions box. This line represents 100 per cent size
• Select the Tape Measure tool and click on each end of the line; 100 will appear in the Dimensions box
• *Before doing anything else* simply type into the Dimensions box the actual size you require your drawing scaled to: thus 50 would be 50 per cent, 25 would be 25 per cent, 10 would be 10 per cent, and so on. If you need the rivet head 2mm across, then enter 5 (as we normally draw everything x10 size)
• A box appears: click Yes to resize your model
• You will need to zoom in to see the tiny rivet

Scaling box.

- Re-measure the rivet head with the Tape Measure tool, which should now be 20mm in diameter (x10 required size)

Re-save your rivet head as File>Save As>a Rivet Head 2mm.skp. Put the actual size in the filename as above, then if you have rivets of several different sizes you can easily identify them.

This technique can be used to scale up and down. You can use the Tape Measure tool on the actual object to get a figure in the Dimensions box: simply alter that figure to the one you require. Just remember it scales all your model equally. To scale in just one or two axes you must use the Scale icon along the top of the screen.

MAKING THE RIVET HEAD A GROUP AND A LAYER

The computer can draw your rivet head faster if it is made a Group. To create a Group, proceed as follows:

- Select the model or the part of the model you wish to make a Group (it will turn blue)
- Right-click inside the selection and choose Make Group from the drop-down menu

Sketchup always draws a wire frame around Groups to show you that they are a Group. Clicking anywhere inside this frame will select the whole Group.

- To make the Group into a Layer, add a Layer called Rivet Head to the Layers menu at right of the screen
- Select the Rivet Group and click on Rivet Head in the drop-down Layers menu at the top of the screen

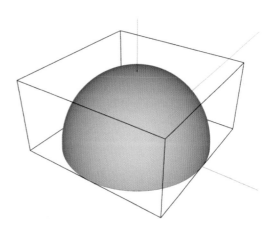

The rivet as a Group with a frame around it. Clicking on any part of a Group selects it all.

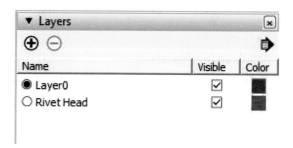

The rivet head added to the Layer menu.

- Test if you can make this Rivet Head Layer invisible by unticking the box next to its name in the Layers menu at the right of the screen

Save your Rivet Head as a separate Sketchup file: File>Save As> b Rivet Head Master

USING THE RIVET HEAD

Whenever you need to use the rivet head in a drawing, save the current drawing and load the Rivet Head master drawing (or a scaled version of it).

You can now copy it to another drawing by selecting Rivet Head (it turns blue), then using Ctrl C to Copy it. Re-load the current drawing and Ctrl V to paste the Rivet Head into your current drawing. It is easier if you have scaled it to the correct size first! Then place it as required on your drawing.

Rectangle 10mm deep drawn by the rivet.

This technique is worth remembering. Just as you can copy and paste text from one text document to another, so you can copy and paste objects between Sketchup drawings.

The sizes quoted are based on 4mm scale; adjust as required for larger scales.

- Begin by re-loading your rivet
- Select and scale your rivet as described above to the desired size
- Use the Rectangle tool to draw a rectangle about 200 x 400mm
- With the Push/Pull tool, push the rectangle to a height of 10mm
- Find a viewpoint where you can Select the rivet without any of the rectangle
- Select the Move tool and hover over the rivet until the green circle is on the base ring of the rivet

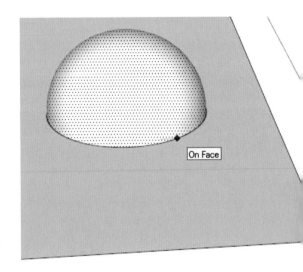

The rivet placed on the rectangle.

- Holding the left mouse button down, move the rivet to the rectangle face to get an 'On Face' box, and then release the mouse button. This ensures

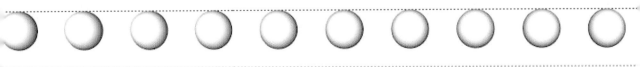

Line of rivets.

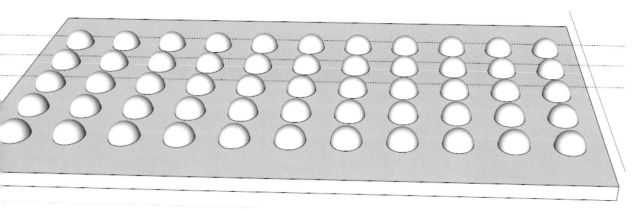

Rivets on the surface of the rectangle.

the rivet is on the face of the rectangle and not hovering above it
- Use the Move Tool whilst holding either the left or right arrow keys whilst moving. This ensures the rivet stays on the rectangle's surface

Now that you have your rivet on the surface of the rectangle you need to move and copy it as needed.

- Use the Tape Measure tool to draw a guideline for the first rivet position and along the ends if needed
- Select your rivet and move it to one end of the line as required
- Use Move +Ctrl to copy the rivet to the other end of the line
- *Immediately* enter /n (and tap the Enter key) into the Dimensions box, where 'n' is the number of rivets you require between the two end rivets
- You can repeat /n with a different number until you have the required effect

Note: An alternative to using the /'n' command to space out the rivets between the two end ones, is to copy the first rivet by the desired space between the rivets and use the *'n' command to copy the first one 'n' times.

Save your work as File>Save As>a Rivet Test.skp.

- Select the entire drawing

Export as an .stl file for printing: File>Export STL>a Rivet Test.stl.

SIGNAL FINIAL

By drawing different outlines, this technique can be used for a simple signal finial. The square base can be added as a separate layer. Remember you can use the Scale tool to stretch and reshape your model if your proportions are not quite right. This finial would print successfully on most FDM printers.

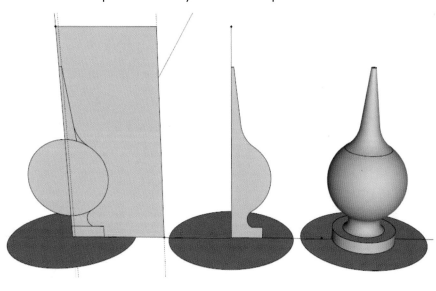

Stages in drawing a signal finial.

CHIMNEY POTS

The chimney pot as pictured below is easily redrawn and resized to suit different types of building. Use the Push/Pull tool to push down a circle to form the hollow centre.

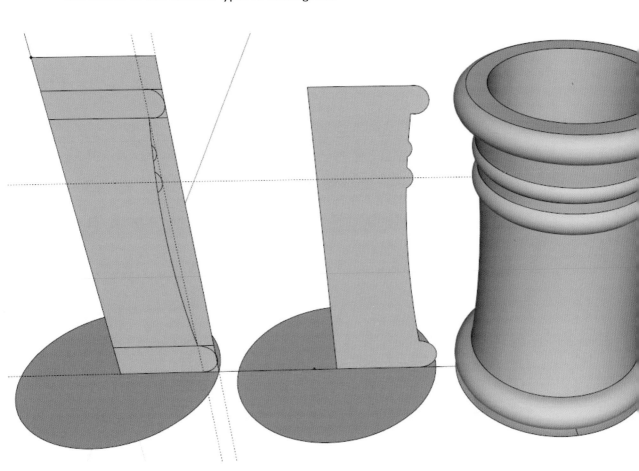

A simple chimney pot using the same technique and the Follow Me command.

WORKMAN'S HUT

Layers can be even more useful in 3-D, where each 'layer' can be regarded as a separate object.

First, re-run Sketchup to load the default Laser3-D template in 'Top-Down' view. You will draw a small hut where the walls, door, window and roof are separate layers in Sketchup. Each can then be printed individually in different coloured filament if required. I always print my prototypes in white as it is easier to see the detail in this colour.

3-D printing is best done from the build plate upwards without overhangs and with sufficient material in the first layer to make it stick to the build plate. You will therefore draw your hut as it looks, but rotate some of the parts once the drawing is complete so they will print better on your 3-D printer. Proceed as follows:

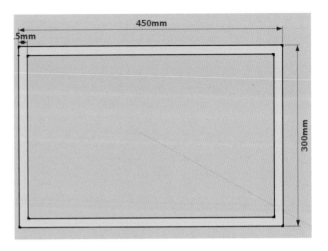

Basic shape of the hut.

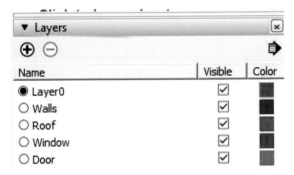

Layers menu with hut items added.

- Add the following four layers to the Layers menu: Walls, Roof, Window, Door. Remember always to draw on Layer0 (round circle chosen)
- With the Rectangle tool, draw a rectangle 450 × 300mm
- Use the Offset tool to draw a line 15mm in from each edge
- Switch to Iso view (the Iso icon is a house)
- With the Push/Pull tool, pull up the walls to 280mm
- Use the Tape Measure tool to add guidelines as shown, 150mm up from the top of the wall and vertical centreline
- With the Line tool, complete the triangle for the pitched roof
- Use the Push/Pull tool to push the end in 15mm

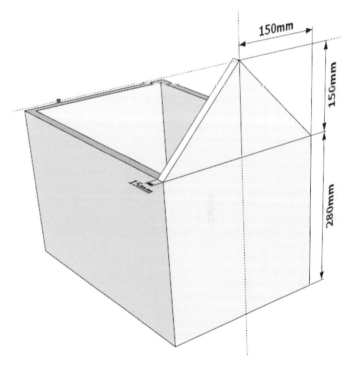

Walls pulled up and the triangle for the roof drawn and pulled to 15mm thickness.

- Delete the two horizontal lines (inside and outside) so the ends are one surface
- Repeat at the other end, as illustrated overleaf
- Use the Tape Measure tool to draw the guidelines for the door and window openings

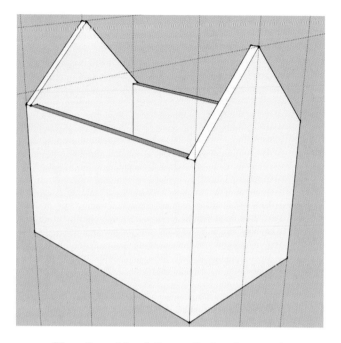

The other side of the roof triangle complete.

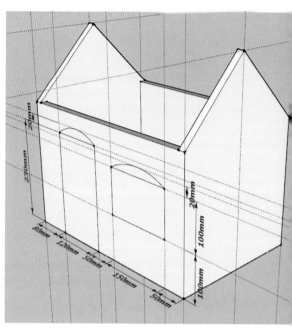

Walls measured for the window and door.

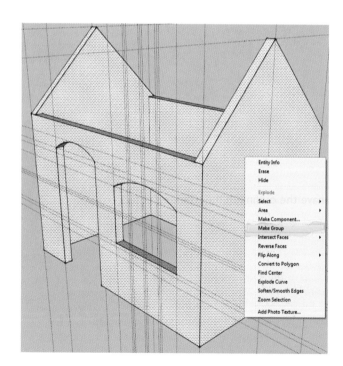

Window and door 'pushed' into openings, and then all the walls selected and made into a Group.

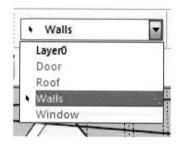

Walls Layer selected.

- With the Rectangle tool draw the two rectangles for the door and window
- Use the two-point Arc tool to draw the curved tops
- Delete the horizontal line on the window and door
- Use the Push/Pull tool to push them both 15mm into the wall to create the openings as shown
- Select all, then use right-click and Make Group
- Go to the top drop-down Layer menu and click on Wall to add the whole of the Walls Group to the Layer Walls. Turn this Layer off and on to check

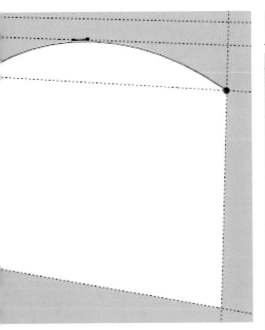

Outline of window frame.

Note that when you now click on the walls they have a frame around them, denoting they are part of a Group. To add to the Group, right-click (or double-click) on it and select Edit Group. When done, click anywhere on the background, then save it as File >Save As >a hut.skp.

You could simply draw your window frame as part of the building (wall), however this would limit you to printing it with the building. By making a separate window frame you have the following options: you can

- print it flat, thus overcoming any overhang problems
- print it several times for larger buildings with several windows
- modify it for different building styles, and save under a different name
- print it in a different colour of filament

Continue drawing the hut as follows:

- With the Layer Wall visible, use the Line tool and two-point Arc tool to draw over the window frame

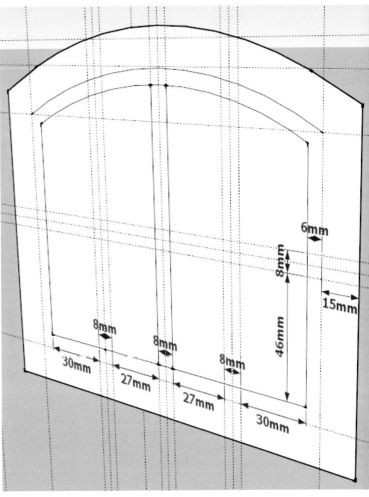

Window marked out for frames.

- Make the Layer Wall invisible again to check you have the outline of the window
- Clean up the drawing space by deleting the existing guidelines using Edit>Delete Guides
- Use the Offset tool to create an extra line 15mm out from the window, and another 6mm in from the window
- Use the Tape Measure tool to mark out for the bars as shown
- Using the Line tool, draw lines for the bars as shown in blue above
- Begin with the two central vertical lines…
- …then the four horizontal lines (two either side of the vertical)…

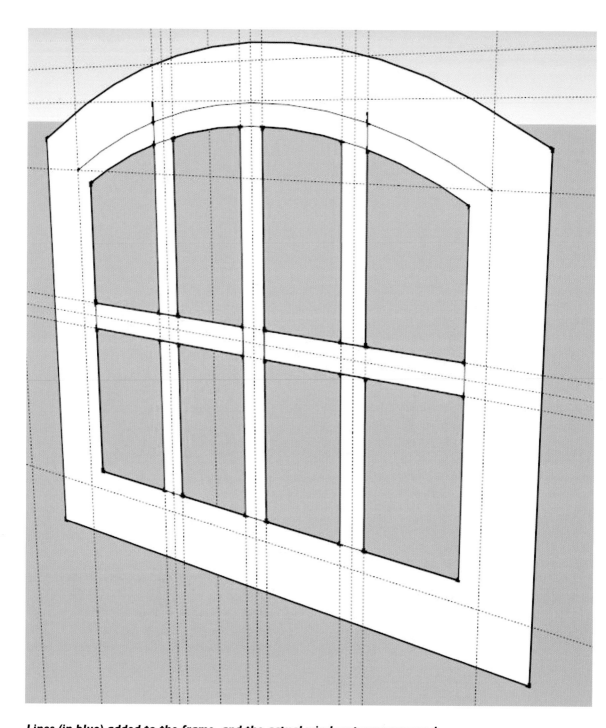

Lines (in blue) added to the frame, and the actual window panes removed.

• ...then the eight other vertical lines (not crossing the horizontal lines). If your vertical lines 'snap' to the top curve rather than staying on the line, continue them beyond the top curve as shown, and then delete the unwanted extra line(s)

• Now select each window pane area in turn and

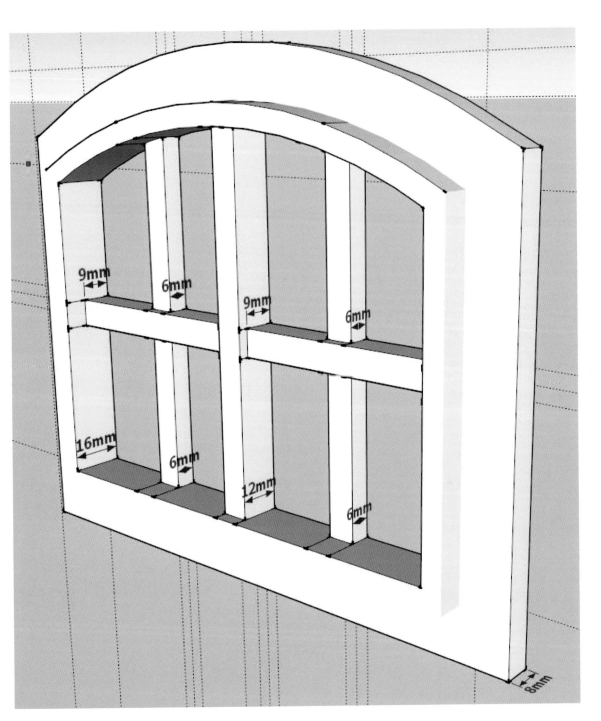

Window frame pulled out differing amounts.
Pull out the thickest first.

delete it as shown. If these are deleted after the frames have been pulled up, your 3-D printer slicing software (and/or Netfabb) may put them back in!

• Use the Push/Pull tool (and use the Ctrl key to get a +by the cursor for each pull) to pull up the various parts of the window frame as shown. Pull them out in order, as follows:

Edit	View	Camera	Draw	Tools	Window	Help
Undo Explode					Alt+Backspace	
Redo					Ctrl+Y	
Cut					Shift+Delete	
Copy					Ctrl+C	
Paste					Ctrl+V	
Paste In Place						
Delete					Delete	
Delete Guides						
Select All					Ctrl+A	
Select None					Ctrl+T	
Hide						
Unhide						▸

Deleting the guidelines to make the drawing clearer.

- inner frame 16mm
- outer frame 8mm
- vertical centre bar 12mm
- horizontal bars 9mm
- remaining vertical bars 6mm

Sometimes you end up with a lot of unwanted or confusing guidelines, for example those from the window when starting to draw the door. To remove a single guideline, select it by clicking on it (it turns blue) and tapping Delete on your keyboard. To delete all existing guidelines select Edit >Delete Guides, as shown.

Ensure you clean up your drawings before trying to print them. Rotate the window so you can see its back. Select and delete all the lines drawn on the rear surface to obtain a 'clean' single surface, as shown in the picture.

Cleaning up your drawing by removing unnecessary lines can help it print properly.

*Making the window
a Group.*

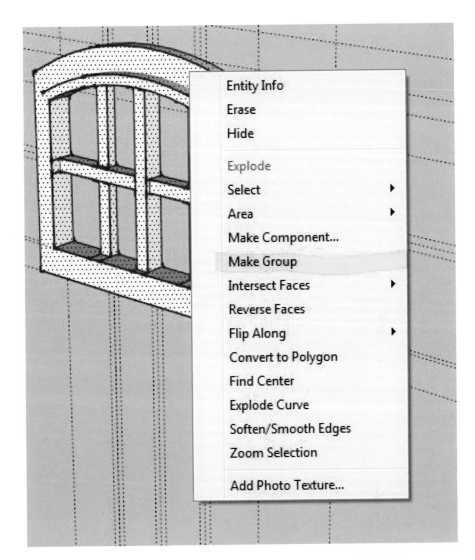

Leaving these lines drawn on the surface can confuse both Netfabb (which could fill in the window panes) and/or your 3-D printer 'slicing' software, and may produce unwanted results.

Whenever possible, try to remove unwanted lines on your drawings as you proceed. If Netfabb fills in holes or spaces, then try re-drawing them using a different sequence. This, I'm afraid, is part of the 'dark art' of 3-D drawing!
- Finally select all the window frame, and right-click to get the menu above
- Select Make Group
- Click on Window from the drop-down Layers menu at the top of the screen

*Making the window a Layer using the Layer
drop-down menu.*

You have made the window frame Layer Window: now try making it invisible by unticking the box in the Layer menu. You now have two separate Layers: Wall and Window.

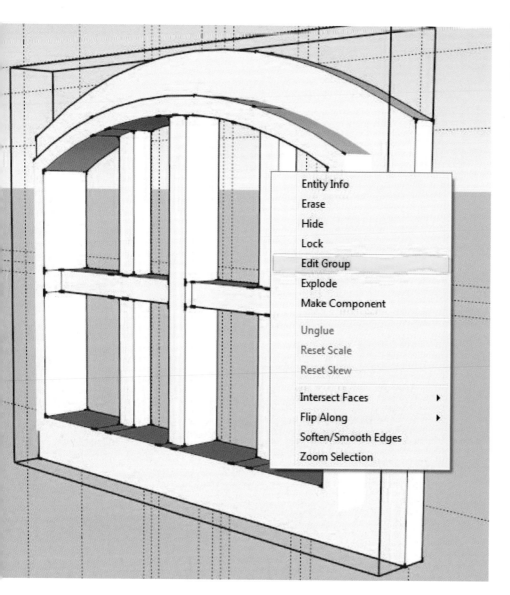

To make alterations to a Group, right-click and select Edit Group.

Although our window frame has been drawn to the exact size of the opening, it will not fit! This is because each layer of filament used to make the model is pressed on to the layer below, and it is squeezed outwards a little.

- To reduce the size of our window without reducing the size of the whole model, you must first double-click on the Window Group to make it editable. Note how the window is displayed in a grey frame to denote it is a Group and is editable

- To reduce your window use the Tape Measure tool and click on each of the bottom two corners in turn. You should see 180 appear in the Dimensions (or Length) box
- Simply change this to 170 and tap the Enter key
- You will see a box as shown with the question 'Do you want to resize the active group or component?' Select Yes
- With Select chosen, click anywhere on the back-ground to return your Group to being uneditable. The frame around it should return to blue

Scaling the window frame Group to fit the opening.

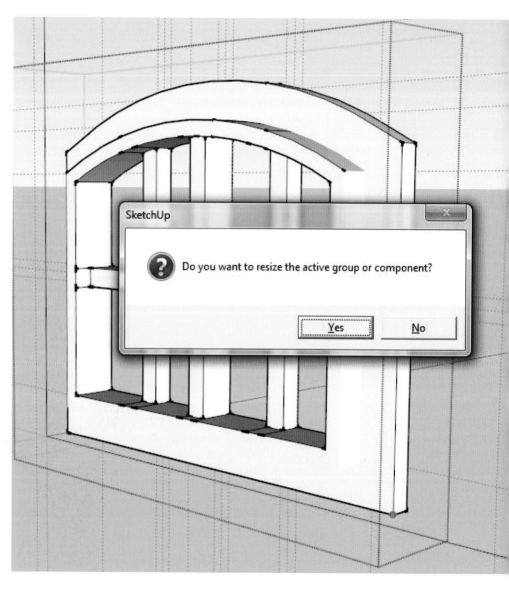

• Now re-measure the bottom of the window with the Tape Measure tool: it should read 170. You have taken 1mm (remember you are drawing x10 size) off the width of the window and proportionally off the height. Your window should now fit the opening; if not, repeat this process using smaller/larger numbers

Warning: If you do not select to edit the Group first, then Sketchup will ask if you wish to resize the model. However, doing this would resize all items of the model, which is useful for changing the whole model to a different scale, but not for reducing the size of single items such as windows!

Now save as File >Save As >b hut.skp.

Now that you have made a couple of objects a Group and a Layer, from now on I shall simply say 'Make Group' and 'Layer xxx', where xxx is the Layer name.

• Make both the Wall and Window layers visible, and click on them in turn. Note how objects that are 'Grouped' are shown with a 'frame' around them when selected. The window sticks out from the walls because of the way we have drawn it, but since it will be printed separately, this is OK

Remember: When you draw on a Group you are drawing a separate layer (as on a new sheet of tracing paper), not on the Group itself. To edit a Group and make changes to it you must double-click on it (or right-click on it and select 'Edit Group'), make your changes, then click anywhere on the background to close the Group again.

- With Layer Walls visible, trace around the door sides and bottom with the Line tool, and the curved top with the two-point Arc tool; the door opening should go solid
- Turn off the Layer Wall visibility
- Use the Offset tool on the front face to add a 15mm border outside the door frame and a 6mm border inside the frame, as pictured
- Use the Tape Measure tool to draw a guideline 15mm up from the bottom of the door frame, and the Line tool to draw a horizontal line 15mm up from the bottom of the door
- Select and delete the three lines that form the bottom rectangle of the door, as shown
- Use the Push/Pull tool to pull the inner door frame (6mm wide) 16mm deep
- Again with the Push/Pull tool pull both the outer frame and the actual door 8mm deep
- Use the Circle tool to draw a small 3mm circle for the handle
- With the Push/Pull tool, pull out 4mm for the door handle, as shown
- Make your door a Group (select it all, then right-click >Make Group) and assign it to the Layer Door (drop-down Layer menu >Door)
- Finally reduce the size of the door to fit by editing the Group (double-click on the door)

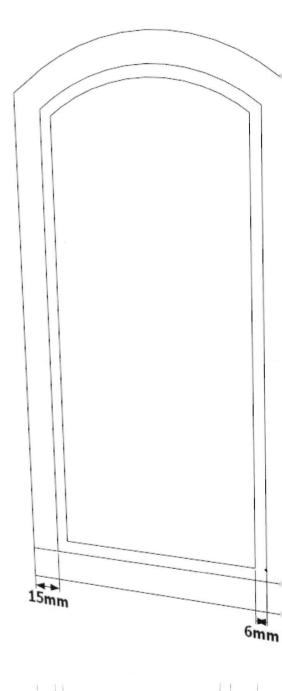

ABOVE RIGHT: *Basic door traced from the walls and with two offset frames drawn.*

BELOW RIGHT: *The bottom of the door with a 15mm deep rectangle removed.*

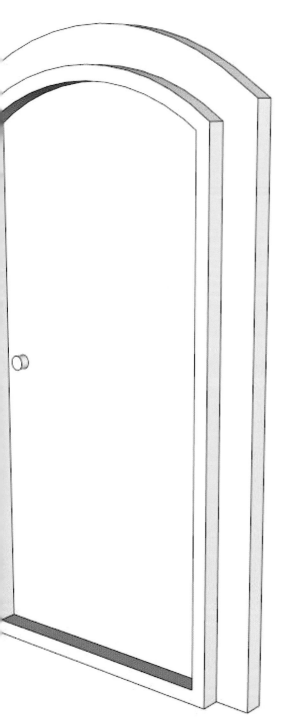

Door with inner frame pulled out 16mm.

- Use the Tape Measure tool along the very bottom of the door (150mm) and reduce this by entering 140mm into the Dimensions box
- Click Yes in the box that appears (Re-size the Active Group)
- Click on the background to close the Group

Save as follows: File >Save As >c hut.skp.
   Now for the roof, using a new tool:

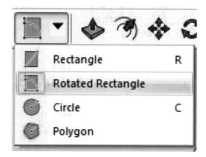

Rotated Rectangle tool.

- Make just the Walls and Roof Layers visible
- Select the Rotated Rectangle tool under the Shapes menu, as shown. This enables you to draw a rectangle at any angle (normally they default to being drawn on one of the three axes)
- With the Rotated Rectangle tool selected, click in turn on both outer ends of the roof apex and then the near lower corner of the roof, as shown. A sloping rectangle will be drawn over the roof, and the roof area should turn blue, as in the picture
- Rotate your hut and do similar for the other side
- Make the Layer Walls invisible, and with the Push/Pull tool+ (and the Ctrl key tapped to get a + by the cursor), pull one side inwards 8mm
- Now rotate your roof as required and do similar with the other side (remember the Ctrl key and the + sign)

Now remove the extra horizontal line near the roof apex and the two short lines at the corners. This is not really necessary, but it does tidy up the roof for further work.

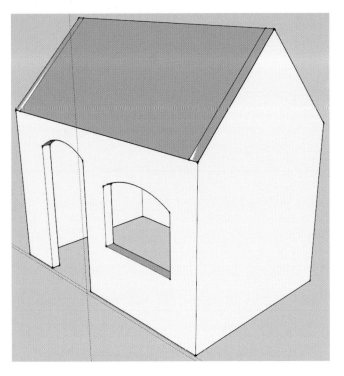

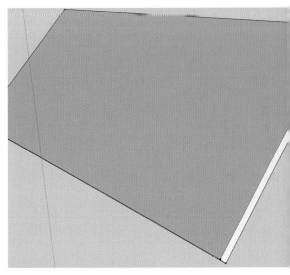

Roof traced over the walls using the Rotated Rectangle tool.

The final roof 8mm thick.

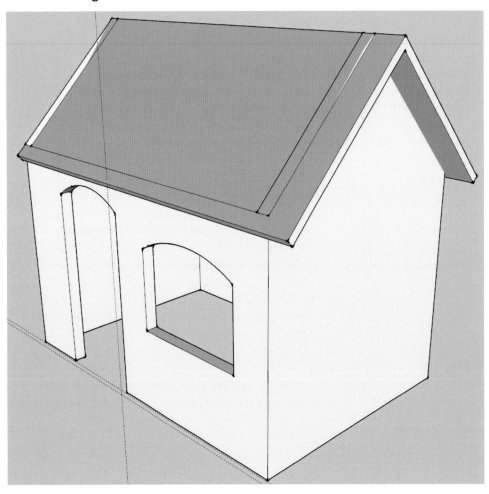

The roof in place on the walls. Note the 30mm overhang is only at one end; the roof will be centred when printed, and glued in place with a 15mm overhang each end.

- Select the Push/Pull tool, and pull out one end of the roof 30mm. This will provide a 1.5mm overhang at each end in the final printed model
- Select all your roof, right-click and Make Group from the menu, then in the drop-down Layer menu select Roof to make the roof Layer Roof

Try making each of the four elements of the hut visible and invisible in turn to check that you have the four Layers and Groups.

- Make the Layer Walls and Roof visible, and check that your roof matches the drawing. Note that you pulled one end 30mm rather than both 15mm to save some work! The lines are those of the walls

You now have a complete hut, but only the walls would print well without further work. Windows and doors are always best printed flat to avoid sagging of the tops or slow printing (tall objects take longer to print). The roof would print 'as is', but the Inner surface would be printing at a 45-degree slope and might sag. You need to rotate each one to optimize 3-D printing.

Before doing this save your final Sketchup model as File >Save As >d hut.skp.

- Make only the roof visible. Rotating the roof is tricky because it is not at right-angles to the way you need to turn it: you need it on its end
- Select the Rotate tool and move to the nearest corner point. Hold down the left arrow key and the protractor should turn green, showing it is aligned with the green axis. Rotate 90 degrees on that axis. The Top-Down view should look

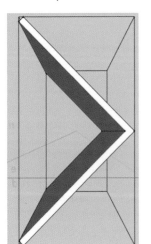

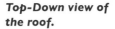
Top-Down view of the roof.

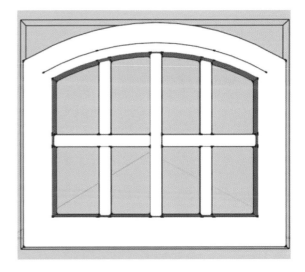

Top-Down view of the window.

like the one shown. You may need to use Undo and try this a few times!

Select the entire roof and save it in a format for 3-D printing: File >Export STL >Centimetres >d hut roof.stl.

- Make the Layer Roof invisible
- Make just the Layer Window visible and do a similar rotation for the window to make it lie flat, only this time hold down the right arrow key to get the red protractor before selecting the nearest corner of the window (in Iso view) and rotating it on to its back 90 degrees. Note the 'flat' side of the window should be its bottom side when looked at from above. Check you get the view above in Top-Down view

Save this as File >Export STL >Centimetres >d hut window.stl.

- Make just the Layer door visible, and rotate the door on to its back using similar methods

Save this as File >Export STL >Centimetres >d hut door.stl.

The illustration shows the final drawing of the hut with the various parts rotated ready for 3-D printing.

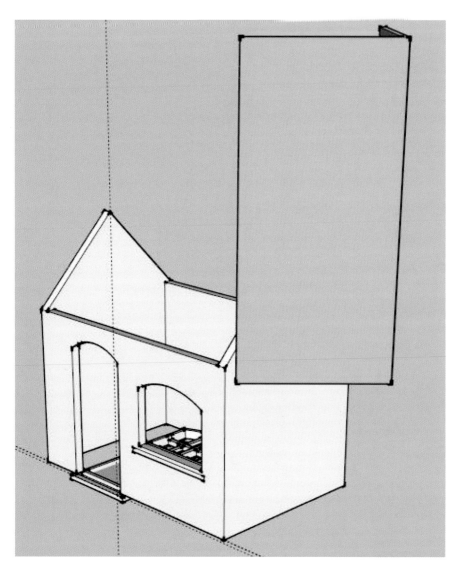

Final Sketchup drawing of the hut.

This is an important aspect of 3-D printing: ensuring that each part is in the optimum position for printing without needing a raft or supports.

To print the hut, each part is loaded separately on to your print bed. You can move these around and copy them (depending on your 3-D printer software) before printing.

If the window and door don't fit correctly, you can re-size and re-print just these by themselves until they do.

If openings such as windows and doors sag badly and are a real problem (and they can be in the larger scales) you have a number of options: you can

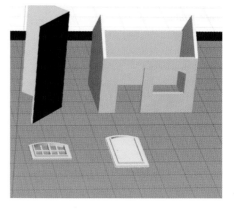

Final parts laid out ready for printing.

The hut as printed on the 3-D printer's build plate. Note that you may get some slight sagging of the curved window/door tops on the walls. Use a sharp knife to scrape this curved to fit the window/door.

- print each wall separately (flat) and then glue them together
- add vertical supports (in the smallest diameter your printer will handle, usually about 1mm diameter, or square, as determined by the Test Piece printed earlier) and cut them away when finished
- print the window *in situ* so the overhangs are less wide

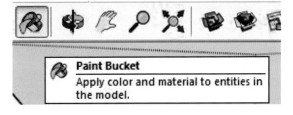

Paint Bucket tool is not for 3-D printing!

WARNING ABOUT PAINT BUCKET TOOL

Now you have successfully printed your hut you can embellish it with roofing tiles and brickwork. You can easily make your roof and walls look realistic in Sketchup by applying a material using the Paint Bucket Tool, as shown.

Unfortunately this is only a photographic rendering and has no depth so it will not 3-D print! Each brick shown is flat. To print 3-D brickwork we need depth, and this is harder to achieve.

See the next chapter, Hints and Tips: 3-D Printing, for more on how to render and 3-D print brick and stonework.

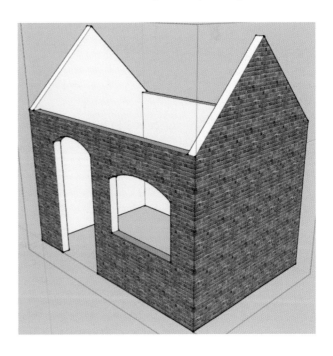

RIGHT: *Brickwork effect using the Paint Bucket tool. It looks good, but will not 3-D print.*

19 HINTS AND TIPS

CHANGING FILAMENT

I always ensure my extruder is hot and then 'load' my filament for five to ten seconds, and let it flow out of the extruder before I immediately 'unload' it. This ensures that all the filament in the extruder is molten.

FIRST LAYER

If your printer software allows it (and most do), make your first layer 10 to 15 degrees hotter than subsequent layers. This helps the first layer stick to the print bed (painter's tape).

ALCOHOL WIPE

Wipe your blue painter's tape with isopropyl alcohol (obtainable from most pharmacies) to 'revive' it and help your first layer stick.

BRICKWORK: PLUG-INS AND PRINTING

Remember that for printing, your brick-/stonework has to be drawn in 3-D. This can be tedious. A plug-in is available for $29 (at the time of writing) called 'Oob Layouts', which enables 3-D brick-/stonework to be added to your drawings. This is available on a one-month free trial from the Extension Warehouse, and is worth installing and trying.

Run Sketchup, and then choose 'Window>Extensions Warehouse' from the menu. Search for Oob Layouts in the Extensions Warehouse, and download the free trial. Install it as for the .STL plug-in described in the chapter on setting up Sketchup.

Oob Layouts allows a high degree of control over the type of brick-/stonework drawn, as shown in the picture. The brick-/stonework will also flow around door and window openings, as well as pre-drawn lintels and window bottoms.

Oob Layouts also has pre-sets for planking, and a number of other potentially useful 3-D effects.

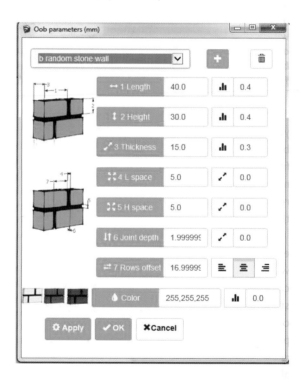

Oob Layouts plug-in parameters, which can be altered to suit the size and type of brick-/stonework required. The right-hand column introduces the required 'randomness' of size. Once a satisfactory style has been achieved the settings can be saved and re-loaded as required. Note all measurements are 10 x larger than required. Try the settings above, and then alter them to your own requirements.

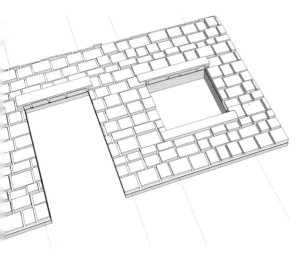

The results from the above settings: an uneven and slightly random stone effect in 4mm scale, which prints flat really well. Note how the door and window lintels and window bottom have been drawn and 'pulled up' first. The stonework flows around these very effectively.

List of pre-sets available in Oob Layouts (those ending in 4mm are ones I have determined and saved as my own pre-sets).

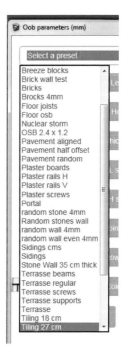

To use Oob Layouts, simply select the area (surface) you would like to cover in stone-/brickwork (it should become blue and dotted), and then run Oob Layouts from the Extensions menu. From the drop-down menu in Oob Layouts you can select the effect you require (and you can define your own sizes and save them for future use), and then click on 'Apply'.

Try Oob Layouts on the workman's hut drawn earlier. You will need to select each of the outside walls in turn, and then use 'Apply Oob Layouts'. You can select the front and rear Oob Layouts brick-/stonework in turn, and using the Scale tool, pull them out wider to hide the corner joins. Use different parameters in Oob Layouts to achieve different brick and stone effects, or use the 'wall sidings' preset, suitably scaled, to produce a wooden planking effect.

THINK FLAT

When developing complex models, always try to break them down into units that can be printed 'flat'. Avoid overhangs at all costs. The G-scale wagon body is printed as one part (it takes about eight hours to print), but the underframe parts, wheels and so on, were printed as separate parts and glued/screwed together.

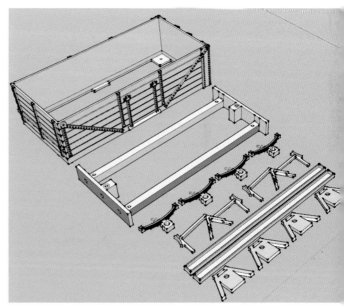

Wagon parts laid out flat ready for printing. Note the bottom of the wagon body is open, with corner pieces that allow it to be screwed to the underframe. For the base I use two layers of Plasticard with lead sheet between to give the model enough weight to run well on the track. I am working on 3-D printed loads!

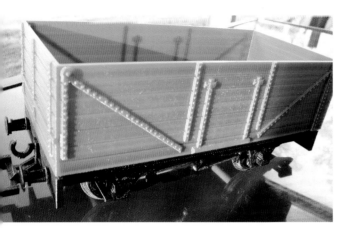

Finished G-scale wagon, entirely 3-D printed apart from metal rods and four washers used for the axles and bearings. Note the use of rivets as described in one of the projects.

By designing and printing different 'bodies', the same underframe and wheel set can be used for different models, including a guards van (remember this is G-scale, so we are not talking fine scale!).

STAYING FLAT

When printing models with large flat surfaces on the print bed, they can sometimes curl up at the edges as the print progresses. This is more pronounced on unheated print beds. Drawing 'pads' at the four corners as shown can alleviate this curling. Cut the pads off once printed. The wagon body shown previously would benefit from this technique.

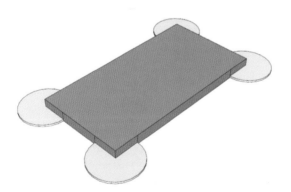

Pads added at the corner to help keep the model flat on the build plate.

BENDING USING HOT-WATER/HEAT GUN

When designing a viaduct, the brickwork under each arch could have been drawn (with some difficulty!) and printed in place. However, I found it easier to print the brickwork flat, and then simply curve it to fit by dipping it in hot water and pushing it into a 3-D printed arch to get the correct curve. I allowed for the thickness of the brickwork when designing the viaduct arches, and measured the length of brickwork required to fit the arch exactly.

After immersing in hot water, the plastic sheet of brickwork for under the viaduct arches is easily formed to shape by the arch itself. Note that the thickness of this sheet has been allowed for in the design of the arch. The brickwork has been drawn using the Oob Layouts plug-in as described earlier.

MAKE SEVERAL SMALL PIECES

Try to break down any large model into smaller pieces, which can be printed flat or glued together in such a way that they add strength to the final model. An example is the viaduct, where arches are printed in two halves, the under-arch brickwork is bent after printing to fit, and the 'facing walls' of the viaduct are printed flat and help strengthen the model. The walls are then printed and affixed to each side.

By making the arches wider at one side, a curve can be introduced to the viaduct. The 'facing walls' on the longer side then need 'stretching', to fit the outer curved side of the viaduct. This can easily be done using the Scale tool in Sketchup.

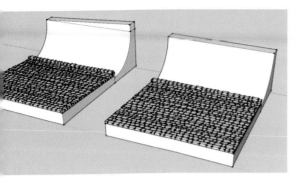

Viaduct arches with 'Oob Layouts' (see foregoing picture) stonework on the main face, and allowance for curved brickwork under the arch. The left-hand example has a sloping top, which adds a curve to the viaduct.

The main facing walls for the viaduct with the arch stonework hand-drawn in Sketchup and 'pulled out' before using the 'Oob Layouts' plug-in to complete the rest of the stonework. The two objects on the left are the two halves of the rainwater downpipes used to hide the joins.

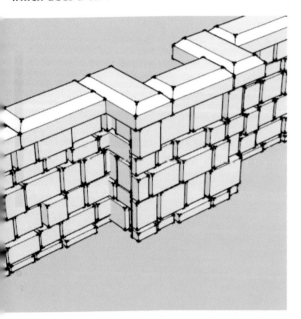

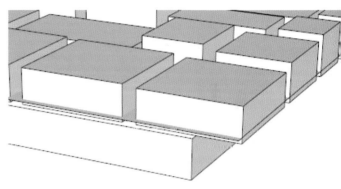

The front corners of the stonework can be pulled out as shown with the Scale tool so that better corners are achieved. It needs to be printed vertically.

The viaduct walling with refuges. One top stone was designed in Sketchup and then repeated and copied along the wall before the 'Oob Layouts' plug-in was used on the other surfaces to complete the stonework. The Scale tool was used on external corners to pull the stonework out slightly to mask the joins. The whole wall section was then printed upside down to avoid overhangs.

The finished viaduct showing the stonework after spraying with Rustoleum 'Texture' spray (see later). Glued together, the various pieces have made an extremely strong 4mm-scale viaduct over a metre in length. The rainwater downpipes hide the joins every third arch.

SCALING

To scale items in Sketchup use the Tape Measure tool to measure the length, height or width of your model. The measurement will be shown in the Dimensions box. Simply type over this measurement with the new number required, and Sketchup will pop up a box asking if you wish to resize the model: answer 'Yes'.

MULTI-MATERIAL MODELS

3-D printed items in PLA or ABS can warp badly if exposed to extremes of temperature, so for items in G-scale destined for the garden railway I construct a 'shell' out of laser cut 3mm acrylic sheet, and then use a gun adhesive to fix the 3-D printed stonework and so on, over the top.

PAINTING

Spray paints sold for painting car bumpers are good to use on most 3-D printed plastics. Primer specifically sold for plastics is also useful. High-build grey primer hides the 'banding' effect of the 3-D printing.

Also useful for buildings, bridges, viaducts and other masonry buildings, as well as platform tops, are the Rustoleum 'Textures' spray paints. These give a fine texture to the surface and very effectively hide any banding.

WEATHERING

There is a range of powders available that can be used effectively for weathering. See the image below. It is important to fix them after use.

These Rustoleum 'Texture' sprays are an excellent textured finish for 4mm- and 7mm-scale stonework and platform surfaces.

Weathering powders work well on both laser-cut and 3-D printed items. I use a cheap, non-scented hairspray to fix them after use.

SUPPLIERS

The following list gives details of products and companies I have found useful for model making with 3-D printers and laser cutters.

SOURCES OF MATERIALS

Blue painter's tape: Dulux Decorator's Centres – search the internet for the nearest; B&Q also sell a version. It helps models stick to the build plate.

Masking tape: Tapes Direct (www.tapes-direct.co.uk) MT7550PR Professional Grade Masking Tape, 75mm x 50m. Use where models have a large surface area on the build plate and are difficult to remove from blue painter's tape.

Double-sided adhesive tape: Tapes Direct (www. tapes-direct.co.uk); DSTPMPM5050 – general purpose, clear double-sided tape, 50mm x 50m. Use over blue painter's tape for tiny models or models in filament that is difficult to work with, such as the rubber-like PLA filament. It really helps models stick to the build plate. It can be used a few times before replacement.

Mountboard: A1 size 1,400 microns (1.4mm), thick black/white sides in a pack of twenty supplied by Rapid Electronics (www.rapidonline.com): order code 06-6154. For all types of model produced on the laser cutter.

Filament: All types supplied by 3-D Filaprint (www.3dfilaprint.co.uk). They sell all types of PLA and ABS filaments, plus several more exotic types. They also sell samples, so you can try before buying a full spool. They sell different grades from 'Reprapper' budget (which I use a lot), through to premium.

Engraving laminate: For items such as signs, control panels; try HPC Laser (www.hpclaser.co.uk), also search the internet. This is plastic sheet with a base colour and a thin, laserable colour on top, which when cut away shows the base layer colour underneath.

Rowmark: See www.csionline.co.uk; it looks like styrene sheet but laser cuts well. HPC Laser (hpclaser.co.uk) also sells a similar material.

Mylar (polyester film): Obtainable from www.stencil-warehouse.com, or search the internet. A very tough plastic film obtainable in different thicknesses. It is used by graphic artists as a masking material. Thinner sheets can be laser cut to incredible detail.

Frisket: (www.everythingairbrush.com) – a very thin, lightly tacky material ideal for ultra-fine masking for spray painting. It can be laser cut and used for masking things such as signal arms for spray painting.

MDF and plywood: For laserable grades see www.hobarts.com

Isopropyl alcohol: Obtainable from your local pharmacy.

LASER CUTTING MACHINES

HPC Laser: See www.hpclaser.co.uk for the hobby laser machine LS3020, which is like mine. However, note that even as I write they are no longer listing my machine, but are quoting an upgraded (and more expensive) machine, the LS3020 LSCT. This has a more modern operating system and works with newer versions of Windows.

Internet: Search the general internet or eBay for 'laser cutting machine'.

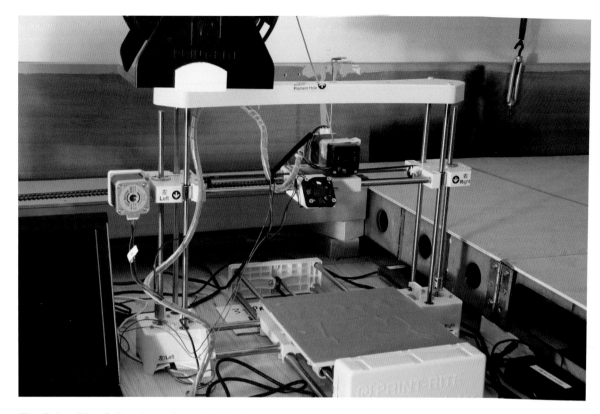

The Print-Rite 3-D printer from Hobbyking, as used by the author.

3-D PRINTERS

Robosavvy: (www.robosavvy.com) – they sell a variety of 3-D printing machines and accessories. I have found their technical support excellent.

Hobbyking: (www.hobbyking.com/uk) – they sell a range of 3-D printers including the Print-Rite 3-D printer like mine.

Colido: (www.colido.com) – do an internet search for 'Colido DIY printer', which is similar to the Print-Rite printer above but may be cheaper from other sources.

USEFUL WEBSITES

Laser cutting services: York Model Making – www.yorkmodelmaking.co.uk. This company specializes in model railway parts, but an internet search will bring up other companies willing to laser cut from your drawings.

3-D printing services: Shapeways – shapeways.com – will 3-D print your drawing in a variety of materials. Others offer similar services.

INDEX